John Octavius Johnston, Edward Bouverie Pusey

Spiritual Letters of Edward Bouverie Pusey

Doctor of Divinity, Canon of Christchurch, Regius Professor of Hebrew

John Octavius Johnston, Edward Bouverie Pusey

Spiritual Letters of Edward Bouverie Pusey
Doctor of Divinity, Canon of Christchurch, Regius Professor of Hebrew

ISBN/EAN: 9783744720106

Printed in Europe, USA, Canada, Australia, Japan

Cover: Foto ©Lupo / pixelio.de

More available books at **www.hansebooks.com**

Spiritual Letters

of

Edward Bouverie Pusey

DOCTOR OF DIVINITY
CANON OF CHRIST CHURCH; REGIUS PROFESSOR OF
HEBREW IN THE UNIVERSITY OF OXFORD

·

EDITED AND PREPARED FOR PUBLICATION BY THE

REV. J. O. JOHNSTON, M.A.
PRINCIPAL OF CUDDESDON THEOLOGICAL COLLEGE

AND THE

REV. W. C. E. NEWBOLT, M.A.
CANON AND CHANCELLOR OF ST. PAUL'S

LONGMANS, GREEN, AND CO.
39 PATERNOSTER ROW, LONDON
NEW YORK AND BOMBAY

1898

All rights reserved.

Oxford
HORACE HART, PRINTER TO THE UNIVERSITY

PREFACE

IN the Preface to the fourth volume of Dr. Pusey's 'Life,' the Editors expressed their intention of publishing a volume of his Spiritual Letters. They pointed out that their task would not be complete without some such addition. Dr. Pusey spent a considerable portion of his life in dealing, whether by word of mouth or by letter, with the difficulties of individual souls; but in the record of his busy years, no room could be found for any suitable recognition of this side of his work, without unduly interrupting the course of the narrative. It was felt therefore that a small collection of his Spiritual Letters could alone supply this gap in the account of his life. Hence it will be understood by all who have sympathetically followed the long course of the biography, that the present volume is properly a necessary supplement to the work on which Dr. Liddon spent so many years; yet it is issued in a separate form, partly because it is in itself independent, and partly because its contents will appeal to many people who have not had the time, nor perhaps the inclination, to read the other volumes, which deal so largely in matters of modern ecclesiastical history and the tangle of theological controversy.

From the nature of the case only a comparatively small number of the letters which Dr. Pusey wrote on the difficulties of those who consulted him, were entrusted to Dr. Liddon for publication. And even of these some were not of sufficient general interest; some were practically repetitions of what Dr. Pusey had often said: while others again seemed to require so much annotation, that there was a danger lest the necessary notes should distract the attention of the reader to a wearisome extent. Out of the whole number thus reduced, only a very small selection is here published. And they have been chosen partly for their own interest, partly as specimens of the manner in which Dr. Pusey dealt with various anxieties of the same correspondent, or guided different minds in dealing with the same questions. As regards the style of these letters, it must be remembered that no applicant who seemed to need his help was left unnoticed; in fact some of his longest letters were written to people utterly unknown to him. To make time for this vast correspondence under the heavy strain of a multiplicity of public business and literary work, he had often to work far into the night, and sometimes through the whole night. The strain of such prolonged work must have been very severe; and traces of it will be found again and again in a literary style which is condensed and obscure to an extent unusual even in his writings (which on other occasions are not always models of clearness). More especially it will be noticed that his quotations of the Holy Scriptures are written down with a freedom bred of an intimate appreciation and a familiar use, which does not always stop for mere verbal accuracy. It has been thought best to leave, as a rule, all such obscurities and free quotations, as he left them; and not to disparage the intelligence of the reader by the frequent insertion of irritating glosses.

It will be noticed that at different periods of his life, the tone of his letters varies greatly. When writing between 1840 and 1850, he frequently displays a rugged severity, which is to be accounted for only in part by the needs of the person to whom the letters were addressed. They reflect in fact the darkness of that day of trial through which the Church of England was then passing; and in them he lays bare the stern and solemn truths which at that crisis filled his own mind, and by which he strove to direct those whom he was trying to pilot through the storm. In later life writing to the same people, under conditions which had changed so happily, his language reflects more the peace and confidence of the brighter days of the Church.

The title which has been given to this volume, in its more narrow meaning, is really descriptive of the greater part of its contents. It consists chiefly of letters of advice with regard to the trials of the spiritual life. Such trials bear no special marks of time or place. They reappear everywhere in similar forms from generation to generation; and letters which deal with them have therefore a universal and an undying interest.

But with intellectual questions, the case is different; the special form of the difficulties which the intellect has to face in dealing with religious questions varies with almost every decade. Young men of to-day can hardly understand how the great perplexities which confronted their fathers' early manhood can ever have been true occasions of distress. The solution seems to them too obvious and easy. They have inherited the land without passing through that part of the wilderness. Yet the wilderness was great and terrible for many years; and the value of the letters of consolation and guidance which were then written can only be understood by those who fully know the precise juncture at which they were penned. Hence comparatively few of Dr. Pusey's letters on the intellectual difficulties of twenty years ago, and of yet earlier dates, are printed in this volume. Those who are interested in his methods of dealing with such questions as they presented themselves, will find them fully set forth in the three volumes of his University Sermons. In these he is conspicuously the Christian Apologist, the guide of souls in the intellectual unrest of the day, trying to rescue them from misunderstandings of the Truth and from the plausible misleadings of error, and to restate the fundamental verities of the Faith with the clearness of mature study, and the fire of deep conviction and of heartfelt devotion.

On the other hand, the controversy with the Church of Rome is represented here with comparative fullness. It is true that Dr. Pusey has dealt with the whole question in the three volumes of his 'Eirenicon': yet each of those volumes is influenced by its having been written with a special purpose, in consequence of some controversial publication or historical event. But the questions at issue between the Church of England and the Church of Rome remain always essentially the same. In his letters Dr. Pusey deals with those questions more concisely, and quite as powerfully as in his longer work. The arguments with which he reassured anxious inquirers, and retained them in their allegiance, are as valuable now as when they were written. Had they been written in the present day, the polemic element would probably, in the light of recent history, have been more prominent, and the apologetic portion of the argument would have fallen into the background.

Readers of this volume may very naturally wish to know some details of the daily life of the writer of these letters. Externally it must have appeared a very simple existence that he spent at Christ Church; shared only during the last thirty years of his laborious career, by his son Philip, whose death so shortly preceded his own. Each morning at 8.30, when Philip returned from the daily College service in the Cathedral, the household assembled for family prayers in Dr. Pusey's study. He used to kneel at his table with Philip, who was very deaf, close by his side and looking over his book. The prayers were chiefly from the Prayer Book, with the addition of a special thanksgiving which he used every day, and of some prayers taken from 'The Paradise of the Christian Soul' during Advent and Lent. When in health he always attended Mattins and Evensong at the Cathedral, unless prevented by some unavoidable engagement. As age came on, he was forbidden by his friend and medical adviser, Sir Henry Acland, to attend the Cathedral in cold weather, and at last he was not allowed to go there at all. The last service which he attended was on the morning of November 26, 1877. The whole day was spent in literary work, lecturing and preparing for lectures, attending University meetings, writing letters, and in seeing all who came to him. In his later years, he rarely even went for a walk, except when at Ascot in the summer vacations. His meals were of the simplest character. After many years of struggle with his doctor, he was at last forbidden to fast; but every meal was rigidly plain. At his 6 o'clock dinner, there were never more than two courses; there was neither soup nor fish. He particularly desired that there should be no waste at his table, not even of a small piece of bread. This was not only as an example, but because he would not allow the waste of that which so many of the poor needed so sorely. The day was closed by family prayers in the study at 9.30.

But of the inner side of his life, in its relation to God, even those nearest him saw but a few glimpses. The rules with which he desired to govern all his life have already appeared in his biography[1]; and readers of these letters would do well to refer to them as explanatory of many points on which he gave advice to others. This habit of life he kept up so far as he was able into advanced age. The stress of work and increasing years compelled him to modify it to a certain extent. Sometimes the demands which were made on his time by those who sought his help kept him at work beyond all the rules of prudence. His mother would sorrowfully complain in her letters to those who knew him well, that when staying with her in Grosvenor Square, he was out of the house by 6 or 7 o'clock, and did not return to dinner until 9 or 10 at night. On one day she reports that he was out before 7 o'clock, and came back to breakfast at 2.30, having preached at 11: and that he preached again in the evening and sat up most of the night writing letters. Even at seventy years of age he would make appointments for 7 a.m., and continue working until 11 and 12 o'clock at night. Of course in the vacations, when he was at Malvern or in the Isle of Wight, or at Ascot, he was able to take more rest; but so long as work had to be done and his weary body could be made do it, no consideration was allowed to interfere with his doing it with all his might.

[1] Vol. iii. pp. 104–107.

At the age of sixty, it was his habit, when at Christ Church, to celebrate the Holy Eucharist in his own house every day, generally at 4 o'clock in the morning. He had received special permission from Bishop Wilberforce to do so. He used for this purpose a marble slab, which was placed on a small table in his study, on which table stood the picture of the Head of our Lord, supposed to be by Murillo, which his brother Philip brought for him from Spain. This picture now hangs over the altar in the Chapel of the Pusey House in Oxford, and the marble slab which he used has been let into the surface of the wooden altar beneath it. In later years he celebrated in this manner only on Sundays and Saints' Days, as a rule. His son Philip and any friends who happened to be staying with him would sometimes join in this service, if they desired. When celebrating in his own house, he wore only a surplice and scarf; but if he was in a Church or Chapel where the Eucharistic vestments were used, he always wore them.

As regards his books of private devotion, his favourite book for many years was 'The Paradise of the Christian Soul,' which he had with great care adapted for the use of members of the English Church. In later years, however, he reverted to the use of Bishop Andrewes' 'Devotions,' which he continued to use to the end of his life. But any devotional book could contain but a small part of his habitual devotions. He spent a great deal of time in mental prayer, not only 'filling up all the chinks of time' in that manner, as he used to advise others to do; but also he would expand and supplement his ordinary prayers by meditations interspersed with them. In the last year of his life, he gave a friend a copy of Bishop Andrewes' 'Devotions,' saying that it was the book he used himself, and he placed marks here and there through many pages of it to indicate the places 'where pauses ought to be made.' He said that though it was all printed in unbroken paragraphs, many pauses ought to be made by those who used the book, because 'the prayers contained such wondrous thoughts.' Similar pauses he would make when ministering to others. He felt that words awoke ideas which would only be disturbed by passing too rapidly to other phrases. When ministering to one who was dying in his own house, it was noticed by those in attendance that he would repeat the one word 'Jesus' a great many times at intervals, slowly, distinctly, and with great earnestness. He explained afterwards that this was the more valuable help to a dying person. It recalled to him the thought of all the grace and loving help which he had received throughout his life, and pointed him to his only Comfort and Support. It may be gathered from one of his letters that he once spent twenty-two hours in prayer with a person passing through a prolonged death agony, most probably in the use of devotions such as these. With continual prayer he tried to help others, for it was the breath of his own life. Dr. Liddon used to speak of him as 'constantly communicating in prayer throughout the day with his Gracious and Awful Friend': and Dr. Pusey doubtless describes himself, without intending to do so, when he speaks, in one of his Lenten Sermons in 1862, of those 'whose home is prayer, whose labour is prayer, whose rest is prayer[1].' He frequently said that to turn to his prayers was like going home.

Since these letters derive their importance from their subject and their writer, all marks that would suggest the person to whom they were written have, so far as possible, been uniformly omitted. It is obvious that many of them were written in connexion with his great work of founding and guiding the early years of the restored work of Sisterhoods in the English Church; and it is hoped that they will still be of value to such institutions. But Dr. Pusey's advice was sought very widely— probably as widely as that of any man ever has been. With reference to only one side of this work, in a letter to the Editor of the *Times* in 1866, wishing to show the widespread demand for opportunities of Private Confession, he wrote: 'I have been applied to to receive Confession from persons in every rank, of every age, old as well as young, in every profession, even those which you would think least accessible to it—army, navy, medicine, law.' And if those who sought him for this purpose were so numerous, there were many more whose respect and love made them

[1] 'Lenten Sermons,' p. 337.

ask his counsel or desire his blessing on the work in which they were engaged. In illustration of this, one scene may now be described to which allusion could not be made when the last volume of his 'Life' was written. In 1881, when Mr. Gladstone was Prime Minister, he was spending a few days in Oxford; and he called to see Dr. Pusey. The visit was for many reasons an act of the most kindly consideration, and it gave Dr. Pusey the most genuine pleasure. 'Only think,' he said playfully to one of his friends later in the day, 'of the Prime Minister being kept waiting in my hall, while the servant came to ask whether I would see him.' Then he went on to say how very kind he thought it of Mr. Gladstone, with all he had to think about as Prime Minister, to come and call on him; and he added in a tender tone, 'He was so affectionate: when he went away he kissed my hand, and knelt down, and asked for my blessing.' It was their last meeting in this world. The next time that Mr. Gladstone stood at that well-known door in the corner of the Great Quadrangle of Christ Church, it was as a pall-bearer at Dr. Pusey's funeral; and the crowd of men who on that day joined with him in the solemn procession towards the Cathedral witnessed to the thousands of souls who bless God for the help which He gave them through the words and works of Dr. Pusey.

The Editors desire again to express their thanks to all those who sent to Dr. Liddon the letters that are here printed. In nearly all cases, a second permission has been given for their insertion in this volume. If, in any instance, this permission has not been asked, the Editors offer their apologies for the omission. They desire also to express their thanks to the Governors of the Pusey House for permission to photograph the bust which appears as the frontispiece to this volume. This bust is the work of Mr. George Richmond, R.A. A special interest is attached to it as reproducing with exact fidelity the casts which were taken of Dr. Pusey's head after death.

CONTENTS

I
LETTERS OF COUNSEL AND SYMPATHY . . 1–128

II
LETTERS ON INTELLECTUAL DIFFICULTIES . . 129–171

III
LETTERS ON THEOLOGICAL AND ECCLESIASTICAL SUBJECTS 173–291

IV
FRAGMENTS OF CONVERSATIONS AND LETTERS . 293–344

I

LETTERS OF COUNSEL AND SYMPATHY

LETTER I.

To a Mother.

Fifth Monday in Easter, 1847.
[*May* 3.]

You have indeed an anxious, yet blessed charge to rear so many young plants for Heaven. Yours seems Martha's office, tending Christ in those He has made His. Yet it need not distract one, so one endeavour to keep Him always before one. The mode of service, not the service, changes. There is often less time to be alone with God, but so you may learn to be with God in all you do, and do all to Him. Such is the way in which most must be perfected. Few have leisure. It is through and in toil that most must win God. Mary's lot is for most hereafter. Yet Mary's spirit may be amid Martha's toil. You will find, in whatever degree you can practise it, that the habit of committing single actions, again and again, through the day, to God, in their beginning, middle, end, does still the soul very much, and make life a continual living in the Presence of God. Not that I mean that you are not learning this (as all must be learning it), but that where there is much occupation, these two habits, (1) committing single actions or courses of action to God, (2) using short intervals of leisure for short prayers darted up to Him, do replace longer prayers. All life is business or brief leisure, and this provides for both....

With regard to external acts of reverence, I think with you, that any such acts as would excite general attention, as the 'kneeling in going out of Church, out of reverence to the Altar' or our Lord's gift of Himself to us there, are better avoided. At Christ Church, Oxford, it is a transmitted custom for the Canons to turn on leaving the choir and bow to the Altar. Elsewhere, I should not do so.

But the Elements having been consecrated, I do myself think it a part of reverence not to let them fall, or a part of them; although one should wish to do this, so as, as little as might be, to disturb others or myself.

I have had no conversation with your daughter on any subject of controversy; she knows that I think it best for her to avoid all such subjects. And on what you say as to 'the practical shortcomings of our Church,' the only way for any is to make all the use they can of what God gives them in her, own themselves unworthy of more, pray for it, if God sees it good for them, and that He would bless to their souls what they have. God has been so wonderfully good to us, that we may have every hope for the time to come. But, indeed, what I think your daughter would feel, are real privations. To you who have been educated in other times, much would not seem a privation, which must to a younger mind. We never had formerly any idea of anything but rare Communions. Our clergy had become used to the least which our Church allows, and indeed less; for if the Holy Communion is celebrated only four times a year it is impossible for all poor communicants (where there are families) to receive it so often. When the Holy Communion was thought of chiefly as a commemoration, it was natural that this should not be much felt. Indeed, good people came to think it more reverent to partake less frequently, and they were afraid lest more frequent Communion should diminish their reverence. One must respect all such feelings. But it is very different, when people believe it to be 'the Bread of Life,' ' the strengthening and refreshing of the soul by the Body and Blood of Christ,' that in It, 'our sinful bodies are made clean by His Body, and our souls washed through His most precious Blood,' that 'Christ dwelleth in us and we in Him,' as our Prayer Book teaches from Holy Scripture.

When the soul hopes to obtain great grace and blessing through Holy Communion and the increased Presence of its Lord in It, and has known or heard of more frequent Communions, then the way in which It is, in our country parishes often intermitted for two or three months, is very dreary. Everything else a person can replace for himself. If he has been accustomed to Daily Prayers in Church, he can say them by himself, in union with those who say them. But the Holy Communion he cannot, if a layman, obtain for himself. And this is one of the great practical difficulties for many persons now. Persons, e. g., spend part of the year in London. If they have the opportunity and God gives them the desire, they would not do right not to receive the Holy Communion when It is administered (as It may be) weekly. But the contrast, to be for whole months without It, is very dreary. I know not how it is with ———. But in his college weekly Communion has been restored. I know not how often the young men communicate. But whatever a person has been accustomed to, whether once a fortnight, or monthly, or weekly, it is a dreary change to lose it. God is restoring frequent Communions everywhere, or rather putting into people's hearts to desire more frequent Communions, and the Clergy to restore them; but the interval is a time of frequent trouble to individuals. This is the one subject which I should fear might be oppressive at times to your daughter. She does believe the Holy Communion to be an especial channel of the grace of God to her soul; she has found strength and blessedness in It; more frequent Communions gladden her and carry her on; they diminish the risk of depression at other times. Hers is a bright, sunny mind. I do not fear for her. But I do very much wish that there could be opportunities of more frequent Communion for her at home....

If she had this, she would not feel any 'short-comings' in the Church. And since, in the early centuries as in the Apostles' times, Holy Communion was daily, it cannot be thought an undue wish that it should be monthly, or, if God permit, weekly.

There is one other subject on which I ought to write plainly. You say you think it safest to turn the mind altogether from the Church of Rome, its convents, &c. Now, with regard to the Church of Rome I wrote in the last letter. Your daughter's delicacy of health, and her home duties for some time to come, would make it wrong to be anticipating anything for the future. Also, I should not *suggest* any such thoughts. But, having professed to write to [you] plainly, I ought to say what I do think. (1) That although marriage is honourable, our Lord implies that celibacy may be embraced "for the kingdom of God's sake"; and St. Paul (1 Cor. vii. 34) speaks of it, as more favourable for "caring for the things of the Lord only." (2) This was held to be so throughout all the ages to which our Church refers, as the purest. (3) United life, among those who purposed and chose freely to live unmarried (in other words, convents, in their purity), was promoted by all those of whom our Church (in the Homilies) speaks with most affectionate reverence, as the great lights of the Church. The absence of such institutions has been mourned by pious minds in our later Church, as Archbishop Leighton. (4) There are very crying evils among us in our great towns, which can only be remedied in this way. If female purity is to be preserved or restored, and great numbers of our children are to be educated for their Redeemer, instead of (as now they are) for Satan, it can only be (in our great towns) by united efforts of persons devoted to this. I do, then, look with deep interest to the longing which has, for many years, more or less (yet more of late), been springing up in the minds of many young women to devote themselves to God in the service of His poor and of His sick or neglected members, 'His lambs.' This feeling has not originated in anything my friends have written. On the contrary, we were afraid of the whole subject, because, until God should provide us such Institutions, to foster such wishes was only to create a longing, by which people might be tempted out of our Church. What really did give rise to it, outwardly, has been the renewed intercourse with the Continent, and the knowledge and sight (more or less) of the different Institutions there, through which so much good is done so simply and devotedly. But, besides this, I am sure that I have seen in many minds and heard of a deep drawing of God to serve Him more devotedly, which has issued in the longing for that mode of life.

As I said, this is, for some time at least, an abstract question as to your daughter, and so, one on which it would be wrong for her to dwell and upon which her mind will not and does not dwell. Before it could be fit for her to entertain the subject, God may have provided for her in another way, and perfected her for Himself. But I thought I ought thus fully to explain my own feelings on the general subject to you. Your daughter's wish to lead a single life was long before my acquaintance with her: she also knew, not from me, that there is such an Institution in our Church, sanctioned by Bishops; but her duties are plain for some time to come, and she does not wish to look beyond them.

And now I have told you my whole mind, in any way in which it could anyhow affect your daughter. This is not a practical subject for her now. I hope it will not pain you that your daughter has mentioned the subject to me as one which has been for some time floating before her mind. It seemed to her to be giving you needless pain to name it to you, while it was something indefinite and distant. Yet she was sorry that there should be any seeming reserve on any subject upon which you did not know her whole feelings. And now she is glad that your letter (of *part* of which I told her) has removed all reserve, although, before, she kept back this ulterior wish not to pain you.

You will forgive my saying that in the case of my own child, I should commit the matter to God, praying Him to direct her. While a wish is thus at a distance, frequent discussion gives pain and changes nothing. These wishes are not changed by anything outward. Especially, discussion among relatives is very distressing and does no good. Forgive me for saying then, that if the case were my own, I should not mention the subject to any one besides. All you wish *now* for your daughter, she wishes also: she wishes to love and serve and please God better, and you for His sake and for your own. The future then you may fearlessly trust to Him Whose it is. Does not this come under the rule of 'not taking anxious thought for the morrow' which may never be?

LETTER II.

To the Same.

August 5 [1847 *or* 1848].

I have been long wishing to write to you, but delaying it until a freer time, and now there is a subject of natural heaviness for the time, and I trust abiding peace and consolation. It is indeed a solemn, sacred existence which your dear child now has, to have God's messenger within her as it were, to call her whenever He sees best for her. Even I cannot but wish that such as she should abide somewhat longer here, to spread abroad to others that love wherewith God has kindled her heart. And yet when I saw her so growing in deep love for God, as she has, I could not but think that He might be ripening her for something. Whom in His eternal Wisdom He means to take early, in His eternal Love He ripens early. Perhaps He would not so have ripened them had He not meant to take them. I clung round my own dear Lucy; she too was so full of promise; so with the whole power of her soul devoted to God. I hoped it might have pleased Him that she should have flourished in His courts here, to win others to love Him. He willed otherwise,—that she should glorify Him by death, not by life; and she passed away. Yet I could not grieve for her. He Who loved her and had taught her to love Him, chose for her the portion which He saw best for her, and which He had from all eternity fore-ordained for her; and He Whom she had chosen for her Portion has become her Portion, not in faith only, nor in hope, but in truth; not here in the shadow of death, but there in the land of the living. " Thou art my Portion, O Lord, in the land of the living."

And much more, with your dear ——, whose life has been here more matured, and has seen more of its trials, although she could not have a firmer choice or a more faithful love of the One Object of faith and love. And there is a special comfort in this solemn disease which she has (which was also my child's), that it is placed there directly by God's hand. If people catch fevers, or in many cases of consumption or coughs, one would naturally think, 'If it had not been for this or that, she might have been with us still, to the glory of God.' These are the seeds of certain death, whenever they are called out, and, although it is possible, it is scarcely possible that it should be God's Will that they should not. It is, I suppose, so very rare a case, especially with one of so slight and frail a constitution as your dear child, and where the disease is, I believe, hereditary. This is no reason why she should not be careful. On the contrary, one should wish that whenever the messenger should come, it should be evident that He sent it. One should wish too that she should not miss any of the time in which it may please God to perfect her, or make her an instrument of His love to her sisters or to others. But still, I suppose, we must expect that if God continue our own lives a little, we shall witness that summons. And when it comes, it will, I am told, like my dear Lucy's, be a very rapid one. But fear not. It too will be a blessed close. The lamp of faith and love will be trimmed more brightly yet, ere she be called to meet the Bridegroom : and you cannot sorrow when you think that the death of the body is but the opening gate of Paradise, and that she will be in His presence Whom now 'not seeing, she loves.'

It is a solemn existence for those around her too, that,

however long God may continue her here, there is at any time but a little space between her and death. Perhaps, whenever the time comes, a fortnight or three weeks of actual severe illness may close her life. And so her sisters will learn, I hope, to prize her, and act towards her as one who might, at any time, within so short a time, be out of sight. It seems an additional blessing to herself also, to know beforehand that there are within her these seeds of death; for as they say that, at all times, we should aim to do actions as though it were the last time, yet it makes this more sensible when the last time may be at any time so near.

Fear not. He Who has so loved her 'will provide' what is best for her. May He ever bless you all.

LETTER III.

ON THE DEATH OF A CHILD.

No one but a mother, who has had her last-born child taken from her, can know what the loss is. What any one can say is so on the surface. And they grate or seem unfeeling out of simple ignorance. Everything must seem very hopeless to you. It was so to me, humanly speaking, when God took [my wife]. I dared neither look backward nor forward. I dared not look back to those eleven years of scarce earthly happiness. Onwards life looked so dreary, I could not bear to think of it. So I bound myself, as our Lord bids us, to the day, and I resumed my work for God on the Monday after that Saturday, when her body was committed to its resting-place. I used for some time (I know not how long) to see, on my way to Cathedral-prayers, the white of the pall wave, as it had waved with the wind on that Saturday at that particular spot; and I used (as I have done since) to say a Collect for her, as I passed to and fro by her dear resting-place; and I kept the hour when she gave her spirit to God. And so God kept me on day by day. It seemed as if I was in deep water up to the chin, and a Hand was under my chin supporting it. I thought I could never smile again. . . . Many felt very lovingly for me; but it was too deep for sympathy. It was all on the surface, and the wound was deep down below. I remember when dear J[ohn] K[eble] came first to see [me], I turned the subject and spoke of other things. He wrote and said he must have been very wanting. I said, 'it was my own doing, I could not bear it.' So I lived on, my real self sealed up, except when I had to sympathize with deep sorrow, and then I found that my letters were of use, just because I owned the human hopelessness.

But then, it must be only 'human' hopelessness. Since God chasteneth whom He loveth, the deeper the chastening the deeper the Love. And so God has some great work for you, in you, since His hand has been so heavy. But He will, I trust, give you joy in your other children; but you cannot anticipate now what He will do. "What I do thou knowest not now, but thou shalt know hereafter." "No chastisement for the present seemeth to be joyous, but grievous; nevertheless, it afterwards yieldeth the peaceable fruit of righteousness to them that are exercised thereby."

Act day by day for the day. Thank God each day for all the blessings of the day, all the promise which you see in any of your children. I was frightened, when I saw your troubles so apparently taking possession of your mind, that God's great mercies in the recent conversion of —— and the impulse for good which He gave —— seemed to be so hidden behind them. God teaches us by St. Paul to be (1) "careful for nothing"; (2) to "make our request known to God in everything"; but he adds (3) "with thanksgiving"; and then he promises (4) "and the peace of God, which passeth all understanding, *shall* keep your hearts and minds." St. Paul does not say it as a wish for them. It is an absolute promise. Do the one and God will do the other. All who have tried it have found it so. So many forget the "with thanksgiving." Take God at His Word, and you will find it so. In eternity, by His mercy, you will find that even your daily trials . . . are mercies. God would, by them, make you what He would have you. They are so many corrections of pride. Without them you might be sweet, loving, tender; but you would not have meekness brought out. The religious proverb says, 'There is no humility without humiliation.' Moses, from the fire of his middle age, was made the 'meekest man on the earth,' by the continued ingratitude and bickerings of those 600,000 whom God sent him to deliver. Almighty God . . . observes you, is ready with His grace to help you if you will, says of you, if you are meek (so to speak), '—— took that meekly for love of Me.' This is what He expresses by the things being 'written in His book.' You are under the Captain of your salvation. His Eye is upon you. One great battle which you have, is to learn meekness. . . . Each [trial] is a chip to mould you to that likeness of Him, Who says to each of us, "Learn of Me, for I am meek and lowly of heart." Take them so, and God will infuse sweetness into the bitterness.

. . . What a great mystery life is! God sends us into the world, to form us amid life's daily nothings and trials for that character which we are to have throughout eternity; and every trial is like the blow of the statuary which makes the unshapen block take the form of beauty which He wills for it.

LETTER IV.

To a Mother on the Death of her Son.

Whit Monday, 1865.

Fear not. He Who in His everlasting Love made your boy for that home, has disposed all things well for him. Our shortcomings do not injure the purpose of His Love. One's comfort is in the absolute knowledge of God. It is to us mysterious why He should have taken those who seem so full of promise. God only knows. We only know His purpose of Love, and that He Who made them in His eternal Love knew, when He made them, how and when He should perfect them. You have then nothing to fear of loss to him, and, while your diligence will be quickened to those who remain and who may have to pass through this life's storms, you will think of him as having attained that place around the Eternal Throne, for which God in His Love created him.

It is indeed a sorrowful gap, one which makes a mother's heart ache for many a year, and which is never perhaps quite filled up, except in the habitual thought that God has given you the privilege of bearing one who is, in ceaseless adoration, loving and praising God, and who, in that same love, is longing for the coming of you all to the bliss which he himself knows. The thought of having one whom they love in Paradise, often, by God's grace, draws to Him the brothers and sisters who remain. May God the Holy Ghost shed abundantly His comfort and love in all your hearts.

Do not think yourself unresigned, because of the bursts of grief which there must be. These wounds of His Love would not be so healing, if they were not so deep. Only look to Him. The meek look of sorrow to your Father is resignation.

LETTER V.

SYMPATHY ON THE DEATH OF A DAUGHTER.

All Saints' Day, 1868.

I did not write to you in your former sorrows, because I only heard of them so long afterwards. I have just heard of your last. Alas, alas, what a world of sorrow it is; and God has visited you very sorely. It is sad to think of you, as relates to this world, like a tree with all the branches hewn off. Yet your store, though lessened in this world, is increased in Paradise; and there, by God's mercy, we hope soon to be, and to find those, with whom we had to part for a while. To me too it is happy to think of your good daughter, perfected, as she is now. How much more to you!

God comfort you, my dear friend, in this your last deep sorrow, as He will. "Heaviness may endure for the night, but joy cometh in the Morning." And night is coming for us too, so that the Morning is not far off. And meanwhile, the deeper the sorrow, the deeper His Love.

Meantime, I am glad to hear that you have one, as Ruth to Naomi, to soothe your bereaved age, as far as human tenderness can.

LETTER VI.

TO A HUSBAND ON THE DEATH OF HIS WIFE.

It is then, the close of a life here, of great singleness of purpose and devoted service of our Lord.

It is a sad break to you, after all these years: but so God has appointed that, in this world of sin, every departure from it should involve suffering, and that the greater, the more beautiful the soul was which He removes. One thought which you have, my dearest ——, is, that it is but for a short time. You are but seven years short of the threescore years and ten; and although a mother is perhaps the most invaluable of the temporal gifts of God, He has continued the gift to your children, far beyond the usual time.

But you too, as well as I formerly, have at last to close your eyes, and say, 'Thy Will alone is good, O my God: Thy Will be done.'

God bless and comfort you and yours.

LETTER VII.

SYMPATHY.

November 11, 1873.

There was only time to write to —— yesterday, before the afternoon post, and I thought you had rather I should write to her. There is, alas! so little to be said. The Comforter alone can comfort. One only thing I know; I dared not to look forward, not a day, nor an hour. I neither dared look backwards nor forwards, but bound myself to the present instead. This differs with many, but I am sure there ought to be no looking forward, unless God makes a change to be a duty. I remember —— lying on her sofa, unable to move, recently a widow, with her nine young children, so changed I knew her only by her widow's cap; and she said, 'In the morning I know that God Who brought me to the morning will bring me to the evening, and in the evening that He Who has brought me to the evening will bring me to the morning.' It struck me as so simple and so true.

LETTER VIII.

To a Husband on the Death of his Wife.

April 22, 1879.

You have, I trust, had every consolation which you could have had. At our age, partings cannot be for long: we have only to prepare for the Great Meeting. Bodily suffering has, since our blessed Lord's meritorious Sufferings for us, been so sanctified to the soul, that one cannot but reverentially sympathize with those, whose friends have died with more than usual bodily suffering. Much more when she, who is now out of sight, was so near as she was whom you have just lost. I have seen in several experiences, and heard in others, how God has blessed the soul through them in ways which others know not of.

I am glad that you have . . . living close to you. . . . I could only wish that they could be to you, what my son has been to me these many years. Solitary, in one sense, a widower's life must be; but I trust that it is in God's good Providence that your son has seemingly no occupation which should interfere with the ministering to your remaining years. . . .

LETTER IX.

TRUST IN GOD.

1865.

Do not lose courage. You have been doing things for God, and God has loved you and loves you, and would not let you rest without loving Him more. You know that the only remedy is prayer. Do not think about the dullness—that your heart is not stirred by what used to stir it. Give yourself, whatever you are, to God; 'Good or bad, I am Thine'; 'I am Thine, O save me.' Hold fast to God with your will. You know that He has said, "Whoso cometh unto Me, I will in no wise cast out." We come to Him by our will. Without Him, we could not will to be His.

Do not analyze whether you do a thing to 'satisfy conscience or out of love for God.' Say to God often, 'For Thee alone.' Pray Him to be the End of all your ends, and do each thing, by His help, the very best you can.

Resist all ideas that you are unable to pray. The power to pray comes with praying. You know, Of ourselves we know not what to ask, but the Spirit helpeth our infirmities. But He helpeth us when trying to pray, not when we are not trying. You think that you *will* be unable; but this is imagination only; while you are weighing whether or no you can do His Will, you are by yourself; and you know very truly that you cannot. Kneel down to pray, asking His help, and He will pray in you. God tells us in Holy Scripture that He will help you; He does not give us a private assurance (as it were) what He will do. But when we are in act trying to do His Will, He helps us.

Do not dwell on past failures in themselves; but tell God, 'Would, O my God, I had not, in this or this or this, offended Thee.' And He will make it as if it had not been. Fear not. Jesus intercedes for you ever, and He is Almighty.

May He bring you safe through your troubles and bless you.

LETTER X.

Delayed Answer to Prayer.

December 11, 1879.

God be thanked and praised for His goodness to ——, and in him to you. Now you know that He was hearing you while you were sick at heart, that He seemed not to hear you. He was doubtless waiting the time, when the last motion of grace which would fix him would be effectual; but was giving him, all the time, the graces to which he would most respond, or saving him from what he might otherwise have fallen into, or re-recalling him, if he stumbled.

So now you will thank and bless Him not only for this last goodness, but for all the rest, which you feared that He did not give him.

LETTER XI.

Sorrow and Controversy.

Ascot, October 20, 1880.

My pleasant time is to be over on Saturday. My infirmities have been a great hindrance to our seeing one another. I have given up hearing long sentences, though your voice is so clear; for fear of misunderstanding what is said.

I have written what I could to poor ——, for it is soothing to have one's hopes echoed. "Out of the deep" issued in "O Israel, trust in the Lord; for with the Lord there is mercy; and with Him there is plenteous Redemption."

I have written a useless letter of remonstrance to ——, saying that in all this agitating there are two parties whom we leave out of consideration, of very different importance: but One of very great weight; with the other we have a very intimate relation;—Almighty God and ourselves.

In our early Tractarian days, we used a prayer out of Daniel ix, with other prayers of humiliation and for internal unity. J. H. Newman drew them up at my wish. Now we seem to do nothing but bark at and devour one another.

But there is no use in complaining, except to God.

LETTER XII.

VOCATION.

November, 1877.

The one question is, whether God calls us: it is not whether we feel fit or no. If God gives us the call, God will give us the grace. We may under-estimate ourselves, as well as over-estimate ourselves. St. Paul said, "Who is sufficient for these things?" If St. Paul, how much more we? The question is not as to anything in the past or present; but as to the call of God. If God calls us, He will fit us. When God put our soul into the bodies which we received of our parents, He had His own special purpose for each of us. He willed each of us to be saved in doing our own appointed work. He had us and our whole selves to be formed in our own special way. We sometimes hear of a person mistaking his profession; of his being, e. g., a good lawyer spoiled, a good man of business spoiled, i.e. he had missed the employment of life for which God adapted [him].

I cannot tell what your calling is; I know only certain outward dispositions: hold up your soul as a sheet of white paper to God, for Him to write on it what He wills. He has promised to hear prayer: say with St. Augustine, "Give what Thou commandest, and command what Thou willest." Do not hurry, but pray Him to teach you.

LETTER XIII.

SELF-CONSCIOUSNESS.

1844.

I may have given you too many rules at once, and so it might be better to concentrate yourself on some few points, to get rid of this all-destroying self-reflection. You never can make any solid progress, until you have uprooted this. It may be unfit that you should, else you might make even good minister to evil, and become worse through what would in itself have been good. It is the worst form of idolatry, setting up yourself as the idol in God's stead, and using any good thoughts from Him to deck out your idol; referring God to self instead of yourself to God.

I wish I knew how to help you, but it seems too deep for me. One only can help you. You seem to want a re-creation of your inner self, a revolution which shall turn you round, so, as I said, to make God, instead of self, your centre. It is a great work. This thought of self seems so to have rooted in you, and twined round all thoughts and words and actions. However, all is gained if you are conscious that you have a great work before you, and that you cannot of yourself do it, and wish it done or begun in you.

I do not say this to discourage you. If you desire and pray earnestly that this rooted thought of self be plucked out of you, all is well. Accidental falls there will be, and this should goad you on to more exertion. . . .

Society is not the place for looking devout. You had better make it a place of recreation altogether, only in the fear of God, than try to obtain a higher tone of mind, and then see what people think of it. Better to do common duties in a common way than attempt things higher and then abuse them to idolatry. You should think yourself unfit for it, until you have more self-mastery. Avoid any outward action in society which may betray any inward good feeling.

You ask for penance. I suppose the severest would be to bind you to tell some of the party the foolish thoughts you had in relation to themselves. I am not going to lay this upon you, but if you would shrink from this, you may realize the more how great the foolishness. I would only say then at present, use daily Ps. cxxxi, and picture to yourself your Lord saying to you, "Verily, I say unto you, they *have* their reward;" and think on for a while what it is to have the reward so as to have none in store. Pray daily for humility, and try daily to do certain acts of humility. Check every rising feeling at once. . . .

I suspect one source of wrong with you is having been able to enter into the thoughts of others, and make them intellectually your own, without making them part of your life and acting upon them; you would thus be thought unduly of, as though you acted as you spoke, and your speaking (as Mr. N[ewman] says in the 'Lyra') makes acting otherwise 'a sin against the light[1].'

---

[1] 'Lyra Apostolica,' lxvii, line 12.

LETTER XIV.

FEELINGS.

[1844.]

You must not allow yourself in morbid or misgiving feelings. Seek to do what by God's grace you can; continue acts of repentance for past failures; sorrow for present shortcomings; and then commit yourself and your all to a loving Saviour, Who has borne so long with us and had compassion on us.

The immediate occasion of this is that, I fear, there is something unhealthy about your sorrow and self-reproaches; there may be a secret impatience or irritation that you cannot at once be what you would, which is not true penitence or humility. We are what we have made ourselves; and we must pray God to unmake and remake us, and must not be vexed if, while we are pulling down the old decayed wall we daubed over, the dust fly in our eyes, or bats and unclean creatures flit about us. Only let us strive that they do not nestle again, and the loathsome sight of them may do us good.

LETTER XV.

SELF-ESTEEM.

Perhaps you have too many rules, and it might be better to set in good earnest about some. And yet I hardly know what to part with. But do be very earnest about speech. You know not what snares you may be preparing for yourself, e.g. by your conversation with Roman Catholics; it seems all parade of self on holy subjects, and unconsciously cherishing discontent as to your own Church. Try to set before yourself, that to seek man's praise is to lose God's. The following happened a few years ago. A clergyman[1] sitting, I think in his garden (I forget whether in a sort of dream), saw a neighbouring clergyman, a popular preacher. He asked him the hour. A[nswer]. 'Half-past one. I have been in Hell half an hour, because I loved the praise of man more than the praise of God.' The next day another asked him, 'Do you know that that devoted Mr. —— is gone to his reward?' 'When did he die?' 'At one, yesterday.' Such is the outline of the history. It was told me with the name of the clergyman who saw it. This love of praise eats out the good of everything; you are casting out with your own hands any treasure you may acquire, and taking in sand to sink your vessel. Do then be resolute as to this. When you have made an offering to God, do not

---

[1] This incident was wrongly supposed to have occurred to Dr. Pusey himself. It was mentioned in the July number of the *Nineteenth Century*, 1884, in an article on 'Apparitions.'

ask for it back again to sacrifice it to self. Such things as 'hinting at self's abstinent living and unworldliness in town,' what are they but a more refined worldliness? How much better when people in simplicity enjoy self and are thankful, than seemingly to give up self in order to make self-praise one's end!

I trust that if you are in real earnest about this, other things will prosper better. While this lasts, everything may turn to poison, because into self-esteem. It may be that God withdraws His sensible Presence in devotion, because, until then, there may be an unfitness in your having It, and you might be doing yourself harm. This self-love is the right eye which must be plucked out. While this lasts, you may be like a person who is tied, though by one chain, and allowed, as it seems, to walk on, yet it is, after all, a mere weary walking round and round the one place to which he is fixed. That place to which you may be fixed, is self. Break this and, instead of this weary round, you may walk on freely to God.

I know not whether you are in anything attempting too much, e.g. as to dress. I have seen persons in station much above yours in very simple dress. It may be again that you are making a snare for yourself, by thinking that you are doing great things; whereas, after all, how little a sacrifice would it be, did not self-love magnify it. If one thinks of the Day of Judgement, or the shortness of life, how utterly contemptible are all these poor things, how utterly [contemptible] even in this world's estimation. We are now reading Ecclesiastes; try to realize its lesson, that everything is vanity and vexation out of God.

I can hardly answer your question about expenses. I should rather say, Try to obtain the habit of thinking what is spent upon self, as the necessary compliance with infirmity.

LETTER XVI.

Parental Claims.

November 18, 1874.

You must not expect 'the course of true' heavenly 'love to run smooth' any more than earthly love, which the proverb says never does. God always allows trials to come, to test sincerity, and to make us the more prize His gift.

To bear this hindrance will be a channel of grace to you. If you have not written to your mother, you will write to her a loving letter, acceding to her wish to stay until spring. Spring will soon be here, and a cheerful acquiescence in her wish will leave a pleasant remembrance in her mind.

Over and above God's usual way it is natural and loving in your parents not to wish to part with you, unless for something which they would *understand* to be for your happiness: and it is natural that your father should not understand what is new and foreign to his habits of thought.

So do not think . . . that any strange thing has happened to you. Your father naturally wishes to be satisfied that this is a mature wish on your part since it is contrary to your early tastes.

It may make you the more sorry for having lived once for this world to think, 'Had I always lived to God they would not have doubted about me now.'

Pray God much for real humility, and that you may know your own nothingness.

LETTER XVII.

THE RELIGIOUS LIFE.

November 7, 1874.

I am thankful that God has fixed your choice on the religious life. Letters say so little, that perhaps I am unduly alarmed about you. Perhaps what frightens me is that you seem so certain about yourself. There seems to me a sort of hardness, which I should wish to see melted. 'How,' you will think, 'can there be hardness where there is so much love?' Well, perhaps the fire and the iron are side by side, and the fire has not yet changed the iron into steel by penetrating it. And I suppose that it is pride which keeps them apart. I wonder whether you have thought not only of the habitual but of the actual grace necessary. It always seems to me that if God gives you the grace to choose a good thing, then you think that your strong will would do the rest. I have to-day seen a mind of that sort, strong love and a strong will: but somehow the faults come from that strong unsoftened will, in details.

The 'passionate love for Jesus' cannot be too strong. What a strong, fiery, passionate love St. Paul's was! He was on fire with love. Yet how pliant he was, whenever he could be! He retained his individuality, but it was like iron at white heat, transparent with light, glowing with the inward fire: pliant, yet iron still.

I would have you anxious for nothing, . . . except for

the grace of God. Whatever of natural good qualities you have will remain all the safer, when penetrated by that grace. St. Paul retained all his individuality. So did St. Peter and St. John. One sees the individuality, even when they wrote, inspired and, as it is said of them, "full of the Holy Ghost." No right course of action will destroy those natural graces of which you wrote, individuality and ideality. You will be yourself still, but ensouled, I hope, with the grace of God.

I write this the rather now, because some think that 'obedience' interferes with individuality of character. 'Obedience,' the wise man says, 'speaketh victories.' It interferes not with individuality, but with self-will. There is always scope for whatever ability God may have given any one. Self-will only misdirects energy; and obedience is so helpful, because we are so full of self-will.

I think that you had better go at first to St. Saviour's, where, I think, I gathered from you that God gave you a call through —— . . . You will have to be accustomed to look away from things outward, and to discern Him Who is invisibly present. And one may even be helped to concentrate one's soul on His Unseen Presence, when one is away from things otherwise beseeming It[1].

Do write to ——, if you have not written in the interval. I think that your health would probably be better amid practical life, doing something for our dear Lord. There is always work fitted for the strength or weakness of each.

I do not think that there is any good in waiting. The work of grace goes on in and through acting.

God bless you.

[1] i.e. things reverent.

LETTER XVIII.

Religious Occupations.

[1874.]

In thinking over the account of your occupations, I rather seem to miss occupations involving the showing of love. The only one apparently is the teaching of your little sister. Your mother is (you say) very independent; you are, if I understood you right, rather apart from the rest. Your chief occupation (sacred embroidery), though it is for the glory of God, and for the honour of His Sacrament, is still solitary, involves no sacrifice of your own will, or giving way to others. It is so far a mode of life, which would rather foster a habit of following your own way, dislike of being put out, in fine, self-will and selfishness, because except your occupation with your little sister, it does not draw out love. But acts of love increase love; love, without acts, dies out.

I should doubt not that the visiting the poor (as your physical strength may permit) would be a good to you, because it would increase your love. Only you would not visit them in your secular relation, but as those whose outward lot our Lord chose for Himself, and who are the special bequests of our Lord to His Church, the representatives of Himself; above others, of such is the kingdom of heaven. You would go to learn of the good among them; anyhow, they are all better, I doubt not, than the corresponding characters in the wealthier classes.

I feel more doubt in saying anything about your sedentary employment, because of the illness which you had.

But doing Church embroidery cannot be the business of life, unless it be the means of gaining a livelihood, the state of life to which it should please God to call any. I should have suggested an office of love (as intercession for others) but that it might be a strain if simultaneous with other employments. Yet ejaculatory prayers, i.e. little thoughts or prayers darted up to God in the midst of one's every day's occupations, increase very much our treasures of prayer, and, if they were for others, would return into one's own bosom, in the way also that they would increase in us that 'most excellent gift of charity.' Do you know the 'Society of the Love of Jesus'? It was begun some (I forget how many, twenty-three perhaps) years ago, so that there should be no moment, night or day, in which some of its members were not praying to God for the conversion of sinners. So whenever you should pray for their conversion, you would be praying with others. And God has heard their prayers in a way which seemed to me beforehand miraculous. Only all Grace is miraculous.

Will you also set yourself to think, for what end God sent you into this world? God has His design for every one. Each soul has to be formed for its own special beauty in the Heavenly courts. No soul is like another soul. Most souls of women are formed through the duties of wives and mothers; others through 'the religious life.' I know not, of course, what God may will for you. But give yourself wholly to Him, and pray Him to teach you how you may best please Him.

The ejaculatory prayers would, I think, prevent that aching, under which you suffer. A soul which is not often with God in its occupations is, as it were, in an exhausted receiver, and aches because it is exhausted, having been away from its Life, God, Who made it for Himself.

God bless you.

LETTER XIX.

EXAMINATION OF THE WHOLE LIFE.

Wednesday after 2nd Sunday in Lent, 1844.

I hardly know how far I spoke of self-examination. Did you ever endeavour to examine your whole life, as if you were then to give an account of it to God? [Did you ever] try to recollect every sin you could, tracing along each course of sin, of omission or commission; or examining, year by year, what you can recall which was amiss in each; e.g. if vanity was one, in how many acts it branched out; or negligence in prayer, or sloth; or resistance to the motions of God's Holy Spirit leading you onward; or doing out of respect to man what should have been done to God; or early neglect of duty to parents; if you were ever the occasion of any other's doing wrong; if you have ever been unsubmissive to the Will of God, or loved creatures too much; or neglected or been careless about prayer; or as a child been ever guilty of untruth; or had dislike to any one, or repeated ill of others, though true; or judged hastily, or put bad meanings on actions which might have a good one; or wherein you have been vain, whether of things worthless, or even of things in themselves good; or envied God's gifts to others; or wished yourself other than you are, or shrunk from doing right out of fear of man, or preferred yourself unduly to others, or been vexed when others were praised or noticed and you not; or wished to be thought better than you are; or excused yourself unduly; or wasted the money committed to you; or taken undue delight in things pleasant to any of the senses; or neglected opportunities of good to others?

Briefly, self-examination is generally divided under the Ten Commandments, and (as great sins not coming plainly under them) pride and sloth. Envy would naturally come under the tenth, as anger under the sixth. Then also there are sins of omission.

I believe that some such self-examination, as in the Eye of God, and praying for His light to search all the corners of our heart ("Look well if there be any way of wickedness in me, and lead me in the way everlasting"), solemnly desiring to know one's self and see one's sins as far as one can bear, will to any who had not made it, disclose much of themselves, show perhaps how sins have not been single actions, but connected, e.g. how self-indulgence has been connected with irritation, vanity, or, it may be, with envy; showing at once the aggravated character of any sin, or the mode of remedying it; or, looking far back, one shall see sins, which one had so forgotten that one could hope they had never been, and yet, if one look steadily at them, they have been; or one may see the same evil tendency shaping itself according to our years, and taking some more subtle or refined form, as we grow older, so that we scarcely see that it is sprung from the same root of sin.

Lent is a solemn time for some such self-examination, if it has not yet been made, and especially with the view to see your sins more as God sees them. It may much deepen humility, and earnest desire to gird yourself more to do God's Will, and set you in the way to know yourself more thoroughly.

LETTER XX.

Daily Self-examination.

The best way of self-examination is by dividing the day into two parts, examining yourself first about twelve, then in the evening, when not too tired. This prevents so large an accumulation, which it is difficult to disentangle. Some good questions for self-examination were published a year ago at Toovey's. But one who is thoughtful about himself knows what to inquire about. It is very useful at these solemn seasons to go over one's whole past life, and try to recall to one's self what sins one can, and class them, and confess them from time to time (as on Friday) before God, with some penitential confession as Psalm li. A list may be made intelligible only to one's self by the use of abbreviations. Thus the two first letters of the place where a sin was committed will mark it. These lists are very sorrowful, but very useful in keeping up continual penitence.

LETTER XXI.

Rules for the Spiritual Life.

For One living in Society who was Hoping to become a Sister.

1. To keep the eyes to the ground in God's House, with the feeling of the Publican, and as having sinned by letting them rove, and thinking of man instead of God there.
2. To speak against no one, remembering one's own sins.
3. Not to speak of self.
4. To meet any rising feeling of self-consciousness as often as you can with prayer, as, 'Lord, teach me what I am in Thy sight.'
5. If ever praised, make an inward act of self-abasement.
6. If tempted to think better of yourself than another, 'Set this Thy servant higher in the kingdom of heaven than me unworthy.'
7. Never interrupt another in conversation, and allow yourself always to be interrupted.
8. Study to see all good in others, especially —— :
9. And how pride has corrupted any good [in yourself].
10. Seek occasions to obey —— and to show respect to her.
11. Never dispute if you can help it.
12. Habitually think how every one may be higher in Heaven, may be less a sinner than you.
13. Do acts of humility—wait on yourself.

14. Learn to use prayer in dressing, that you be not found 'unclothed.' Think of the unclothing of the grave.

15. Avöid things which lead to self-display; there can be no need to act charades nor to go to balls, surely; much less to waltz.

16. Pray before entering into conversation, 'Set a watch, O Lord, &c.' (Bishop Andrewes), and that it be 'to the glory of God.'

17. Never use the word 'Dio' in songs except in devotion, nor sing what you do not believe, what is not real.

18. Make some rule as to money which shall involve self-denial, and give what you give in penitence, as having wasted it.

19. Check laughter, as having an earnest work in hand, your own salvation.

20. Be very watchful against exaggeration, and anything which leads to it.

21. Fix (for a month) some hour (e.g. 6) after which always to rise as soon as you awake; (if tired, lie down to sleep in the middle of the day, or go to bed earlier), but keep to hour of rising: (sleep about seven hours, not less).

22. Put off the hour of prayer for nothing of your own; so as not to make a stroke more with pen.

23. Move the moment you are required, so as not to give way to sloth.

24. Speak more slowly.

25. Put nothing in a ludicrous point of view.

26. Say nothing which you think would tell except to God's glory:

27. Nor try to condense things so as to speak vividly.

28. Say plain things in a plain way.

29. Try to speak as in God's Presence—seek not yours, but His.

30. Do not speak against anything.

LETTER XXII.

Spiritual Advice.
August 20, 1838.

I am very glad that you have summoned resolution to write to me, and, though I did not anticipate it (as I did not know on what you were going to write), readily feel that you must have had difficulty: for it is a solemn and earnest thing to write about one's self, and there is a feeling of reluctance annexed to laying open one's self in any degree, as a caution that it is to be done rarely, and only when required by some adequate object.

On the subject upon which you write to me, my general strong impression is that all comfort ought to be of 'God's giving, not of man's taking,' i.e. that it is not our end, but a reward or an encouragement given by God, from time to time, in greater or less degrees, in glimpses, more or less vividly, as He sees good for us; and that the attempt to secure it for ourselves, not being the temper of mind which He sees good for us, ends generally in a false excitement and a fictitious state. I recollect being struck with a saying of Bishop Taylor's, that, 'to look for comfort in prayer and to be anxious for it, was like following our Lord for the loaves and fishes,' or something like this. And Scripture speaks of 'peace' as the direct gift of God. St. Paul begins all the Epistles which he begins in his own name (i.e. all except the Epistle to the Hebrews) by praying for it as God's gift, as much as grace. "Grace be unto you and peace from God our Father and the Lord Jesus Christ," and this is so fixed a form that he varies it only so far, as to the Galatians, to say "from the Father," and to Timothy and Titus he adds "Grace, *mercy*, and peace." St. Peter uses nearly the same form in the Second Epistle, "Grace and peace be multiplied unto you through," &c., still in the passive form, as a gift conveyed to them; and so far in the First Epistle also. St. John in his Second Epistle, as addressed to an individual, uses the same form as St. Paul to Timothy and Titus. And this doubtless was an Apostolic blessing, and they were conveying on, by virtue of their office, the blessing which they had received from their Lord, "Peace I leave with you, My peace I give unto you; not as the world giveth give I unto you:" which seems to be implied by the uniformity of the words used by different Apostles; and indeed the Seventy had the direction to convey it. "Into whatsoever house ye enter, first say, Peace be to this house," as I think also the words "Peace be with you" are a blessing pronounced by the priest in all liturgies; and our other benediction, "The peace of God, &c." (from Phil. iv. 7) conveys the same. Again, when "peace" and "joy" are said to be fruits of the Spirit, i.e. worked in us by the Holy Spirit, or the words "joy of the Holy Ghost" (1 Thess. i. 6), "were filled with joy and the Holy Ghost" (Acts xiii. 52), the same truth is conveyed that Christian joy and peace are worked in the Christian directly by God. They may be lawfully the objects of prayer; but we can no more work them in ourselves, or arrive at them by any process of the understanding, than we can at any other of His gifts.

A good deal of mischief as well as of discomfort has been caused by overlooking this: people have gone about to establish their own peace as the Jews did their own righteousness, and so have missed the 'peace of God.' This is eminently the case with the Wesleyans, whose whole theory is built upon the necessity of having and obtaining peace, and who seem to think that there can be no false peace, and so frequently produce or continue it. The same is, in its degree, the case with the so-called Evangelicals (we may call them *x* to avoid names): and Dr. Arnold's theology, in which you were educated, has a good many *x* ingredients; and one of these is to look to joy and peace, or the feelings, as something in themselves, something to be analyzed, used as a criterion of the spiritual state, acted upon directly, instead of being a result, a reward, or an instrument to lead people on to more faithful exertion. I should not then make it a question, 'whether the words of encouragement or of reproof are meant to apply to my case,' i.e. not I think what you mean by this: for most both are needed, the reproofs to quicken and to keep them vigilant, or to make them fill up that which is lacking, and correct what is yet amiss, or deepen their repentance for what has been so. And so I should think that the fear of being a castaway was sent into many minds from time to time, or doubts whether they might not be falling back, to make them gird themselves up more strongly and press on more vigorously, and so eventually escape being castaways, and obtain a brighter crown. So that I should think the practical way, when any of these feelings come over one, was to see whether one had relaxed in any plan of action which one had formed, or given way to anything amiss; or to sift things, which one was in the habit of doing, to see whether there was anything amiss in them; and to set about correcting these, leaving

> 'Present rapture, comfort, ease,
> As Heaven shall bid them, come and go:—
> The secret this of rest below [1].'

One thing I think I can point out in your present mode of life, as unfavourable to spiritual comfort, and that is

[1] 'Christian Year,' Morning Hymn.

the exclusive pursuit of a professional object; you say, 'I make it a rule hardly to look at these books, except on Sundays, and am as much as possible engaged with medicine in some shape or other from morning to night.' This you seem to have proposed to yourself, as a duty, as I did once in a somewhat similar case, when I was at work at Arabic abroad, and wished to shorten the time in which I was engaged in a study bearing so indirectly on Theology. But I should say from my own experience, that the engrossing pursuit of any study is unhealthy to the spirit, because engrossing; that one becomes unawares engrossed with the means in a degree instead of the end, that the mind (as the very words imply) cannot be in that disengaged, free state, sitting loose to the things of this world, that it ought; that, in fine, it is an unnatural state, and so disarranges the mind, making it restless and unquiet, throwing it off its balance, and making it feverish and distracted. There seems to be a degree of self-will in proposing to do in a given time more than we can naturally do, which is chastened by consequent disarrangement of mind. If it is necessary for a given end, and that end is also necessary, and to be accomplished by our means, then, of course, the self-will disappears; but one ought to be very sure of this, and then seek to cure it by other means—self-discipline. One very obvious one is continued mental prayer not to be engrossed by that wherewith one was occupied; but this will not do, if one is all the while occupying one's self more than one ought to be, because one is then praying against the consequences, which have been annexed as a warning against what one is doing. I should rather, in your case, recommend the diminishing the degree of occupation, and employing it, at intervals if possible, in religious exercises. An hour a day gained in this way would be an act of faith, and, if given up readily (supposing that under the circumstances, which I do not know, it seemed right) would, I doubt not, have an accompanying blessing. The observation of the ancient 'Hours,' or the chief Hours of the day, 9, 12, 3, if it were but for short prayers (such as are in Bishop Cosin), learnt by heart in relation to the wants of those hours, is very healthful.

And now, since you have made me in a sort a spiritual adviser, I will mention two things to you, and you will not be mortified at my naming them, or at my having seen or heard of them. Not to keep you in suspense, I would say at once (with all affection for your general character), that there is one prominent fault, which people least like to be charged with, though so many have it, over-self-esteem, or to speak very plainly, vanity. Knowing very little of your early life, I have no grounds, as I have no reason to judge, how much of a fault this is; nor could I say precisely, on what it turned, what was its principal subject. I might suspect, perhaps, even 'personal appearance,' or something about the person or connected with it, was a subject (as it is a most capricious quality, and they said of an eminent German linguist, Schlegel, that he was vain of everything which was his, down to his elbow-chair). This you can tell far better than myself: whether it be this, or conversation, or general ability, or acquirements, or whether it floats about different things, it will in some shape or other, constitute your trial for some time. And it is of course a very important one, because it has a tendency to corrupt everything we do, by infusing self-satisfaction into it. It is easier to write than to say this, though you will believe I have some reluctance even in writing it; but having seen good sort of people in whom it has grown up even to advanced life, and knowing what a bane it is to spiritual progress, and a hindrance altogether, I could not but think it right to name it. It is often useful that a person should know that any given quality is perceptible to others; it makes them realize more the degree in which it is in them; and I doubt not that, in earnest as you are about yourself, you will set yourself vigorously to correct it.

The other point I have heard of only, and cannot tell wherein it exactly consists; it amounts to this—I know not whether in disputing, or speaking, or objecting—you have said 'strong' latitudinarian things, which have given pain to serious people. I could be sure that you had done this; I do not know how long ago it was, but I imagined it recent. Perhaps you saw that what you said about the inscriptions on the Cross in the Four Evangelists pained me; it was a sort of pain which I do not shrink from, just as you would not from the sight of anything physically painful in a patient: I should be sorry if you were less open with me in consequence: but there was a sort of off-hand, matter-of-course way, which pained me. You will recollect that I answered strongly, not as to yourself, but as to the scheme, which used such arguments. (I have offended in this way formerly myself, I know; so one ought to be the more patient as to the same in others.) Now, you have changed not only your habits of mind, I imagine, but your views in some sort on Theology: you do not adopt those which we aver to be Catholic, but you have probably parted with some which you held, or hold them less peremptorily, or have modified them, and hold others which you did not hold. In a word, your mind has been undergoing a change. But this ought to make you less decided as to those points which you still hold, but which belong to the same peculiar school, some of whose opinions you have modified or abandoned; you ought, at least, to hold your mind in suspense, and not maintain, or give vent to them, except for the purpose of gaining clearer insight, not in mixed societies as matters of discussion, but privately and quietly. For if they be untrue (as you must suppose possible), then as far as this goes, you would be (though ignorantly) yet upholding or circulating untruth, perhaps bringing it to the knowledge of those unacquainted with it, or impressing it on those who know it, or retarding those who are getting rid of it. This necessity of uncertainty upon some points need not make you fear forming a sceptical habit of mind, so that you but distinguish between what is Catholic and private; having found one modern teacher in error, in whom you placed confidence, does not at all involve doubting what has been held not by one but by all. But, besides the possible injury to others, you must do certain injury to yourself, if what you thus speak of is erroneous. For it is not the way to obtain fresh accessions of truth from God, to utter things which (though you know it not) are against His Truth; and the more, if they be such, as, if untrue, are irreverent also, and strike sober-minded people as being such. Thus, I have seen cases, in which the habit of talking against those who held what they called the 'literal inspiration' of Scripture, did the whole mind a great deal of harm, and put it in an irreverent state; as, on the other hand, if it be true that there are great depths in the sayings of the Bible, and manifold truths may be evolved out of them, this way of speaking would indispose a person to receive it [them], and so keep hidden from him much truth. Secretly also, but necessarily, this theory involves regarding much in the composition of the Bible as human, as the theory of the Fathers looks on every jot and tittle as Divine, and the whole as in a higher degree Divine; whereas that other system unravels the Divinity of Holy Scripture, some making the history, some the arguments, others the moral sayings (as the Proverbs), others what does not seem to them good (as the Canticles), human, and having in the end no criterion of Divine and human, but their own private judgement.

My advice then on this head would be, (1) not to speak of any of these subjects for mere theory or argument's sake, but for edification: (2) to put restraint upon yourself in mixed societies: (3) which is involved in these, to be very watchful for what end you speak of them: (4) to endeavour to keep your mind in suspense as to the theories of moderns, which you have reason to think *may* be at variance with the teaching of the ancient Church.

I have now written, as you asked me, 'very plainly,' and I trust, and indeed doubt not, that this plainness which one would use the rather in correspondence, will open the way for unreserved intercourse, when it pleases God that we should meet.

LETTER XXIII.

THE SAME.

Feast of St. Luke, 1844.

I have regretted much not being able to write sooner. You must not be weary, nor mind the 'buzzing of the flies.' People never dread a gnat more than when they hear its shrill note by them; and these thoughts, it may be, are permitted, as I have often said, in order that you may hate them more, and your self-satisfaction which occasioned them, than you would if not tormented by them. It may often be difficult to decide whether there has not been a momentary acquiescence; but if you doubt, reject them by an act of the will, as soon as you can, and pray for humility. And generally I should think a strong contrary act of more avail than mere 'driving them away'; e.g. when some self-congratulating thought comes, if it is simply repelled, as you say, it 'keeps coming back again,' but if one can fill one's mind with some contrary thought, either out of one's self (as God's Immensity and Majesty and Glory, so as to become nothing in His Presence, and make some act of it, or of the Day of Judgement, and how tinsel what has won man's praise will then seem, picturing to one's self our Lord's awful Majesty viewing one through and through); or within one's self, as past sins; again picturing one's self to one's self (with good Bishop A[ndrewes]) as something 'leprous and defiled, a stinking carcase full of sores from head to foot,' this self-gratulation would not find where to settle upon, or would make us sore if it did.

I think your perplexity about 'entertaining' thoughts arose from your confounding consciously and unconsciously. There may be too so many shades. The thoughts, e. g., may be entangled before a person is aware, or the pleasure may have been felt and dwelt upon, before the mind was awakened to its being an act of self-gratulation, or it may have been admitted momentarily, or when it returned, it may have been received because it was troublesome to get rid of, or some excuse may have been made—all this short of persisting in a thing knowing it to be wrong. . . . Going on with what you were doing, when knowing it to be against rules, because of the awkwardness of breaking off, is not so heavy, as doing it wilfully from the first.

Do not be discouraged at failures; you had a large field of weeds to clear; it is much if some are resolutely plucked up and seem to have disappeared, even if the rest seem as tangled as ever. Only take fresh courage for the rest, and take care that they do not occupy the ground you have cleared from the others.

I am very glad of the 'feeling happier to be left quiet and unnoticed.' You must indeed be on your guard that this be not (as has been said) like one of the monstrous fish at the bottom of a pond, which lies still, and so the lake seems pure and clear until the bait is thrown in; then it springs forth, defiles the lake, subsides again, and after awhile all seems clear. However, I hope this is not so with you, but that you have laid the Cross upon the monster's head, and will not take it off again, so that it should have power to revive. But one must not trust feelings: e. g. one might, from weariness, or temporary distaste, or because the persons one is with are not calculated to call one out, or from some feeling of humility for the time, like 'to be left quiet,' and yet forget all, so soon as one more to one's taste, e. g. —— and an occasion of displaying sympathy, should present itself. Yet such feelings are rewards; treasure the memory of the 'happiness of being left quiet,' and love to be more with Him Who gave it you.

It is very dangerous to do anything indirectly for effect, even if it be to convey the truth. It is unreal and so bad. If desirable, it would have been far better to have explained yourself simply to those you 'love and respect.' The probability is that what you did, you did unnaturally, because you were doing it for an end, and so the less succeeded. After all, one must be glad to take such crosses, except so far as it is contrary to edification. In the end, people will see whether we love our Lord; and after all, what they say is but too true, that we have too little love or trust of or in anything but self; and so what they say may teach us humility.

I think for the present, if you do tell of self as an example, speak of it in the third person, as some one you know. But although self comes the readiest to mind, what a sorry example it is, at best, so that when the thought comes to speak of self for edification, at least make the effort to think of something more edifying. This would tend to take you off self.

When away from home, do, in matters of duty, fasting, &c., whatever you would have done at home; only not as a great thing, but as a simple duty, thinking as little of it as you can, and how everybody would do it better than you, had they been taught. If you do not think much of it yourself, the unpleasant remarks will pass off without much impression.

Try against this 'going on in a routine.' Rouse yourself in the midst of doing things, in order to do them better and to God. Do not talk long together, without collecting yourself in God's Presence. This is very drying. If it be ever so brief a direction of the thoughts to God, or a prayer to speak aright, it gathers up the mind again from being dissipated in outward things, which is so great a hindrance to love and devotion and all good.

God bless you, and God be blessed Who is giving you His grace: be diligent to use it faithfully.

LETTER XXIV.

THE SAME.

Ember Wednesday, September, 1844.

It would be good to try to make your rules of marking self-conscious thoughts stringent, if so you might make vanity a subject of humiliation. Thus, if you were to fix in your mind what a hideous thing vanity is, like the frog or toad, unsubstantial, unsolid, bulky, inflated, loathsome to touch or sight, and then as soon as a self-conscious thought came into your mind, think 'This is what I am making myself.' Or picture to yourself the court of Heaven, all lowly and humble in the sight of the glorious Presence, and yourself, how unlike them; or that if you have by God's grace done anything good, you are casting it away with your own hands; or that you are stripping yourself of the robe of righteousness and making yourself an object of shame; or think of our Lord and Saviour as a little Child for our sakes, and bidding us to be like Him, that we may receive Him; or that the gate of Heaven is low, and that the lowly only who stoop can enter it; or that you are actually abasing yourself and losing, if you obtain Heaven, the place which God purposed for you; or if, by God's grace, you are doing anything really good, that it is God's gift and would have been much better but for former and present failures, whereby one has lost God's grace in part and the insight into Divine things, in a word, one is but the wreck of what one might have been by His grace; or say the Gloria Patri and add, 'and shame to me'; if vain of outward appearance or anything external think of the grave, and internal deformity through sin; make some picture of yourself to yourself, as of a body in which each sin was a foul, loathsome ulcer. A vain person must be much more foul in the sight of the Holy Angels.

Above all, contemplate early in the morning our Lord in His humility, and pray for the grace of humility through the day, and to be less unlike Him.

Then meet all thoughts *quick* in some of the ways I have named or any other, or those in the former rules, so that the very temptations to vanity may become means of humility; or reject and detest them before God, and disown them as soon as you can, praying for lowliness.

Try to make a certain number of definite acts of humility through the day;—as, on the sight of nature, 'All things serve Thee but I'; 'Servants obey us, we disobey God; they condemn us'; 'The poor are rich often, we the poorer and yet taught and fenced so much more than they.' Make at least seven such acts in each day, seven times taking occasion to humble yourself, internally or externally.

Be very careful of contrary acts, speaking of your own good or others' ill (there has been a good deal of talking of self).

Be very careful about acting against conscience, or when you suspect yourself to be wrong.

The idea of dress seems almost to be a monomania with you. Which dress does our Lord commend, that of John the Baptist or the gay clothing of kings' houses? How was Dives clothed? What is all dress but the fig-leaves, and so a token of penitence and God's pardon of sinners?

If tempted by others' praise, or to court it, think how absolutely ignorant people are of your real self, and how you are losing the praise of God. You cannot seek God's praise and man's.

Often in the day compare yourself with others to your own disparagement. See the good only in others; the evil in yourself.

Confess yourself interiorly unworthy of everything, as having wasted God's gifts and by reason of sin, of the light you see, the food you eat, of all God's creatures.

Confess any fault, if you can without scandal or undue pain.

Beg pardon.

Recollect that we are 'corrupt' by nature; we confess ourselves so; but what of foulness does not that word corrupt contain!

Recollect that the praise of men is the greatest snare, shame and contempt our Lord's portion. . . .

Let this be the object of your struggles, your daily prayer, your meditation. There are some very valuable instructions in Rodriguez on 'Christian Perfection,' vol. ii, also the 'Meditations' in St. Peter de Alcantara which I spoke of, and St. Ignatius' 'Spiritual Exercises,' only I do not know what these last are in, besides Latin.

God bless you.

LETTER XXV.

THE SAME.

November 27, [1844].

I do trust that you are on the whole making progress. You do not always distinguish between thoughts suggested and consented to, or between the relation of thoughts of self-esteem and that undercurrent of consciousness of what is amiss, which when you write to me comes to the surface. You must not depress yourself unduly or despond: there may be a degree of pride or temper even in dissatisfaction with self. But again, you may be tormenting yourself unduly with what is the remains of former sin. Thus, it is quite a nature with you to fill up half-sentences with your own praise, or expect that they should end in it, or interpret things or looks to your advantage, or see the one favourable point which will enable you to answer self-examination to your advantage, &c. As well might one recovering from a long illness expect to walk strongly, or one awakened out of a sleep to shake off the impression of a long dream at once, or one who by habit had contracted a limb to put it down straight, as one recovering from mental self-indulgence not to be haunted with the phantoms of it. As I have often said, this powerlessness is part of the chastisement, perhaps according to some immutable fitness in God's wisdom, certainly one of the most efficacious ways of teaching us to loathe former sin. It is like the sight of midnight vanities, masks, tinsel, &c., in the coming day. And so now that the day, I trust, has been let in upon your mind, these spectres are allowed to haunt you, that by the light you may see how hideous and miserable things were which, when darkness was upon your eyes, you could neither see, nor yet know that you were blinded so as not to see them.

Let them be then a part of your humiliation. Meet them, as you are trying to do, with some opposite thoughts; lament yourself before God that you are such, that you so set up self as an idol in His temple, your heart, that you cannot chase it away, that in the time of darkness the bats nestled there and, now you feel them to be unclean and defiling, you cannot drive them away, but they flit before your eyes, and obscure His light; in a word, regard this as a loss, do contrary acts as much as you can, pray God to remove it, lament it before Him, and so go on, more anxious not to give way to such thoughts than to be free from them. Accept them as humbling, just as it is better for a person from whom any personal advantage is passing away, to look steadily at what is replacing it, in a glass, than to turn away.

But be very careful as to overt acts: these perpetuate the evil and are the more displeasing, now you are aware of their sinfulness. Try to make very strict rules, at least, as to some one point, and fence it by penance, until you have in some degree gained it. Thus, not to speak of self. The 'speaking of self in an ordinary way at home' is very mischievous. It keeps up a continual atmosphere of self. The rule ought to be peremptory, except in answer to questions. Complaining as to self, as of cold, headache, stupidity, &c., repeating what self does, or what happens to self, is continually fanning that self-consciousness, so that it more readily occurs to tell something of self, to use self as an illustration, &c., than of anything else.

To speak of self's acts of poverty, &c., you know, is to 'have your reward.' 'The change of dress' was bad as an overt *act*. Alas for dress! I have just heard of a whole family of a clergyman which has scarcely or has not shoes, stockings, blankets; they sleep on straw, and for seven weeks had no meat; and then we are thinking of petty self-denials!

It shows that you have not made much progress in humility only to see it in the poor. They, as a matter of course, are our superiors. We cannot reach their self-denial when they give one penny. Again, that you can more easily prefer strangers than those you know well, shows that you are but on the threshold. However, it is much to be even there. But it is in despite of appearances that we must think others better than ourselves, think of this one's affectionateness, that one's straightforwardness, a third's gentleness and so on, whatever quality they have more eminently, and contrast it with self. And then think of God's mercies to one's own soul, and one must be covered with confusion at the sight of any one.

I do hope you are making progress, but set yourself specially to gain humility, without which God can bestow no grace upon you.

Take care about abridging sleep; it injures devotion. About the occupation, notwithstanding your deterring account of yourself, I should not have been afraid to send you more, but I suspect it is finished. Will you kindly send me what you have, and I can tell better.

God bless you and this holy season to you, that Christ may so dwell in your heart by His Spirit as never to leave you.

LETTER XXVI.

THE SAME.

Second Wednesday in Advent, 1844.

I almost hope that you are improving, notwithstanding all you complain of and some bad overt faults. You are plainly stirring, and so, I trust, will gain the victory. Your former self-love must have been most excessive, and you must expect much toil to get rid of such a slough; but, courage! These tormenting thoughts of self may be the very process whereby you are to be freed. Only reject them; mind not whether with the 'upper' or 'inner' self: whether you can feel that you do it or no. Do it with your will, if every other power be tied. I am glad to see that you have made the discovery about S[urin][1]; I absolutely felt perplexed in putting it out; the doctrine is so high that I thought people would not see how it could any way be consistent with the ordinary duties of life. I wished people to feel their way towards it, and then to find that you could fancy that you had attained! Very earnest persons have spoken of it, as setting before them an ideal of what they had not known before, something to look and aim at afar off. I can only think that you have not yet got even the ideal of it, or else mistake some passing thought, or glimpses, for the possession of the reality.

[1] Surin, 'The Foundations of the Spiritual Life,' translated and adapted by Dr. Pusey.

What I should still press upon you are—

(1) Extreme vigilance as to overt acts, speaking of self, saying anything which can draw praise of self. Make a special examination of this, and appoint a penance (not too severe) for the breach of it.

(2) Meditate on the privations of our Lord (as Avrillon will suggest), or again of His holy Mother, of the prophets (Heb. xi), and pray for shame at being so unlike them.

Be very careful not to take praise unduly, and if not at the time, disown it, if you can, afterwards. To allow one to think you 'pale at the thought of the Passion,' untruly, is hypocrisy.

Do not worry yourself about self-conscious thoughts; as, when it comes to you afterwards, that you have done a thing well; only give God the praise, say, 'Glory be to the Father,' &c., quick. It seems to be a sort of temptation to you, to disgust you with trying to do well, as if it were of no use, this sad self-consciousness marring. Do as well as you can, by God's grace, and then give Him the glory. Pleasure at doing well is meant as encouragement.

I should think the laughing was partly the result of former levity, indulgence in the ludicrous, &c. It remains often as a disease. Cultivate serious thoughts, and what an earnest world this is, in which your own salvation, and that of all around you, is at stake. Think what Hell is. Now especially meditate, if but for a short time daily, on the Second Advent, and

> 'The black and yawning lake
> Of restless endless pain,'

and pray for yourself and others that you may escape it.

Do you dedicate the whole day and all its actions in the morning to God, and then pray that courses of action be to His glory, and at the beginning of each?

The best rule as to quantity of food is, 'always to leave

off (if ever so little) hungry.' I have seen the rule too, 'if towards the end of a meal fresh hunger seems to come on, be aware that it is a device of Satan, and break off at once.' Never complain of food; but if it be nasty, take it 'as fittest for me.'

About dress I have given rules before; 'try to recall in what Dives was drest.'

How much better all 'self's mean things' are than you deserve: how we ought to dread lest we have 'our good things in this life'! How one is ashamed to be as one is, in this weather, with all the cold and privation around us! And yet, if one's bones do not ache at night, or one has no rheumatism, one cannot be like the poor.

If the 'tear' come again, thank Him heartily for it, Who hath stricken the rock that the water should flow. Own yourself a dry and barren land. Use words of love to God with your will, if you cannot with your heart to our Saviour on the Cross.

With regard to balls, if you earnestly think that they are bad for you, tell your Mother so; tell her they fill you with vanity, levity, and whatever other evil they do you; tell her this and any other grounds you have against them privately, with all earnestness, and pray God beforehand, and at the time, that your mother may consent to what is for your good.

I really have very little to say about indulging in warmth this weather; only do nothing against conscience, and for every comfort thank God.

I think self-denial ought to be a matter of your own conscience: there might be subtle self-deceit in accepting 'niceties,' even offered by your M[other].

Just now, I must employ myself in arranging materials I have, not looking out for more; and you too might well be employed in digesting for self. However, for reading, you could not do better than take some course of study of Holy Scripture, with St. Chrysostom in the Library of the Fathers, and if in reading over, e. g., his Homilies on St. Matthew, you were to mark passages which you found useful to the poor (looking to yourself first), it might turn to account by-and-by.

And now may God ever bless you, and teach you 'heartily to despise yourself,' and love Him, that you may gain Him in endless bliss.

LETTER XXVII.

THE SAME.

Second Sunday after Christmas, [*Jan.* 3], 1847.

I do not recollect what rule I gave you as to speech except the two old ones, *to make it your aim,*—

(1) Never to repeat anything in any way to the disparagement of another, *unless duty require it.* Ask yourself before you say anything of this sort, 'Is it a duty to say this?'

I think I said, if this end in your not speaking of any one, so much the better, but I did not mean to give this as a rule. I think if you aim at keeping the other, God will give you grace to speak aright of others, when you do speak.

(2) The other rule may be *to aim,* 'Never to speak of yourself unless charity or the good of your own body or soul require it; and when you speak from your own experience for the good of any one, use, as much as you can, the third person.'

The hindrances to your becoming a Sister of Mercy seem, by your account, to be likely to be the same at any future time. It seems a question whether it shall ever be. I hope it might be right to say or write to your Mother, that you are weary of the temptations of the world, that you fall into the same faults over and over again, that you do not see any progress in yourself, that you long to be out of the way of what are to you your besetting temptations, and then, in calmness, without excitement, to live to your Saviour; that you are sure that it would be best for your soul, and that she, out of love for you, would not put a hindrance to what you feel to be for the good of your soul and would save you, by God's grace, more than anything else, from your continued falls; that you might still come to your Gr[andmother] or her, should it please God that they were very ill; that you know that your Mother would part with you for anything which should be for your happiness, even if it were to go to India and she might never see you more; that this, you are sure, would be, by God's mercy, for your present peace of mind, and the good of your soul, and your eternal happiness. Lastly you might tell her that the wish has increased upon you hitherto, and ask her to name some time when, if you should be of the same mind, she would give her consent.

Pray God [as] earnestly as you can, and perseveringly, to bring you to the S[isterhood] and to direct your Mother's will.

Your note reminds me, that another rule was to try to collect yourself in the presence of God, before every conversation, and five times during any evening spent in the society of others, with thought of the five Blessed Wounds.

Also, to aim more and more to 'offer single actions, or at least courses of actions to God'; in a word, 'not to begin anything without some momentary lifting up the heart to God.'

Aim to 'think, before everything you say, Is this according to the Will of God?'

Wish to know or not to know anything, as it is the Will of God for you.

Refrain your eyes, as much as you can, from curiosity. (Recollect, 'death entered in through the eyes' and curiosity).

Do not despond, though these are 'long lessons to learn.' If you have learnt them in some degree ten years hence, if you live so long, it will be much to have lived for. They are learnt amid repeated forgetfulnesses.

LETTER XXVIII.

THE SAME.

[1849.]

As to the two wills. We cannot help having them. It is the combat of the flesh and the spirit. In fast-days the flesh is glad to escape pain; in Easter probably you put too much upon it, and it would have been better to have allowed the half-hour to pass, which is all which St. Charles Borromeo thought needful for reverence sake, after Holy Communion, and so to have taken food. It is not good to turn Easter Day into a fast, when you feel it such. Reverence does not require it. Better to take food and thank God. And so on other days.

What I meant to advise you generally was to think less about yourself, to analyze your own feelings less, to look to words and actions, and for the rest to commit yourself to your Lord, owning that you are full of imperfections, but praying Him more and more to fill you with His love. The less you reflect on your inner self the better for you now. Look to the outward expressions, go to God in all your needs; whatever you feel you want, ask Him, and then do not dwell upon your own imperfections. You are God's child. Do not let those thoughts keep you from Him. You should think less of yourself, and more of your Lord. This gloominess hides His Face from you, because you do not look to It.

What I meant by 'simplicity' is, doing things as a little child, as far as you can, without self-reflection; do simply and straightforwardly what you think right to be done in God's sight; do it for Him, and then leave it with Him.

———'s rule is too rigid. We should not, of course, be keeping a debtor and creditor account with God, as if certain acts were acceptable to Him, others not, though not sinful. All are imperfect. The best are what are done with most trust in Him; yet one cannot say that He does not accept what is done out of an habitual state of grace, though not with prayer at the moment.

LETTER XXIX.

The Same.

I do not know Fénelon well, nor how far any of the mysticism which was pronounced faulty may be in the books you have. But tell me before you adopt any new practices out of it; and so long as you use it only to enforce more deeply what you tell me of, you may use it safely.

Try to throw yourself into ——'s mind, to see what is good and beautiful in it, and to sympathize with it.

You will recollect the practice of throwing yourself into other minds and what is said, and not to illustrate it out of self, nor think of it with regard to yourself, except silently to learn from it; but think of it in itself, or in reference to Holy Scripture, and see how it may be developed, not what there is in yourself relatively to it.

On hearing Holy Scripture in church, try to listen to or to read it, as God speaking to you, especially in the Gospels. It would be well every day, in your devotions, to read meditatively some short passage for at least five minutes, which you might gradually increase, listening to God in it, and speaking to Him on occasion of it.

I do trust that you are making progress by His grace. You should not read any controversial part in F[énelon]. It is not directed against us.

God bless you ever.

You may ask any Sister to help you, or ask any who leads you to talk of self, not to do so.

Pray daily for increase of love to your S[isters], and observe what all the occasions of seeming indifference are, and so pray for more love at the time and do something loving.

Love and every grace and every good feeling grow through prayer and then doing the acts of it.

LETTER XXX.

THE SAME.

[? 1850.]

I do not think that increased fasting would benefit you. Its objects are (1) to bring down exuberant strength of body (which you have not); (2) to obey God's appointments through His Church (this you do); (3) as self-denial. But in this last way, other things would be far more of self-denial. Anything which checks over-activity of mind is far more of self-denial, than anything done to the body. I doubt whether this would promote what I wish, the mind of a little child in you.

I could not suggest to you to use any prayer, as to leading me to think that what has been passing in you has been the work of God's Holy Spirit. (1) All the details which you gave me, bore to me the character of its having been the working of your own mind. I never saw this more clearly in any case. All things which you told me with a different aspect, told to me in this way. (2) There cannot be one way for one, one for another. It is not, as in the drawing towards a life, that all are not called. It is not a question between what is higher or lower, but between right or wrong. It is right for us, whom God has placed in the English Church, to work out our salvation in obedience to her, and availing ourselves of the blessings which He has in store for us in her; else it would be wrong in all to abide in her. Since she has the full Truth, and the grace of the Sacraments, and the Power of the

Keys, and everything necessary to salvation (and to us especially the Cup), it is right to stay. We have only to be diligent in working out our salvation. We have everything to further, [not] anything to hinder it.

Believing then that it is fully the duty of us all, to abide in the Church where He has placed us, I could not be convinced as to any other, by anything which would not convince myself. In St. Augustine's time, as I said, miracles were wrought to convince the British Church to give up the then ground of separation, the keeping of Easter. They are not now.

I should think that it would be better (if you were not otherwise wanted) that you should give half an hour of your recreation-time daily for special devotion to our Lord, that you might so love Him as to have nothing else but a desire to do everything in simple childlike love,

In haste for to-day.

LETTER XXXI.

Over-Introspection.

[1851.]

My strong impression about what harasses you, is that it has chiefly arisen in discontent with yourself. You earnestly desired to be freed from your infirmities, and you hoped that under this or that outward circumstance, you would succeed better. Hence your speculations about a Benedictine Convent; and then you indulged your imagination, as is your wont. All this was wrong, and could not, so far, but lead to perplexity. One ought to lay one's faults entirely to one's self. God's grace is not lacking to us, if we are not lacking to it. I think that this dissatisfaction has in different forms been at the root of your disquiet. You have been vexed with yourself and so disappointed.

I was going to write to you about those things which trouble you. I doubt whether you do not distract yourself, by attention to feelings and emotions, which, if not allowed, are not yours. It is well that you should know what is in your mind, and that I should know it: yet you are not displeasing to God, because there is that in you which is displeasing to you, because it is in itself contrary to God's Will and would be wrong in you, if you consented to it. There may be too much contemplation of what is faulty in one.

Then too a good deal of what you complain of is nature. I mean neither good nor bad except as it is coloured by other ingredients. Eagerness, impetuosity, are qualities which may be sanctified. St. Peter, St. John, and St. James had them; yet these were they whom our Lord took nearest to Himself.

I think almost you might do better, if you did not think so much about your manner. Throw yourself into another's mind, and you would not be rude and rough. You think of showing kindness to them. What probably you need to see, is what would be kind to *them*; i.e. I think you have not studied other minds enough, being always busy about your own. Whereas, I think that if you were to observe yourself less, you would learn that self-forgetfulness which you really want. Yet you have been learning it.

I wish you could forget your feelings altogether and look to acts. You would learn to 'behave properly after Holy Communion,' not by schooling yourself, but by frequent inward aspirations. Be not mortified, if these be not so frequent as you wish, but pray that they may be more. You should be natural, simple, as a child. Again, you would become more 'loving' not by trying to *be* so, but to *do* acts of love, to study what is most loving to do or to say, by having others in your mind at the right times, not by dwelling alone in your own separate inward cell, but by interchange of natural acts and words of love.

But do not brood upon yourself, but, as I have often said, let every feeling that you are 'unlike what your Lord would have you' issue in a breathing of the soul to Him that He would make you what He would have you. He has done much for you: He will finish His own work in you.

Write to me more fully what is in your mind.

God bless you.

I wish in that conversation with —— you had confined yourself to sympathy with her, not advised her, nor interpreted God's Providence to her. It may be as much His

Providence that she should be sheltered in your peaceful home, surrounded by the gifts of God's grace, having all which she needs so bountifully around her, to detain her where she is, and where she is a source of blessing.

To give up your own will is better than abstinence from meat. You only purposed to do it, if you could. One dare not tamper with your health.

LETTER XXXII.

Spiritual Advice.

November 18, 1881.

I do trust that you are making progress in 'religious indifference,' not in the usual sense of the words, but indifference to all which affects self except in thanksgiving. I think that the

'Le Rien ne se trouble de rien'

of St. John of the Cross would be a good study for you. Only one must not have only the thought that one 'is a nothing' but also,

'Rien partout—Rien en tout—
Excepté Dieu toujours et en toutes choses.'

But still one must have fixed in one's mind that one is 'a nothing.' Why should 'a nothing' fuss about 'anything'? It is always self which is vexed, and there is nothing too little, in which self may not put itself out. . . . It is one's own will, which God allows to be crossed by the will of others. And so about 'a Sister putting herself forward.' If she does, she does herself harm, not you or any one else. She is, as I have often said, your benefactress.

Take great care about sharp speeches. It is a good rule, 'If anything comes to your mind which seems a good answer to anything you don't like, suppress it.' There is sure to be something of self in it. It is pride putting down pride.

I am glad that you are attending to little things. For they occur oftenest. And the rule is as to very little things, "Do all to the glory of God."

God bless you and make every little thing a step nearer to Him.

LETTER XXXIII.

THE SAME.

February 16, 1882.

I have written to —— as you wished. I am very glad that your last Confession in January was 'quiet and simple.' Simplicity is a good sign in you. But I must press on you, that very frequent Confession implies very great earnestness to *exterminate* some fault. Thoughts one cannot help. They may be mere temptations of Satan, or things which recur to the mind from old associations. The remedy against them is very often to take no notice of them. For to fight against them brings them. But words are our own. (1) Why should one *ever* speak evil of any one? God says, "Speak not evil one of another." (2) Why should we *ever* pronounce any judgement against any one? Our God and Judge says, "Judge not, that ye be not judged." (3) Why should we *ever* complain of anything which comes in the way of God's Providence? To complain of anything is to be wiser than God, Who loves us better and more wisely than we can love ourselves, and Who makes all things work together for good to those who love Him. He says to us, in all His dispensations, "What I do thou knowest not [now]; thou shalt know hereafter."

Set yourself absolutely to extirpate these three faults, and may God pour His grace into your soul.

LETTER XXXIV [1].

GRATITUDE.

Feast of St. Stephen, 1877.

I only received your letter and ——'s this morning; but I had the intimation of the news which you kindly wished me to have on Christmas Day, on the day. . . .

It took away my breath to see such a list of names, and to know that they gave to this particular charity out of love for me. I prayed for each individual, as far as I could at once, and will as to the rest; and will spread out the list before God at each Celebration for some time to come, and pray Him to bless them.

—— says that Mr. —— has great plans, if it should please God that he should come back. I never look beyond the day: everything beyond is dreamland, with which I may have nothing to do, except as any may be permitted, from the other side, to pray for any details here. I fear that it may not be so—I forget how I was going to finish this.

The young ladies who look to go into religious houses have so many more wants than they had thirty years ago, that I fear they will not be satisfied, except when a resident Chaplain supplies their requirements. In the first zeal all which they wanted was to give themselves to Christ as their Spouse; Confessions to cleanse them for His frequent

---

[1] This letter and the following one refer to the gift of £2000 for the Ascot Convalescent Home, from some personal friends. See Life of E. B. Pusey, D.D., vol. iv. p. 342.

Communions, in which He would give Himself; counsel how to exterminate their leading fault or faults, how to become more pleasing to Him. Now the brave go as missionaries, the rest seem to like the luxuries of devotion. But perhaps God will give us a stray lamb now and then.

Will you tell your husband that I want to get up the cry 'Liberty of Conscience' against those who would oppress and stifle it. The misery is with the pedantic copiers of Rome.

God bless this coming year to you and yours.

LETTER XXXV.

THE SAME.

January 4, 1878.

It nearly took away my breath, to hear of all the love of those loving hearts, who gave to that particular work at Ascot for love of poor me. I could do nothing but pray God for each of them, as long as I could, meaning to continue this and spread the list before God (though in a different way), as Hezekiah did that sent to him.

What a wonderful thing love is! And yet it would be more wonderful, if it were not wonderful, since "God is Love."

I will, please God, continue to spread out that list before Him at Holy Communion, and remember individuals, as I can and the son you so love.

LETTER XXXVI.

A CALL OF GOD.

Do not be dejected because I told you truth. You cannot set about mending unless you know what there is to mend. If you know it and set about it, asking for God's grace, He will give you the victory.

Since your F[ather] does not bid you stay, and would on no account influence you, your course is clear; there are others to cheer his old age. 'God' (you and I too believe) has called you. To ask others is to throw a doubt on that call. Listen to no one but to what you believed to be God's voice. It cannot be selfish to follow God's voice; only when you have followed it, take heed not to be selfish in the life to which it leads. Beware of selfishness to those who are to be your Sisters. You should have the supernatural love of grace. God will give it you, if you ask Him perseveringly.

God will help you though you will not see your progress.

LETTER XXXVII.

A Rebuke.

It is old proverbial advice to 'Let bygones be bygones.' If there had not been great practical wisdom in it, it would not have become a proverb. You work yourself up into anger by thinking of things in the past.

The centre of your faults is your self-conceit. There is some absurd conceit about being a lady. People's estimate varies. I was walking in rather a broad alley in London, and asked some question about my way. The person whom I asked directed my attention to one standing behind a greengrocer's stall, 'If you ask *that lady*, she will tell you.' No one who has any real rank thinks anything of it. They are just those on the lower verge, who think of it. A popular writer gave to one of his characters the name of 'Mrs. Proudie.' She was supposed to be a Bishop's wife. I hope that there are not many 'Mrs. Proudies' among our Bishops' wives. I never met with one. But it would be good for you to remember the name of 'Mrs. Proudie,' and not be a 'Miss Proudie.' If you give yourself airs, you become a 'Miss Proudie'; for Religious, even if they had rank, forget it. Ladies are only known by their more delicate-shaped hands and refinedness of manners. I know not how it is that your manners are so unrefined. I suppose that it is because you think much of yourself. Have you ever heard from your brothers, when schoolboys, the word 'bumptious'? It is a schoolboy term. It expresses the character of one who thinks much of some quality or circumstance about himself or herself (it might be some natural or accidental advantage as they think it), and who was always showing it in his or her manner, generally ludicrous, always overbearing. This exactly expresses what you are. You used to be so to me. Do you remember contradicting everything which I said, until, at last, I required you to listen and contradict no more?

Our Lord bids us "Judge not." You do.

LETTER XXXVIII.

SELF-ABASEMENT.

Maundy Thursday.

I cannot write much to-day, having tired myself yesterday.

I will only say to-day, 'Think of our Lord this evening and to-morrow amid all the horrible blasphemies which He endured for love of *you*': (for St. Paul says, "Who loved *me* and gave Himself for me"; what He suffered and did for all, He suffered and did for each of us). Think of this, and think of Him saying to you from the Cross, "Learn of Me, for I am meek and lowly of heart," and pray Him to make you what He died to make you.

You would not wish to be abased on the Great Day; then do not exalt yourself here.

Long that He would make you His disciple, Who said to those who had left all to follow Him, "Except ye be converted and become as little children, ye cannot enter into the kingdom of Heaven."

Be not startled then or offended if I bid you now pray Him to convert you and take away all 'self' from you, that you may be wholly His.

LETTER XXXIX.

Repentance.

I did not mean that you were to try to recall past sins in detail, but, without looking to them individually (unless God should bring any one or more before you), that you should pray for deeper repentance for everything in which you had ever displeased God.

This you do, whenever you say the Litany, 'That it may please Thee to give us true repentance.' I thought that in Lent it would be well to make this a special subject of prayer, that God would make us hate past sin as He hated it, even while forgiving us, His poor sinners.

It is saying, again and again, "God be merciful to me, a sinner." Every time we say this sincerely makes us more of the same mind with God, in hating and grieving for whatever He hated in us, even while He loved us; and He remembers each against the Great Day of Judgement.

God bless you.

LETTER XL.

VOCATION.

June 4, 1878.

One line to correct a central mistake, which I trust it will help you much to remove. Your business now is not to ascertain whether you are fit for the life, but by God's grace to fit yourself for it. God called you, being in many ways unfit, to fit you for it by His moulding grace. Picture yourself to yourself as an unformed block of stone which the Heavenly Artificer is shaping day by day for that form, which He in His Almighty love purposes for you, and let everything which you do not like be one touch of His Loving Hand to take off some edge which interferes with your becoming what He would make you.

God bless you.

LETTER XLI.

HUMILITY.

September 20, 1881.

The first stone in every building is humility—honestly to own your own nothingness. You are wishing for something large. You answered, and honestly, 'Yes,' when I said, 'You want more elbow-room?' Unless any one have dug deep by humility, and so reached the living Rock, their humility is but like the house of cards, at which children play: each storey is carefully fitted together, and placed on that below it, but the higher the little builder raises it, the more certain it is to fall.

You have large ideas. The greater the temptation to think something of yourself. I hope, for your sake, the work will be very small at first. The Devonport Mother began alone, and worked some twelve hours a day; then with a single Sister. However, the Bishop of —— has, of course, his own plans, and you may be 'a nothing' in simply following them out. A very thoughtful person said, 'I hate a splash.' Oaks grow from acorns; but grow slowly; not like bulrushes.

I dare not think about bodily penances. They fall so unequally on different frames. Better, I think, pray for true repentance for whatever there was of self in whatever you were unintentionally concerned. Self is so likely to thrust itself into everything which you do.

Pray God that you may really feel yourself nothing.

LETTER XLII.

THE CONTEMPLATIVE LIFE.

April 7, [1881].

I do not think that God *has* called you to the contemplative life. What is your conception of it? How many hours do you think that you could spend in the day in prayer? And in what prayer, vocal or mental? What would be the object of that prayer? Your own closer union with God, in what is specially called 'contemplation,' or in intercession? And if both, in what proportion? Would your idea be of the life direct to God, without doing anything for your fellow-creatures, except by intercession through the Great Intercessor? For what length of time are you at present enabled to pray to God, unbrokenly? You are a member of the 'Company of the Love of Jesus,' of which Ascot is the centre. Have you great interest in these prayers for our fellow-sinners, and do you pray them with fervour?

Will you, in your answers, put down these questions, one by one, and your own answers under each?

I do not see any good in 'fancy work,' except that it gains money for the poor. But all enclosed Orders, I believe, do three hours a day of 'fancy work.' All the old Brussels lace was, I believe, the work of the enclosed Orders, after a pattern of which they were in exclusive possession. Subjects of meditation or ejaculation were provided for those hours of silent occupation. How have you been employing the time in which you have been doing yours? You might have employed it, according to the ideal of the 'Society of the Love of Jesus,' in praying Him for the souls which were in sin. Did you?

You seem to say that you must either lead a life wholly contemplative (whatever you mean by that word, whether the life of the 'mystica' [*I* do not use the word in any depreciating way]) or 'strain every nerve' in the practical life of active charity. For most persons a mixed life of prayer and active work is best.

But according to your account, I do not see why yours might not be the contemplative life now. Your 'paltry 12½ hours a week' among them would leave you more time than any enclosed Order, I believe, has. But I should think that it must be in consequence of some supposed want of physical strength of yours that you can have so short a time. The visiting time of the Sisters of Charity used to be six hours a week-day, i.e. about three times what you speak of.

What made me speak doubtfully about Ascot was a prospect that if there should be a quicker succession of patients, there would be some active work among them so as not to leave you wholly to yourself. But I will wait your answers to my detailed questions.

God bless you.

I have my misgivings, whether your mind is not so criticizing, that Mr. —— may not be right, that no plan would suit you, which you could not do in your own way, i.e. that you must have the direction of any work. But then the working under the direction of the clergyman would be inconsistent with this, for your judgement might clash with the clergyman's.

By doing work with all your might, I meant as far as in you lay. I thought that you had not thrown your heart into your work, and depreciated that mode of work, because you had not the idea that it was for souls, not for bodily wants only. God corrects our self-will continually, by giving us checks. He will not let us serve Him in our own way. Most is done when we do or think we do least.

God fits us for Himself and His love by [our] doing work (whatever it is) which He gives us for Him. There are 'snares and temptations' everywhere, to be overcome by His grace. "I can do all things through Christ in-strengthening me." Our chief enemy we carry about us everywhere, 'self.'

The picture which you draw of your alternative future is vehemence in the one way or the other.

One more question: How have you employed your time in going to your cases? It gave good leisure for prayer. You might have been praying to God, all the while, for any object, either those whom you passed, or yourself, or those whom you were to visit, or for souls generally. One with whom the contemplative life was a picture would. This was the outset of the life of St. Catherine of Sienna. Did you?

God bless you.

LETTER XLIII.

SAINTLINESS.

Easter Day, 1847.

'Why,' you ask, 'are we not saints?' Pray God earnestly to empty self of self, and not to do anything to foster self, and He will give you the love of Him. The soul must be empty, in which He can dwell fully. 'Empty me, O Lord, of self, and fill me with Thee.' Self chokes the mouth of the bottle into which He would pour His Love. He loves the soul which in silence waits on and feeds on His Love, and gives back His Love to Himself. Let this be your battle, out of love for Him to exterminate self-love, to have more room for His.

You may go to Holy Communion at M[argaret] C[hapel] after Tuesday; but pray then, as you now desire, that His Love may fill you, and so fully as to displace self-love.

Your only penance now must be in speech, to utter nothing consciously fostering self-love, and to pause before speaking to pray, when you are in danger or perceive yourself so to be. God bless you and fill you with His Love.

LETTER XLIV.

Spiritual Advice.

Thursday in Sexagesima, 1847.

I think you had better not put down in your account these self-conscious thoughts. It is indeed a miserable power of the former self, that it should have power to cross the mind at such a moment; still you could not help it, more than a lame man that he cannot walk. One only can give perfect soundness. Pray that He displace this self-love with love of Himself alone. And try to forget self and take no notice of it, except to pray for Heavenly Love.

I am glad that your Mother persevered in asking the question, because it would have been wrong to go to the Sisterhood without her knowing it. However, I hope you meant to tell her beforehand, though not then. You may go there, as far as relates to leave from me, when and as long as you will.

I hope the distractions you speak of were rather the effect of sleepiness. Spiritual writers speak of it as deranging mental prayer.

You should take care not to fall into a habit of refusing to expect evils, even when apparent. Some people harden themselves against all sorrow, by refusing to believe it beforehand, and acquiescing in it selfishly when it comes; secretly wishing to escape pain both ways.

Is it not inconsistent to wish for anything (the watch) and at the same time to wish to give up all?

You will recollect that your great mortification is to be in speech. I have often said how we fix our feelings by it. One self-conscious speech does more harm than very many unconscious self-conscious words.

You must try to obtain rest really now before Lent, and if there was any wilfulness about those four nights, take it as a penance.

I cannot give you a rule for Lent; it is a physician's office: you have experience of former Lents, and know your present strength.

LETTER XLV.

The Same.

Fifteenth Sunday after Trinity, 1847.

I do not think you should adopt constrained silence in order to avoid faults. That would not mend it. Only try more and more to collect yourself before, and in, speaking: pray God to keep your speech; try to correct the faults you are told of. It may be a long battle, but by God's grace you will win at last. Outward slowness will be a help to be on your guard.

Those thoughts may indeed be of use, as showing in part what you are, i.e. that self is ready to put itself forward, in every possible form; in part what but for God's grace you would be. They are not sin; it is but the foul matter issuing from that deep ulcer of self, which God is healing. As He deepens your love for Himself and others, it may by His mercy dry up. You may tell me anything you observe in yourself. Yet you should be careful not to attach too much value to it. (1) Because your mind might be so likely to imitate what it has read of, and to imagine what it wishes, that you might readily deceive yourself. (2) The real test of growth in God's favour is progress in grace, subduing of self, not even God's gifts, if real. (3) If real, self-reflection is likely to destroy it. Quiescence is absorption in God; to think of self is to awake. Bless God for all His love to you in recalling you wherein He has recalled you:

and be not curious about His gifts. But humble yourself; and think what grace you might have had, had you been faithful.

'A very few words' will expand into an ocean of prayer through the love of God. Be not anxious about many prayers, but about praying much.

You may wish and ask to receive Holy Communion with your own poor people.

Take great care not to let anything interfere with appointed prayer, except charity, and then pray and do the act of charity too. It is, as it were, looking that God should wait for your leisure, instead of waiting on God.

You speak of 'several hard letters.' Are they letters which it is best for you to receive?

When hurried by the children, pray for them.

LETTER XLVI.

THE SAME.

Seventeenth Sunday after Trinity, 1847.

Rules, suggesting devotional thoughts, are binding in the principle, not to the very thoughts.

Daily mortification may ordinarily be slight, to keep up the habit. . . .

What I meant about prayer on distraction was, not to make a definite act of contrition and asking help, but to endeavour, instead of thinking, 'I *must* fix my mind,' [to say] 'God help me!' I mean, to make the brief mental act which must take place, when one feels a distraction, 'prayer,' not 'resolve.' It had better be a simple act of prayer for help; a twofold act is distracting. I mean, an instantaneous act, then throwing the mind into the prayers. Do not notice what you are doing at the time. If you do not recollect afterwards, let it pass. The more you feel your dependence upon God at all times, the more, I hope, will these 'scarcely conscious acts' be multiplied. Involuntary distraction is infirmity, not sin.

It is best to read something for the morning meditation, although you should not adhere rigidly to it, if you find devotion in something else, or some one point of it.

If any one say anything implying God has helped

her through you, praise God for it, inwardly owning yourself unworthy.

I think you had better not bind yourself artificially to any plan about using the Ps[alms]; you might be occupying yourself intellectually in finding out meanings, instead of using them devotionally. *That* would be the object of spiritual reading: in devotion, use them in any way which God gives you, making your chief object to say them to God, in whatever meaning. I suppose that too much of the prayer of very many is intellectual, giving the mind to the meaning of the words, instead of begging of God.

You would be less liable to be distracted in the silent use of the Lord's Prayer and Creed, if you were to repeat the words to yourself, saying them as devotionally as you can, undistracted even by the sound of your own voice.

It is better to avoid being curious about outward things; the more you will learn to be inward.

LETTER XLVII.

THE SAME.

Octave of the Epiphany Night, [1848].

At last, I can write a little. I think it would be better for you, as to food, to have a certain rule (your whole Rule is an abstemious one), and then not to heed these occasional thoughts. Your head is always at work, and so I should think that they probably were part of the unceasing working of your own mind.

As I before said, what I wish to see uprooted is this overt reference to self. The subtler you may not be able to escape for years, the overt you can, at once, if you will do as I say. (1) Pray against it. (2) Actively endeavour to throw your mind into other things, so as to find illustrations out of yourself. (3) Resolutely close your lips when anything as to 'I' or 'we' comes to you.

Never mind feeling sore at being told of faults. The proud flesh will feel the caustic; only be glad that it is applied, and pray for humility.

It cannot be right to think of right things at wrong times: so if such thoughts come, you may bid them wait, or give them to your Guardian Angel to take care of for you, if right.

Recollect that what seems faulty may spring from something quite different from what you are thinking of. If you see faults, which you are not charged or have no calling to remind the Sister of, pray God to give her grace, and so leave it.

You need not mind asking about things of self, really for edification. The first 'alphabet of religiousness' is to unlearn self, empty yourself of yourself, and so God will fill you: still yourself, and so you will know what [it is] to be 'hushed' and 'gathered up' in Him. But all you can do, is to take heed to overt acts. I must have often said, 'Choke these, keep your grasp upon them, and self will die for want of breath.'

As to eagerness and excitement, this too, I hope, will die, the more you learn to commend single acts to God, and think what it is so to do. We cannot but be still, in what we are doing to God. It is self which is so restless.

As you are less distracted about many things, and restrain your own over-activity at all times, or labour more to do all things in God, and gather yourself up in Him, you will, I trust, be less distracted in His House also.

It is true, to do things for God is very different from loving Him or having faith in Him. We may forget God in the very things we do for Him. Much which we hope is of grace is of mere natural activity. We can only gain love by prayer, and inward doing and bearing things for God, and concealing them when we may, that so God may be our sole End.

Do not look back at former years with regret. I doubt not that you have been making progress, though this deep disease of self is as yet unhealed. Such acts as naming yourself to the poor woman, seem essentially contrary to the spirit of the rule 'not I' but 'we,' and to imply that she might be right in preferring you to others, which is contrary to all humility.

Do not think so much of getting rid of self-conciousness

as of fixing your thoughts on God. People become, in affections of this world, 'absent' by having their minds riveted on some object. They forget things around them in it. To desire to forget a thing fixes the soul more on it. As I have often said, they are those endless acts which strengthen self-consciousness. Your mind in daily acts revolves around yourself. Everything suggests something as to self. And the expression of this stamps the feeling deeper. Go forth out of self. Even your 'craving to seek His Presence in your heart' may aggravate it. Seek Him, not His sensible Presence, but to love Him more devotedly, ardently, alone, nor for any present comforts to yourself in being assured that you love Him, but because He is the Infinite Object of all love.

The best way of preventing the feeling of wishing to know what another has is (1) (what you did) to think it best for you, because you know it not and cannot : (2) to pray that that other may grow in grace in it, and live to God's glory ; so will you forget self. If you were transferred to Heaven with these feelings, how would you not wish yourself in the place of each, as they were nearest to our Lord and His Love, instead of being thankful to be lowest there.

Do not long for 'fervent Communions' (this is still reflection on self): but rather that you may indeed be made one with Christ.

All resolves itself into this one thing, 'absence of self.' To have our thoughts and acts His, must be His gift: all we can do is to pray, put down self, and act on His suggestions when we know them.

Your consciousness or not of others' presence in devotion will depend upon the way you act. As before, do not try to act directly upon it, but say the Psalms, &c., to our Lord, and of the presence of others you may be conscious as of the Holy Angels. Think of 'mistakes' in reference to our Lord only, and yourself as an ill-taught, forgetful child, yet a child.

Your friend —— said, 'An excited nun seems a contradiction.'

—— had better make no account of thoughts and temptations: only use some prayer in them. They are the devil's, and as good Archbishop Leighton says, 'will be imputed to him,' not to her.

'Loneliness' is often the portion of those whom God loves most. What like the loneliness of St. John, or the Blessed Virgin after the Ascension?

Self-praising thoughts, self-preference, &c., need not be confessed unless yielded to or acted upon. Treat it as folly (it is), and think yourself a fool for having them, and so pass them by; as you would any other folly, or any of those incoherent thoughts which cross the mind when half asleep. You only fix them and make them recur, by dwelling upon them.

I think probably one reason why you feel this life harder is, that you are under rule, instead of making rules for yourself, which had excitement in it. But also the even simplicity of the life may make it harder.

Those who love any human being intensely, are conscious of his presence, even if they see him not, are with him even though absent; the thought mingles with their thoughts whatever else they think of, they do all with reference to him, the love of him makes them do all they do better: they can play, sing, speak better, can do things beyond themselves, feel no fatigue; it diffuses gladness over all: nothing is irksome: no pain felt, or gives a thrill of pleasure: it is gladness to suffer for him. One surely need only think of what we are, to know what it is to have the 'thought of God'; but to know the 'sweetness of God' must be His gift to those whom He overstreams with His love.

To do things 'purely to the glory of God' is to have no respect of self, no by-ends, no wish for praise, but to desire to do it just as God would have it, because He wills it.

If a thing is of moment, the mind should be given to it, as in teaching, visiting the poor, &c., with the raising the soul to God at intervals on the continued thought of God; but you should not have a separate train of thought, as you may in things mechanical or nearly so.

You should pray individually for the poor under your care, if they continue the same and are not very numerous. But this is not always possible, e.g. for clergy.

You will find a beautiful description of being 'hushed,' in St. Augustine's conversation with his mother just before her death [1].

I think I am now at the close of the questions of many notes; if there are more, ask me.

God bless you and empty you of yourself that He may fill you with Himself.

---

[1] See in St. Augustine's 'Confessions,' Lib. Fath., Oxf. Trans., pp. 174, 175.

LETTER XLVIII.

THE SAME.

Rogation Monday, [1848].

What you write of is part of that intense disease of self: but be not disquieted. Nettles are beaten to death by being continually lashed: a disease wears itself out continually throwing off what is loathsome: whatever is odious to you, does not hurt you. Pray for the Sister, whom you are inclined to grudge self-d[enial]: suppose there are reasons for what you do not see: quell the rebellions: the best victories may be where there has been 'hardest work': do not mind how many dints there are on the shield, so you do what in you lies by prayer and self-subdual to repel the enemy. Be not surprised that you have these conflicts; but take them humbly as a matter of course; even while you say, "Who shall deliver me from the body of this death?" . . .

It is the beginning of humility to feel that we can do nothing for ourselves, and so to leave off complaining that we have 'no real, deep sorrow for sins past,' but pray for it and for love, and avoid anything, any acts or words, which may hinder it.

LETTER XLIX.

UNBELIEVING THOUGHTS.

Feast of the Purification, 1881.

I have been up to the lips in work, and so delayed day by day all other writing.

And now three weeks have elapsed since the date of your letter. What is the form which it takes now? Is it still that continual jabbering against faith? Satan cannot understand faith and love; only the knowledge of his own doom. And so he subserves the ends of God, in giving Him the occasion to conquer in His own. You remember St. Catherine's 'Where wert thou, Lord, when I had those thoughts?' So even to St. Catherine of Sienna it must have been a perplexity. And it was her favourite grace against which he jabbered. And yet she was puzzled, and could not make out that they were not her own. If she was so puzzled, much more may you be. So then take our Lord's answer as said to you, 'Where art Thou, Lord?' 'In thy heart, else thou wouldest not hate them.'

But the less you think about them the better. Do what you can for God in His poor. He says, " Blessed is he that considereth the poor and needy. The Lord shall deliver him in the time of trouble."

So He will deliver *you*. Satan can only be an occasion of good to you.

God bless you and through trouble or through joy lead you to Himself.

LETTER L.

DOUBTINGS.

August 4, 1880.

I did not suppose that the devil would leave off whispering his 'ifs' at once: the more attention you pay to them, the longer probably he will continue them. They answer the purpose of his malice in plaguing you. To suggest doubts about faith altogether or any portion of it, is one of his known devices. Pascal was an instance. Pascal's advice was, 'Take no notice of them, but do some contrary act of faith.' If Satan found that he could disturb neither your faith nor your peace, he would leave off. For his pride makes him hate to be baffled. When Job had stood his malice and blessed God when he hoped he would curse Him, he left off. He departed from our Lord for a season when he had failed, hoping to prevail another time.

It is a very simple temptation, and not uncommon. 'What if it is all a dream!' has been suggested to many. The object is to prevent its becoming chronic, which, if you let it take hold of you, it might. The way, then, is to act quietly. The cross on the forehead, as I told you, has great power, the forehead being the seat of thought; Satan fears it. Or to make a short profession of faith, 'Lord, I believe all which Thou hast revealed,' or 'I believe in God the Father, &c.,' standing for the whole Creed. It should be very short, so as not to relax the energy with which you begin, or to give Satan time to say, 'No, you don't.' They must be temptations of Satan. We hope that these assaults on faith were permitted by God in answer to your prayer. God would not Himself take away His own gift of faith. He does all which His Almighty power can to keep this faith in us. But He may allow us to be assaulted as He did Job, intending that we should be conquerors. I told you some known and approved ways of fighting. You had said to me some such words as, 'I must, as before, grasp my own nettle.' What is *your* way of ridding yourself of this temptation? It may be overcome by prayer. But beware of pride. God may be permitting it to cauterize pride, by showing you how helpless you are. It is not to be overcome by folding your hands, but by prayer and fighting. You may have some ways of fighting, of which you have not told me. What do you do against this temptation? But fight you must, and humble yourself before God.

LETTER LI.

THE SAME.

August 10, [1880].

Almighty God could allow you, in answer to your prayer, to be buffeted, tempted with thoughts against faith. He could not take away your faith. It is, we trust, in answer to your prayer, that He has allowed this mist to come over you. The thoughts which Satan puts into one, seem often so much ours, that we cannot distinguish them. St. Catherine of Sienna, having been assailed by thoughts contrary to her favourite grace of purity, complained to our Lord, 'Where wert Thou. Lord, when I had such thoughts?' The answer came, 'In thy heart: else thou couldest not have hated them.' Archdeacon Manning (as he then was) asked a poor villager, who was troubled with thoughts against faith, 'Do you ever say, Get thee behind me, Satan?' Villager: 'No, Sir, I dares not say that: but I do say, The Lord rebuke thee.' He fought against it, and so must you. God has heard your prayer in allowing the mist to come over you. He would not paralyze your will.

The 'price which you have to pay' is to accept the mist of having the doubts put into your mind. God has put you into this battle. But He bids you fight. He conquers in His own: He Himself is crowned in them, whom He crowns. It is not your duty to analyze yourself, as you describe yourself as doing. Any temptation might find an echo in your heart but for the grace of God. It is a saying, that we have the germs of all the deadly sins in us. God has been very merciful to you in letting Satan tempt you in this way, and not in others which might have been more distressing. But He says, "Resist the devil, and he will flee from you." It does not depend upon you, how long the mist will last. This is in God's Hands. But as long as He allows it to last, you must believe that the sun is behind it, although you do not see it, and all around is damp and clammy. You are not 'resuming your offer' by fighting. God accepted your offer by putting you into the battle. The mist will last as long as God wills, and, as long as it lasts, you have the battle to fight. Not to ask help of God would be unchristian. The devil tells you this, and you must not believe him.

Never mind your feelings. The trial must be dreary. Dreariness is part of your trial. If all were bright within, then temptation would be but summer clouds. You do believe in God. It would be Satan's lie, to say that you did not. I fear that you hug your temptation, as if it were part of your offering, or not your temptation only, but your inaction under it. Jesus, your Redeemer, is no dream. It were blasphemy and ingratitude to think it. The 'if' is giving way to the devil. Fight, as others have fought. God met Job, Face to face, but *after* that, by God's grace, he had conquered. While he had to fight, God helped him without his knowing it and unseen.

Do everything just as you would have done if Satan had not put the 'ifs' into your mind. They are his, and the malice of them will be ascribed to him, not to you. But if you omit a prayer in consequence of his temptation, you are *in that instance* defeated.

I did not mean any one sort of pride, but all: all self-opinion. Of course, you who are in this mist about what the heathen believed, cannot judge about anything: but chiefly I suppose that the suffering which you offered yourself for, God sent in this particular way to heal your pride, that you are assailed with doubts about which even heathen consciences saw clearly. As for leaving you alone, you are one of the most necessitous of all my children, and to leave you alone would be to leave you to sleep on the snow, which is death.

LETTER LII.

VANITY.

September 1, 1880.

Your letter awakens in me the apprehension that you may really be indifferent to the state in which you are: which would be the way to become really indifferent to the loss of God and to lose your soul. You must fight and pray earnestly, and reject the thoughts as not your own. You must tell God, 'I will to believe': 'I believe with my will.' 'I disown all these blasphemous thoughts which deny Thy Existence and Thy Goodness.' You are so miserably vain, that it might minister to your vanity to be in any way different from others.... Your great battle must be with vanity. Self is your idol, and everything may minister to self. You could be vain at one moment, that a person pays attention to yourself, however inconsistent it may be with your habit: and vain at the next, at indignantly repelling him. You have no conception of the extent of your vanity. God has given you a certain degree of natural ability. I do not know its extent. But you told me when I saw you at —— that your head had given way amid hard reading. How hard, I, of course, do not know: for I do not know that you told me the books. But this implied, that you had not a strong head. And as I said once before, cleverness is something very petty. It is the quick perception of single points: it does not imply any great grasp; rather it excludes it. You may speak of a clever boy, because, having his faculties still undeveloped, he sees single things quickly and clearly. To speak of a clever man or woman would be a disparaging term. It would imply want of grasp or compass. But this cleverness is a great temptation to vanity. The single remarks strike persons, and they admire them. Some smile shows it; and the person goes his way and is self-satisfied and his vanity is nourished. And these petty tributes may be the more numerous, because they *are* petty.

Now just watch yourself for the little occasions in which you think yourself cleverer than another. Perhaps you won't call it clever, but something more solid; a true perception of things. Set yourself against any supposed superiority to any one. One grain of love is better than a hundredweight of intellect. And after all, that blasted spirit, Satan, has more intellect than the whole human race. And remember that to plume yourself about anything is robbing God.

What distressed me in your letter was that you still spoke of 'I cannot believe in God,' which is speaking as if Satan's lie were true. You must not take his lie into your own mouth. Again, you say, 'gives me more time for blasphemous thoughts'; say, 'gives Satan more time for putting blasphemous thoughts into my mind.' I was afraid too that you liked talking of having these blasphemous thoughts put into your mind. It is something unusual.

J. Keble's remedy for having a good opinion of one's self is, 'Recall to yourself the thing which you would be most ashamed that people should know': and his humility is admired even by people of intellect. It is not the 'Christian Year,' or anything else which he did, has raised him to the place around the eternal Throne, which God prepared for Him.

Now don't be vain of having this commonplace letter, because I have taken pains with it.

LETTER LIII.

EVIL THOUGHTS.

January 4, 1877.

Your confessor's advices are right. Satan, as he cannot now lead you into sin, torments you, as you describe. And God permits him to do this, in order to call out in you a deeper repentance for what displeased Him in the past. We should, none of us, know the gravity of past evil unless we were tormented with memories of it, when broken off. It is a great law of God, 'Whereby a man hath offended, thereby is he punished.' Whether it is pride, self-esteem, love of human praise, anger, or any other sin, we bring temptations upon ourselves, which we should not otherwise have had ; and (it has been beautifully said) ' God forgives the past sins, and now pities us the more, because we have brought trials upon ourselves, which we should not have had unless we had brought them upon ourselves.'

Do then, as your confessor advised, take no notice of those thoughts, except to humble yourself to God for what brought them. Say some such prayer as, ' Would, O my God, for love of Thee, I had not so offended Thee! ' Do not examine yourself about those thoughts, whether you consented to them or no, but only whether you said the prayers. Do not try *not* to have them ; but simply turn your thoughts to something spiritual. Think of the souls of those you live with or meet, more than of their bodies. A soul in grace is said to be so beautiful that we should die if we could see it. Think of our Lord as in that inapproachable light of glory, so that you could not discern His Features for that ineffable glory. Own also to God, that you deserved all this torment which harasses you: accept it as less than you deserve: pray Him that through it you may hate the more all which occasioned it. Be not impatient to get rid of it; only desire that you should love God more, Who has forgiven you, and hate that past self. He may lead you through fire and water, but He will lead you at last to that wealthy place, which He gave His Son to purchase for you.

May He bless you in what way He knows.

LETTER LIV.

THE EFFORT TO LOVE GOD.

August 19, 1864.

I am thankful to hear that you had recourse long ago to the remedy, which I thought would be a relief to you. I think that you have not perhaps brought home to yourself, how great and complete God's goodness was to you in it. In it, He pronounced, by His Minister's voice, the forgiveness of your sins, as much as if you could have heard Himself saying to you, "Thy sins are forgiven thee." Henceforth the guilt of sin is removed: the memory of sin is only healthful and for your growth in His Love. 'Much forgiven, much love.' It is of His great Love that He has brought to your mind what people so commonly think so little of, sins of omission. He would have you love Him more for having forgiven them. But this is the very thing which you complain of, that you have not 'the glowing love' which you feel that you should have for all His goodness. This too is part of His Love. If you had not love, you could not feel the want of it; for love only feels that it does not love enough. But then you know what you have to do. It is a safeguard of humility, to feel that you do not love enough; it is a goad to make you ask for more love from Him Who alone can give it. Love, love, love! It is the thirst of the soul, the only thing which the soul needs. "Ask, and ye shall receive." Jesus has pledged His word to you. Do not ask much for *sensible* love. But set out with this, that He has merited for you by those bitter Sufferings on the Cross, the forgiveness of your sins; that He has forgiven them, blotted them out; that He died for you as much as if there had been none besides to die for; and then thank Him and bless Him and ask Him for exceeding love for Himself Who so loved you. I said, 'Do not ask much for *sensible* love'; let this come or go, as He wills; but ask Him for a great love. Forget yourself and your own feelings; go beyond them; to think of yourself chills love; but dwell on God; ask of Him for that love which shall be the bliss of eternity. Think of Him, of all He has done for you, thought for you, loved you with all that individual Love. And then, do not think merely, 'how I *ought* to love Him,' 'how cold my love is!' but go to Him Who came to send the fire of His Love upon the earth, and ask Him for His Love.

The memory of forgiven sin, whether of commission or omission, should be humbling, not depressing. In all eternity, we can never love God enough for His forgiving Love. I suppose that one of our feelings, as He unfolds to us more and more of His Love, will be, 'This for me!' It is quite true, that you do not love God enough; it would be a very bad sign, if any one thought that he did love Him enough. In all eternity we could never love Him enough.

I think that you are more likely to find comfort, when you cease to look for it and dwell more on the thought of God's great Love and pray for it. While we watch our feelings, we lose sight of God. There is a great deal of truth in those hymns, 'Just as we are'; only that we are not to be satisfied with remaining 'just as we are'; but to pray for grace and to use it, still feeling our own nothingness and worthlessness and thanking Him Who has had pity on our badness.

I do not know what you include among the 'outward

things which occupy the largest portion of your time.' Life is necessarily filled with a number of little outward things, but the love of God may be the soul of them all, while we thank Him for His continual mercies in all the little daily comforts of life, and ask His grace to please Him in all its little duties. Thanksgiving is a great nourisher of love, and of peace too, as God tells us ; " In everything by prayer and supplication *with thanksgiving* let your requests be made known unto God: *and* the peace of God, which passeth all understanding, shall keep your hearts and minds through Christ Jesus." Observe that *and*; pray, thank, and the peace will come.

As for people thinking too well of one, it shows one, I hope, two things, (1) the worthlessness of all human opinion; they know nothing about one; (2) how great a good is any grace of God which He has vouchsafed to us. Those who see it, for love of His grace, lose sight of all the dark parts, just as people admire the lustre of a jewel, though all beside it has no brightness in it.

LETTER LV.

SUBMISSION.

February 9, 1853.

It is plainly right to give way, in ——'s state of health. Besides, he has a right to refuse. It is in vain for me to think of giving work. There are more hands than heads to look over. Your daughters must look on the patterns of Moses in the wilderness and St. Paul in Arabia, and pray God to fit them to be employed by Him, when He wills. It is much to learn to be content to do nothing when God wills, as a sort of living statue, remaining where its Master placed it.

LETTER LVI.

CASTING LOTS.

February 21, 1840.

I should dread the casting lots: it might be that I had not faith enough, and do not see that *we* have a right to employ them in so solemn a matter. I should have thought the better way would have been to have postponed the subject for a time (until after Easter), and using Lent as a time of humiliation, pray God to enlighten one's mind, and to put into it the thought which He knew to be best. It might be a subject of prayer before receiving the Holy Communion. I should have been afraid of the casting lots, lest it should arise from a wearisomeness of indecision, instead of waiting patiently for the time when He would enable one to decide according to His Will.

I will try, when I can, to give you a better opinion: as it is, I should be afraid of it.

LETTER LVII.

THE SAME.

February 25, [1840].

I cannot come to any other conclusion about lots. Were you to try them, and they fell out one way, I should be thankful—if the other, *I* should not be satisfied. It seems to me to be risking the more excellent way. For myself, it seems to me clear to what you are called, though, at first, I did not feel myself entitled to lay upon you what I had never been called upon to decide for myself: my own way of life had looked one way since I was eighteen, and the question which you have to decide was never brought before me.

But I do strongly feel (as far as one can judge for another) that you are being led to be an example, if it may be, of the higher way of life, and yourself to the higher holiness than I imagine you would attain to in the ordinary way. God guide you. I have done, as you asked, sincerely, and was glad that we were near each other at St. Mary's.

LETTER LVIII.

Apparent Failure in Mission Work.
1876.

Life *is* very chequered. They are very comfortable words, "The light shall not be clear nor dark; it shall be one day, which shall be known to the Lord, not day nor night—but *in the eventide it shall be light*[1]." Zechariah certainly is prophesying of the distant future, of which there was no fulfilment at our Lord's First Coming, so it belongs to His Second Coming, and who knows, whether the beginning of it may not be now? Everything is on such a gigantic scale: good and evil seem more active than they have been of a long time. It seems again like the close of the Revelation, where it says, "The time is at hand. He that is unjust, let him be still more unjust (i. e. God leaves him to be so)—and he that is righteous, let him be still more righteous; and he that is holy, let him be still more holy[2]." I remember when I was young, thinking things so stagnant and being glad of the signs of a moral thunderstorm—not such a thunderstorm as we have had. We have a different thunderstorm now. However, God is preparing His own way. "Thy way is in the sea, and Thy path in the great waters, and Thy footsteps are not known," but it follows, "Thou leddest Thy people like sheep by the hand of Moses and Aaron[3]."

It was a bright promise when that former king translated our Prayer Book into Hawaiian, and sent to ask us to help

---

[1] Zech. xiv. 6, 7.   [2] Rev. xxii. 10, 11.   [3] Ps. lxxvii. 19, 20.

him. It was like the man of Macedonia who appeared to St. Paul and said, "Come and help us." It was right, that the people should follow their king in what was good. It is the way in which many nations were converted to the Gospel. Other days are come; and will pass away, whatever may succeed them. But God's word does not pass away, nor anything done for God. Not one 'Our Father' was ever lost. It entered into the ears of God, and swelled that cry, to which His Heart has listened, "Thy Kingdom come;" and it has brought down its 'showers of blessings.' How, we know not, and shall not know till the Great Day. Work on then in bright hope. Not one thing which you have ever done for God, has been lost; not one is lost, or ever will be lost. While we each do the little we can do, we may leave the rest to Him.

LETTER LIX.

SELF-DENIAL AND ALMSGIVING.

Second Sunday in Lent, 1841.

With regard to the mode in which self-denial is to be brought about, different people will arrive at it in different ways; if a person with £3,000 per annum be brought to give up £1,000, he must exercise self-denial (unless he have been saving), he must live more simply somehow; when the collection for the London Churches was made here, one gave up a summer excursion, another (*inter alia*) made an old coat serve the place of a new one. Whether people begin by giving up luxuries, or that which feeds them, comes to the same in the end; one will begin with laying down his carriage and horses, another will find at the end of the year that he must have less expensive servants or fewer; another will find it inconsistent to have his drawing-room tricked out with all sorts of gewgaws, china, prints, &c., which our grandfathers had not, &c. I should instance these things sometimes, in preaching, myself, because I am sure it has a good effect on the mind to get rid of them; but I would not make it my object; if we can get, or rather if God infuse the thought of self-denial into people's minds, simplicity will follow sooner or later; people will see it to be inconsistent to have their fingers covered with rings (which is something βάναυσον also) and to be wearing expensive necklaces, while they are retrenching other expenditure in order to give. I do not want a person to 'give his wife's and daughter's jewels,' but I wish these to learn that it is better to be without them, and with their husband's and parent's leave, to part with them. Some such offerings there were in the Metropolis Churches-Fund[1].

We shall never get real charity without a return to simplicity, first or last. Our want of simplicity is hurting us more than can be imagined. People trick out their drawing-rooms and leave God's house bare; our 'elegancies' are offensive to good taste; if the things are beautiful in themselves, they are too crowded together; but the worst is, they make self the idol. Our young women will not work seats for drawing-rooms or slippers, and Altar cloths at the same time; we shall not have silver corner dishes and handsome Chalices together. God or ourselves must be our first object, and the one will drive out the other.

Why should we speak of 'depriving one's family' of things? Why should they not be equally ready to give them up as ourselves? I am sure that there are a number of difficulties of this sort which Satan raises, to cloud our eyes, but which are like so many phantom-figures which disappear as soon as one touches them. The wife, by God's appointment, leans on the husband, looks up to him, imbibes his way of thinking, at least gradually; let her see that her husband in earnest wishes for greater simplicity, and in nine cases out of ten or ninety-nine out of a hundred, she will help him forward, not hinder him; will take a pleasure in following out his plans; be as glad to 'deprive herself' of perishable things for the sake of eternal, and for her Saviour's sake, as he. Our women are more self-denying, more ardent, more devoted as a body, than we. There is a depth about the character of our English females, which has not been brought out, but which, when 'Sisters of Charity' are formed, and self-

[1] See Life of E. B. Pusey, D.D., vol. i. p. 330.

denial acted upon, will bring glorious days to our Church.

Again, as to servants, it is more difficult, but the simpler a person makes his establishment, the simpler the individuals will be. A large establishment, living by itself, with little or no intercourse with its head, is an unnatural thing, and will generally, I fear, be bad; but there are good servants also, and they will readily fall into regulations, if spoken to as Christians.

I think you must beware how you make amount the test of charity. A person *might* out of £3,000 per annum give £1,000 and yet go on in self-indulgent habits. It is not likely perhaps, that one to whom God had given this grace, would so fall short; but to avoid self-deceit we need both self-denial in detail, as well as largeness in giving, which is something elating. Where the everyday living is simple, the sum actually saved by fasting will be little; yet what a stress do the Fathers, and good Churchmen among ourselves, lay on giving to the poor what is saved by fasting. It is becoming partakers of their want, and making them share our plenty.

I agree with you that we do lose vast sums (as we deserve) by our odious system of flattery. If a person gives £100, no matter out of what income, he is idolized, panegyrized in papers, complimented by the clergy, taught to be satisfied with having done a good deed, instead of being stimulated to further good deeds. We lose for the Church, and do harm to people's souls. We speak like mendicants, who think they have no claim to what they ask for, and so shower down praises for any pittance we obtain. We teach people self-satisfaction and unteach humility. We must learn to act more boldly in our Master's Name and leave it to Him to give the praise, as is due, at the Great Day.

LETTER LX.

SELF-DENIAL IN FAMILIES.

Lent, 4th week, 1841, *Tuesday.*

If I did not mistake you, you seemed to think it hopeless to attempt to induce servants to be contented with less than others had. I suspect practically this is not so. I have heard of great families lately who have been putting their household on an allowance of 1 lb. of meat a head per day. And in the middle classes, regulations, restricting food, are common. What is done for economy may be done for Religion. Your letter making me think on the subject, I proposed to my own to exercise some degree of self-denial during Lent; that the savings should be given to the poor. Those who were allowed butter, gave it up; my mother's two men-servants (London servants), who were accustomed to eat meat three times a day (a sad habit), gave up one, and all agreed only to be helped once at dinner. Our whole savings in the week came to near £1, and a servant expressed a hope that there would be less consumed the next week, taking an interest in it.

I hope they will continue the plan for other fast-days: it is but a small beginning; still, the very notion of self-denial, for the sake of the hungry poor, among servants, is a blessing. I accounted as saved, what was under 1 lb. of meat per head.

LETTER LXI.

THE POVERTY OF THE RICH.

September 16, [1869].

I fear that the poverty of the rich is of will, not of means. And if people give, like ——, they give naturally to their own objects. I thought that ——, according to his principle, would have helped; but he is an instance of 'if riches increase they are increased who eat them.' He used to be liberal till he had wealth. I believe that it is true from the peasant upwards that people give in the inverse ratio to what they have.

But do not ask any one to whom it would involve a sacrifice. Better to keep sacrifices for direct gifts to God. I have incurred the responsibility[1], and I must bear it. I could not ask people beforehand, thinking it best to keep the publication secret, for fear one should be prevented; and people hate being asked to help as to that, about which they had not been consulted beforehand. I should not have asked, but that I have been embarrassed by some wrong dealings; but it will come right. . . .

I am much more afraid for the rich in the Day of Judgement than for our 'degraded' or 'neglected populations' of which people are so fond of speaking. 'Magnas inter opes inops,' and that of the true riches.

But it is very reasonable that they should not give for the De Turrecremata. It is only that what you said woke up that ever present feeling.

---

[1] This refers to the publication of Cardinal De Turrecremata's work on the Immaculate Conception. See Life of Dr. Pusey, vol. iv. p. 181.

LETTER LXII.

REPARATION.

December 1, 1878.

I never liked —— on account of its introduction of the French word 'reparation.' It seems to direct the thoughts to others' faults or shortcomings rather than one's own. 'Zeal for the honour of God, for His Glory, in the Blessed Sacrament,' prayer for increased devotion to, thanksgiving for, reverence to It, or the like, would have seemed to me natural subjects for prayer. 'Reparation,' in our English sense of the word, seems to me something foreign to one, as a negligent sinful creature. If one thought what a single Communion would have been to Elijah, who was so fortified by the type of it, or that one Communion might make a saint, and then thinks of the many many Communions, which one has been vouchsafed, since one's first; how tepid one's best compared with what they ought to have been; what they might have made one compared to what one has been and is—one can but bury one's face and say, " God be merciful to me, a sinner ;" I cannot think of making reparation to God for the dishonour to Him by others. I can only think, 'Most likely with their lights, they are better than I.'

LETTER LXIII.

INTELLECTUAL PERILS.

June 15, 1881.

I am indeed thankful of the account which you give of ——. Work for the love of Jesus among His poor seems to have drawn out the loving side of his character, and to have thrown into the shade what our unhappy intellectual Oxford system fosters. Thanks be to God. May He lead him on.

LETTER LXIV.

THE STUDY OF THEOLOGY.

October 18, 1881.

Sad as it is, I am not surprised at any result of the study of Theology to an unsubmissive mind. 'Either God is wiser than he,' and then he submits; or he thinks himself 'wiser than God, as He has revealed Himself,' and then he rebels. Formerly 'heresy' was the alternative; now, it is 'absolute unbelief.' But Card[inal] Newman wrote to me, 'I had rather have to do with the open unbelief of the nineteenth century than with the hidden unbelief of the Middle Ages.'

I have often said that 'love or reverence for our dear Lord will carry a person safe, and nothing else.' Conceit, as you must have seen, I hope *was*, not is, ——'s peril. . . .

I had added a little note, as to what I believe, to a third edition of 'What is of Faith,' &c. It comes to this.

(1) I have myself no thought as to the proportion of the saved and the lost. I leave it blindly in God's hands, Who loves us, and would not part with any whom He could keep without destroying that likeness to Himself, our free will.

(2) I *do* believe myself the pains of sense, although no one is bound as matter of faith to believe them.

God bless you.

LETTER LXV.
OXFORD STUDIES.
October 21, 1880.

You may, alas! well ask why it is necessary at Oxford to go through all that unbelieving reading in order to gain what are called the highest distinctions and the way to Fellowships. Why should they have to pass through or over all those shallows, at that early period of life? I have done what I could to direct minds from it, since I could not alter the scheme itself; but there is a layer of mind in the University which must peel off before anything can be done. Meanwhile there is a rising tide of believing tutors, who will, I hope, change things. The Theological School is unpopular because the Oxford mind is un-Theological.

LETTER LXVI.
SPIRITUAL ADVICE.
[1880.]

Do be careful about 'jesting on a sacred subject.' I suppose that you mean more than speaking playfully with a serious meaning, i.e. you did not do it for the glory of God. "God," Scripture says, "is greatly to be feared in the council of His saints."

Take care about the day-dreaming. It is such special vanity, and so unreal: picturing yourself as being what you would never be, and robbing God in imagination.

If any one thinks well of you, praise God for it. I suppose that Herod's *was* a very able speech.

If you thank God, you need not mind the pleasure which praise gives you. Only remember that it is people's love, not your deserts.

Now set to work again, and be careful not to resist any check of conscience: for it is God's Holy Spirit.

God bless you.

LETTER LXVII.

PROFESSIONAL DISAPPOINTMENT.

[July 15, 1882.]

It is strange that they should admit the young to a laborious profession, take their best years, and then, in middle age, turn them adrift. It is unlike the time when Nelson could introduce midshipmen as 'England's future Admirals.' However, perhaps the succession was the more certain to those who survived, because the battles cut off so many. So perhaps God has preserved to you your son, and in a more active time of war he might have been taken. We cannot know why things are: we only know (as you too have learned) that God sends all good; overrules all evil to good.

LETTER LXVIII.

THE SAME.

Ascot, July 2, 1882.

The country has lost a good officer, and the Admiralty has been ungrateful. But it does not matter, being the object of ingratitude, if one is not ungrateful one's self. It seems a strange sort of profession, which is to be terminable in the midst of one's years. However, Edward is content. His only fear, when I saw him, seemed to be lest you should be disappointed, after throwing yourself so much into his interests. However, God works through crooked and interested agents, and 'what He does, that is well done.' But this you have learned long ago, and this I hope will be dear Edward's lesson now.

> 'E'en disappointment Thou canst bless,
> So love at heart prevail.'

What a gift it is, 'exact conformity to the Will of God.' It is the vestibule to the life of the Blessed Angels, as our Lord has taught us—"Thy Will be done in earth as it is in heaven."

I am again in this wonderful air. God make me thankful for it.

LETTER LXIX.

THE TRIALS OF CONVALESCENCE.

September 8, 1870.

... As far as your health permits, do begin resuming your former devotions. There was, of course, nothing wrong in interrupting them when ill. Illness has its own ways of devotion, not long or set prayers mostly. Then comes procrastination; or convalescence finds it difficult to say what it can do, what not. But do resume something. By trying some increase of prayer you will be able to tell whether you are yet well enough to prolong set prayers. Do not resume all at once, since you are still ill: but try what more you can do than you now do. This will take off the sense of unfulfilled duties, or that you kept away from God of your own accord. If you are not well enough to add set prayers, then increase ejaculations; or in lying down, look at a picture of your dear Lord; or hold a Crucifix in your hand and long for His Love.

LETTER LXX.
Suffering.
[1877.]

I could not find your letter when I wrote yesterday. The near acquaintance with terrible suffering disposes me rather to congratulate those who have any, only desiring grace for them to bear it, as He wills.

Your infirmities will not hinder the grace of the Sacraments; only in this Easter time as well as in Passion-tide, recall to yourself daily that our Lord's Human Nature was glorified in consequence of the depth of His humiliation. In Easter-tide, too, we should seek to sink more and more into our own worse than nothingness. The 'defiled worm,' which Bishop Andrewes calls himself, never rebelled against God's Will.

LETTER LXXI.
Suffering.
[*October* 27, 1870.]

Try habitually to unite your sufferings with those of our dear Lord. The bones of His Sacred Back must so have been torn, dislocated, severed (the word is), the one from the other: and everything must have been so aggravated by the superhuman sensibility of His Frame. Pray Him to sanctify yours by this. Do this often by brief prayers to Him. This sort of disease seems to be increasing. One who became a Religious, and who, seven or eight years ago, when she chose that life, had all the simple brightness of twenty-one, seems [likely] never again to get up. Another is up for three hours in the day. So you are not alone even in this extremity of suffering. Anyhow, God knows each particular pang. Receive as many as you can from Him, and you will thank Him for all eternity.

LETTER LXXII.

THE TRIALS OF SICKNESS.

January 13, 1882.

I am so sorry to hear of your illness. It must in many ways be a great privation to you. But not one consequence will come which will not be overruled to you by the Loving Will of Him, Who knows all the hairs of our heads and all the beatings of our hearts. He says, "Underneath thee are the Everlasting Arms." So lie still in Them, as a child in its mother's bosom. . . .

You cannot help being harassed: but commit yourself again and again to Him Who loves you, He says, "more than a mother doth." Our Good Lord bless and keep you and bring you by this too nearer to Himself. . . .

Only give yourself again and again to God's Sweet Loving Will.

> 'All is right which seems most wrong,
> So it be Thy Sweet Will.'

God heals us body and soul through oneness with His Blessed Will. I have for my subject[1] this evening the words of Psalm xxii, "He trusted in God." It is literally, "He rolled all on God," like one who has a burden too heavy for him, and he rolls it all off himself and upon God: as another Psalmist says, "Cast" (literally, roll) "thy care upon God." God loves you better and more

---

[1] i.e. the subject of the Hebrew Lecture he was then preparing.

wisely than you can love yourself; so cast every thing upon Him.

Yes, I do know that you 'wish to be very sorry for every thing wrong, known or unknown, in your whole life.' Tell God so repeatedly, mentally. It would tire you to say so long a sentence; but if having once said, 'O my God, I would grieve, for love of Thee, that I ever offended Thee,' you were to say at intervals, 'for love of Thee,' 'for love of Thee,' this would stand for the whole. And every time that you said it, or thought it, God would, as it were, undo it. You do undo it, by willing that it had not been.

I have just sent you the Benediction, which I hope your Guardian Angel will convey to you : and once more

> 'The Cross of our Lord Jesus Christ
> Seal thee as His own for ever.'

'For ever!' What a word! Unintermitting, unending, ever-enlarging!

LETTER LXXIII.

METHODS.

Monday in Holy Week, 1882.

I am sorry that you, and especially dear Mrs. ——, should have nothing but disappointment in me as to his writings. But they have brought out to me the different moulds into which our minds were cast. His was (so to speak) a scholastic mind; mine was, from circumstances, a practical mind. His leading idea was to make things exact: my prominent thought was, 'How will they affect others?' I have been for so many years accustomed to men's scruples, that my first thought is, 'Will this give rise to a scruple?' Thus on Confirmation, as to matter, my thought would be, 'Would people question whether we ought to have been anointed, or had the sign of the cross made anew?' and so on. Again, as to Baptism, whether the word should be 'blessed,' &c.

Then as to authorities: when not employed in Hebrew, I used to live in 'the Fathers': the Vincentian rule was my rule—'What was always, everywhere, by all.' I must limit myself. All additional work extrudes some other: and every question wakes up so many more. I am sure that the looking over these papers would bring me a good many thumps on my head; and after all, it looks very much as if its basis were seven Sacraments, using the word Sacrament in a laxer sense (as one, whom —— was catechizing, after explaining that there were two great Sacraments and five lesser Sacraments, being asked, 'How many Sacraments are there?' the boy answered, 'Seven,' which is not the answer which the Catechism would have suggested.)

II

LETTERS ON INTELLECTUAL DIFFICULTIES

LETTER I.

On the Laws of Nature.

1866.

I THANK you very much for giving so much time to the answer on the great subject, upon which I wrote to you. One thing is, I think, clear, that it [the question of fixed laws] is not properly a theological question at all; I mean, that no Divine truth is in any way affected by it. For if the laws be ever so fixed it only needs that they should have been fixed, in relation to the foreseen condition of His creatures; and the subject of prayer is no otherwise touched upon than the whole subject of God's Providence.

But one point I still do not seem to get at in your paper, the proof of any fixed laws as to minute details; e.g., wind or rain, upon which the well-being of mankind mainly depends.

Taking the analogy of your steam engine, all the 'mutual adjustments of certain invariable forces, inherent among the particles of matter,' remain just the same, which ever way the will of the guiding mind directs it, in *this* line or *that*, with greater or less speed, or even over the rails so as to destroy it. It is not interference with its powers, but direction of them through free-will.

Analogous to this, would be the accumulation of electricity, reduction of temperature, change of wind, &c., which proximately produce lightning or rain. You tell me that the rain which falls in a year in a given place does not much vary; and that the winds from the different quarters blow in much the same proportions. But, assuming these as fixed laws of God, and that they proceed from known causes, still it is not these but the minuter conditions (the coincidence of the rain with certain seasons or of the wind with the existence of something which becomes the instrument of chastisement, as locusts, or that, whatever it be, whereon the travelling of the cholera depended) which directly affect the human race. There might be the same average of South Wind in Palestine, but if it blew when the locusts were in the deserts of Arabia ready to be brought, it would be a terrific scourge; otherwise it would be a gain. If rain be concentrated at seed time, the ground may be unfit to sow; if at harvest it may be spoiled. A hailstorm which should be harmless at one time, might destroy a whole vintage at another. They say that spring-wheat requires a very nice adjustment of dry weather and showers. One year (many years ago) there had been next to no autumn-wheat sown; all seemed to depend on the spring-wheat; just at the very last we had exactly that succession of dry weather and rain which was needed.

Now these minute variations seem to me analogous to the directing of the forces of the steam engine. The general laws which you mention, are doubtless indispensable to the general good condition of the atmosphere. And so far we may assume that there are fixed laws for what we observe to be fixed, whatever the law be (I suppose that there is some law), by which God regulates, that there should be the same proportion of rain or wind. And the fact that there are these laws, naturally suggests the hope of discovering other laws for what you can find no law for at present; in which as you say, 'the deviations baffle all expectation.'

But on the other hand, is; it not equally open to Professor Mansel to say, 'All your discovery has not brought you means of discovering any law as to the *time* when these natural phenomena should occur. They are not then, as yet, any real matters of science at all, since science relates to known laws'? Nay, the very fact that you do discover so many other laws, but have made no approximation to any discovery of any law as to this, is, as far as it goes, a probability the other way, that it does not depend upon any fixed law, but upon the Will of God, just as the inherent force of the steam-engine depends upon the combination of certain fixed laws, but the direction in which it shall go depends upon the will of man.

I am thankful to find, that, though Professor Tyndall put it as a Theological question, it is no Theological question; nay, the existence of a physical system, proceeding, in all its details, upon laws immutably fixed, and yet adapted beforehand in all its minutest details to the moral condition of moral agents, would only be the grander adaptation of this physical world to ourselves, its moral and responsible inhabitants. It would be a grand contemplation if true! So if you or your successors should discover such a system of fixed laws, Theology would only teach us in a different way to marvel at the wondrous condescension of our God and His loving forethought for us.

LETTER II.

To an Unbeliever.
July 25, 1881.

I have read your article in *The Radical* to which you draw my attention. I wish that I could render you any service. But God alone can; and I fear that I am not likely to persuade you to ask Him. Writers of the class, to whom I fear you belong, decry dogmatism, yet none are more dogmatic. I think in that column and a half there are a good many dogmatic statements, a good deal of contempt for those who adhere to the old truths, and yet I have not observed one attempt at proof. You have your authorities. Only instead of Jesus, or John and Paul, they are Theodore Parker, or Lord Lytton, or Carlile[1] or Volney, or Feuerbach. Yet anyhow Jesus, although withdrawn from sight, has drawn men unto Him, and has for above eighteen centuries been the Object of the love of all those hundreds of millions upon hundreds of millions. And more, you yourselves are a witness to Him, in that He prophesied of you.

However in one thing I agree with you, that "Love is God," for God has revealed it. God is Love, and Feuerbach is so far indebted to St. John. Yet before the Gospel no one thought of it. They could think of an Infinite Mind. They could not think of Infinite Love.

---

[1] Apparently referring to Richard Carlile. See Life of Dr. Pusey, vol. i. p. 44.

It is a deep saying of Pascal, 'To love man, we must know him; to know God, we must love Him.' God will give you that love if you ask Him. Nay, if you could only say the sceptic's prayer, 'O God, if there be a God, and Thou takest any heed to Thy creatures, teach me to love Thee,' He would hear you. I knew in early youth one whom all recognized as of keenest powerful intellect, who was a disciple of the then German philosophy (I think that the latest then was Schelling), who so prayed and became a Christian.

God guide you and bless you.

LETTER III.

TO AN UNBELIEVER.

October 14, 1881.

I hardly know what was your object in writing to me, whether to abuse the Church of England for her shortcomings, or to protest against my quotation and profession of our love[1]. The Church of England has a good deal of ground to recover, a good many stray sheep to win back, whom she lost in the stiffness and chill of the last century. But God has infused new zeal and greater love into the hearts of men. And the Church loves and prays for you, although in a way in which you probably would not thank her for praying, but in which I too will pray for you and love you, that He would 'bring into the way of truth all such who have erred and are deceived.'

No one would have excepted against Mr. Bradlaugh unless he had made a parade of taking an oath in the Name of God, Whom he declared at the same time not to exist. It was the mockery which outraged people's minds.

And now let me in love for you tell you the history of one whom in my youth I knew very intimately. He was a student of German philosophy, one well known, whom those who knew him respected, and admired the

---

[1] This refers to a 'Letter' to the members of the English Church Union, in which Dr. Pusey expresses his approval of their use of the hymn:
'Faith of our Fathers! we will love Both friend and foe in all our strife,' &c., &c.

clearness of his intellect. He thought that he never could again believe a miracle. He went to church and heard the Gospels. He believed in nothing, yet the history struck him. 'That would look like true history if it were not for the miracles.' After a time he prayed, ' O God, if Thou takest notice of Thy creatures, hear me.' He became a Christian.

It is little to speak of our poor love. Jesus, your and our Redeemer, Himself loves you (for He died for you), and wishes to bring you back to Himself. But He so loves the free love of His creatures that He will not drag you back as if you were a stock or a stone. He would draw by His love. Say to Him any, the best prayer which you can, if you are a sceptic, or say to God whatever doubting prayer you can and He will hear you. I doubt not that He hears the well-known prayer, ' O God, if there be a God, save my soul, if I have a soul,' if it was all which His creature could offer. So He would hear you if you pray to Him : 'O God, if the faith which I once had was the truth, give it me back again.'

God bless and teach you.

PS. I have no parish, and so none of the 'hinds' whom you speak of contemptuously; but have for now fifty-eight years been in contact with intellectual unbelief, in all its forms, mainly as it has existed in Germany.

LETTER IV.

SPECULATIONS OF 'EXACT SCIENCE.'

December 6, 1881.

It startles me to see what a small basis of fact modern science builds its enormous theories upon. The only fact which I see is, that 'in a thousand years the change in the length of a day is only a fraction of a second; but that the change is always in one direction.' So then it is 'inferred' that a million years ago the day *probably* contained some minutes less than our present day of twenty-four hours. 'Exact science' has surely nothing to do with 'probably's.'

And it is said to be proved that the length of the day must involve a corresponding change in the motion of the moon. Granted. And so, that 'more than 50,000,000 of years ago' the moon was born of this earth.

How do we know that the earth existed 50,000,000 of years ago? So that the theory begins with an 'If.' If the earth existed 50,000,000 of years [ago], then we can conceive that 'the orbit of the moon which is now getting larger and larger,' may have been less and less, until we come to a time 50,000,000 years back, when it was projected from the earth.

It is a simple objection to the theory, that if the moon was originally detached from the earth, it should have been like it. But the writer, too, grants that no two bodies seem to be more unlike; the moon, with those tremendous cavities, which (they used to say) the sun never penetrated, and (as he too says) which has no sea. Still he speaks of 'tides in the sealess moon.'

I suppose that to amuse his audience he was obliged to use poetic language. But what has science to do with such language as p. 105? 'I do not know what decided the moon; but what the decision was is perfectly plain.' In simple language, he does not know why the moon revolves round the earth at all. And I suppose it is insoluble why a body projected (if it was so) from another should revolve round it, and not fall back again, unless a higher Will controlled it. One Agent he omits,—Almighty God. I hope that he presupposes that it was at His Will that all those things which he imagines took place. But for the future, he ignores one event which *may* disturb his calculation of the millions of years in store for this earth, the destruction of this earth by fire, of which Holy Scripture speaks. True, that however God shall bring this about, it does not speak of the absolute destruction of the earth. It may still be "the new earth" which Scripture also speaks of. And he modestly says '*if* it shall last so long'; but what depends upon an 'if,' belongs to imagination, not to science.

However, there is one thought which these speculations about this all-but-boundless time bring home to us: When shall we see God? In old days, when we thought of the duration of this world as 6,000 years, it seemed, at all events, as if it must end a century hence, and that then, anyhow, one should be admitted to see Him. But now that one has accustomed one's self to think of ages upon ages in the past, time in the future also may be—one knows not what. And one knows not what the waiting-time may be. However, "the souls of the righteous are in the Hands of God" wherever they are. These theories may do us the good of doing away with commonplace notions, and make us commit ourselves blindly to Him that He will do with us what He wills.

LETTER V.

COMPROMISING REVEALED TRUTH[1].

[1879.]

I am afraid my opinion of R. Schmid's opinion (as far as it goes) will be disappointing. Whatever good it may do in Germany, I should fear it would do rather harm here. His defence of faith comes to this. Darwinism (however true) does not exclude Providence, hearing of prayer, our Lord's Resurrection, or our own. Plainly not; for it leaves them on one side, except as far as it makes 'Natural Selection' a sort of goddess, development personified; but it is a mere metaphor, for you will remember what he says, that a single instance of clear design in a complicated structure would destroy his system, or the like.

Schmid's defence seems to be directed against the current disbelief in Germany, and it amounts to this, that there are no *a priori* objections to the Providence of God, or His hearing prayer, or to miracles, or our Lord's Resurrection, or our own. But these are fundamentals of the Faith, and stand (as he seems to feel sometimes) so entirely on their own ground that they are altogether apart from any questions about Evolution. It is only the peg upon which he hangs what he has to say.

Then he is living in an entirely different atmosphere, and as the hands get hard by hard work, so his ears have got

---

[1] For Dr. Pusey's deliberate judgement on 'Darwinism,' see Life of Dr. Pusey, vol. iv. pp. 330-336, and his sermon on 'Un-science, not Science, adverse to Faith.'

accustomed to horrid blasphemies by living among them. It would, I think, do people simple harm to read of all the disbelief in pp. 172-200.

Living in Germany, where I fear Atheism has so welcomed Darwinism as doing its work, he has thrown himself into the Darwinian theories, owns that they are still only hypotheses, and takes it, seemingly, for granted that, one day or other, some one of them will be established to be true, and writes of the costs of a wrong relation between Theology and Science, identifying Evolutionism as a whole with Science. He has evidently taken a keen interest in it, and pours out all he knows and pleads its cause. I should think that the result of recommending his book would be to recommend people to learn Darwinism....

I think that in what he says about God working through means, he mistakes the real objection to Evolution as stated by Darwinists. Their system is practically Atheistic. For a First Cause who sets things going and then leaves them to themselves is practically in no relation to His creatures. It is an Epicurean god. A mere First Cause is no object of adoration or love or hope or trust.

With our belief in God, if millions of years passed by during which God created, before He created man, we have no doubt that He created in view of other intelligent creatures besides ourselves. The Darwinians write as if we knew all about it. They multiply aeons upon aeons, during which they suppose the development to have lasted. Of course to the mere Atheists among them, or to those who deny any τέλος of Creation, it is simply a matter of decypherment. Such and such was the order in which things developed. But for those such as Schmid, who believe that there is a God, and that God created for an end, it seems to me strange that they should think that in all those aeons God was doing all this, with no other end than that we should imperfectly decypher that there is an order from lower to higher, and not this only, but that the lower all along gave birth to the higher, and this, too, without any known instance of it. It must often strike one that this our present creation must be for others also. How little we see of it; for ·how little do we give thanks! To take beauty alone, the intensest beauty is what is seen by fewest. The beauty of those masses of flowers embosomed in mountain dells; the almost every-day summer beauty of sunset; the intense varied beauty of cataracts; the unceasing variety of the beauty of light; the depth of beauty in the recesses of glaciers—it was not made for nothing.

Then, too, there is to us something so very anthropomorphic in their ideas of creation. They seem to think that it is some great effort to God to create; that successive creations (or rather one continuous creation) implies successive efforts in God; whereas we, of course, believe what our Lord says, " My Father worketh hitherto, and I work."

In the chapters about the creation of man, his theory translated out of abstraction comes to this, that when God willed that our last ape-ancestress should bear a man, God endowed its offspring with intellectual gifts, wholly distinct and superior to any before, specially as regards its personality, its I, its freedom, its full likeness to God (p. 300). I should think that any Darwinist would treat this as absurd. . . .

We all believe that the book of God's Works rightly interpreted will not contradict the book of His Revelation. Schmid uses this to put minds in a state of readiness to surrender this or that truth, if what is now owned to be hypothesis should turn out to be truth. He seems ready to surrender anything, except the Resurrection of our Lord. Thanks be to God for any degree of belief which He retains in any one. But a state of mind which would be ready to give up the belief in the Fall, and to think St. Paul wrong in his argument about our Fall in Adam and our Restoration in Christ, or to take up with the idea that we are not of one blood, but only descended from different ape-mothers in different parts of the world, is not one which you would wish to cherish. One who was so ready to part with Articles of Faith would part with much more. It would be inverting the relation of Divine and human truth, that what man thinks that he discovers is certainly true, and that God's Revelation must be conformed to it.

I have only read of Reusch's book what I wanted for the subject of my sermon. Development is the fashion of the day. I should think that such a book as Reusch's would be more useful in stopping people from throwing themselves headlong into new hypotheses.

Some of my friends have asked me, 'Should you think Darwinism, if it should become a science, contrary to Faith?' I always think I ought to answer them as well as I can; my answer was meant to be: 'Darwinism cannot become science, because there are no facts.' As for the correspondences in the whole animal creation (and in part vegetable too), you too are old enough to remember that we were familiar with them in our youth and only looked upon them as so many indications of our Father's Hand in all.

LETTER VI.

FRIENDLY CRITICISM.

[? *December*, 1878.]

You need not expect 'severe censures' from me. We have, I fear, been educated in very different faiths. But in these days I am but too thankful for anything which is in the direction of faith. And as such I am glad that you at least demolish that assumption of Fetishism as man's primaeval faith. To me it is strange that people should assume, as a postulate, that we were born in the most degraded condition in which we could exist, and yet be men. The account of Genesis, with which the New Testament agrees, is the more reasonable. Degradation is easier than self-elevation. But that we were *mutum et turpe pecus* is assumed as a self-evident fact.

I hope, as far as you do teach on [Non-Christian] religion, you will keep to this, which is your vocation, and which you so wonderfully understand, and not go off to the Old Testament which (forgive me) you do not understand. I do not think that what you write on this, you write on your own knowledge or thought: e.g. you say that "Thou delightest not in burnt offerings" is a contradiction of the Levitical sacrifices. I think myself that those sacrifices were a wonderful picture of the deserts of sin; but David's words were no contradiction of them, for there was no sacrifice for murder or adultery.

LETTER VII.

Doubts.

March 29, 1882.

It must be a piteous sight to you who have always lived in a home of faith to see so many of our young men drifting about with no definite faith. I fear that they have not brought the realities of their existence before them, or what even Felix trembled at, "judgement to come." They will not look at things in the face. Jesus came with a message to each of those whom He redeemed: 'Believe in Me, for I came from heaven to save you.'

Physical philosophy has nothing to say to this. It tells us increasing marvels about the physical creation. It can tell us nothing more. It is even marvellous how much it can disclose within its own province, while it has absolutely nothing to say beyond or above it. How Creation came into being, how long it shall be, it is absolutely silent. It cannot contradict Revelation, for it moves in a different sphere. It can guess at certain things. People may assume that our little world has existed for millions of millions of years. It cannot say that it had no beginning. Holy Scripture speaks only of 'the *beginning*.' People are only throwing dust in their own eyes when they speak of physical science contradicting Revelation. But if they *will* throw dust in their own eyes, God alone can open the eyes of the blind.

In like way as to Holy Scripture, these things are absolutely certain :—

(1) That the Old Testament tells of things as to Jesus which man could not foresee, and which man could not bring to pass. (I mentioned some heads of these in my Sermon, 'The prophecy of Jesus, the certain prediction of the [to man] impossible.' I was obliged to put in the ['to man'] not to make it too great a paradox.) God won by it one of the most solid minds I ever knew. Entangled by the philosophy of Fichte and Schelling, he thought that he could never again believe a miracle. His was a far stronger, clearer mind than any with whom you are likely to meet. But God won him through the miracle of prophecy. Prophecy was to him the credential of the Revelation of Jesus:—Omnipotence fulfilled what Omniscience could alone foresee.

(2) That the Gospels were written while the events and discourses recorded in them were recent, is again matter of certainty. It has been ascertained as it is not as to other books. A person has no right to say 'It is too much trouble to go through all that reading.' Too much trouble to ascertain whether we have the very words of Him Who converted the world ; Who says that He came to die for us, to save us from God's displeasure, to make us His children that we may be blessed in Him for ever!

It is no large labour; not one-fiftieth part of what they are ready to spend, in order to gain some passing honour, in which they may very likely be disappointed. What if they succeed? A person of talent was converted once by an able man, who asked him gravely what he proposed to himself as to his future. The young man began with his immediate prospects. It was all taken seriously and with the question 'Et puis?' The young man went on picturing his career and was led on by the 'Et puis?'

until at last when he had reached the summit of his ambition, a tender 'Et puis?' brought to his mind the hollowness of his hopes, and he turned to God.

But it is not a large range of reading after all which is required to convince a person that the Gospels were of the date at which every one, till our English Deists, believed them to be written. Nine papers by Dr. Lightfoot in a periodical! Dr. Liddon tells me that Kirchhofer's *Quellensammlung zur Geschichte des N. T. Canons* contains all the important evidence as to the Gospels. But granted the early date, Renan's failure has shown how impossible it is to make a consistent history of Jesus which should not be Divine.

I fear that the hindrance is in truth some indisposition to believe. Some, I think you told me, called themselves 'Agnostics.' The translation of the word into Latin would be what they would not like to take to themselves, 'Ignoramuses.' But what a thing it is for a reasonable creature to profess that he knows nothing about his being; what after a few years will become of him; whether he can do anything to affect his condition then; whether he is the object of the Infinite Love of God Who is Love! It is so unspeakably stupid, more stupid than the most stupid of our four-footed fellow-creatures. I have never come across them. In term-time Liddon would be glad to help them, if they wished to be helped. I wonder whether it would startle any of them to be told, 'God loves *you*' (for He does love every soul which He has made), 'and *that* with an infinite individual Love'; or 'You will never be happy till you love God in return, for God made the soul for Himself, and so it must needs be restless till it rests in Him.' (This you will recognize as St. Augustine's confession after years of wandering to find out the origin of evil.) You who have seen them must know how they can best be roused. They have a suspicion probably, that they are in the wrong; for God doubtless speaks to them at times. Your own firm faith probably startles them more than they are willing to own to themselves. They could not say that a conditional prayer would do them no good. For their own profession is that they know nothing about God. Gain them if you can, to make the trial, and to pray any the best prayer they can. . . .

LETTER VIII.

DIFFICULTIES ABOUT REVELATION.

1853.

The answer about the heathen is, that we know nothing. God tells us what concerns us, not what concerns us not. He tells us what will befall us if we refuse the Light; He tells us nothing as to those on whom the Light has not shined. Our simple duty is to do what He says. He has said, 'Preach the Gospel to every creature.' The Church then is bound to teach; and we individually are bound, in what way we can, by alms or prayers, to aid. How God will deal with those who refuse to hear is with Him. Their refusal opens the state of their hearts to us: He to Whom all hearts are open knows who will hear and who will refuse.

The meaning of 'generally necessary' is universally necessary; but with the understood condition, 'where they can be had.'

We know nothing about the heathen philosophers. Those who loved God, or dimly searched after Him, have doubtless been accepted by Him for His sake Whom they knew not, their Redeemer.

The answer to the question about the Revelation and the Apocrypha is, that the Revelation was only doubted about by part of the Church, for want of information. The doubts disappeared after the Council of Nicaea, when Bishops from all parts of the Church had the opportunity of comparing their traditions. The Canon of the Old

Testament received the seal of our Lord Himself, when He explained the Law, the Prophets, and the Psalms, the well-known Hebrew division of the Hebrew Scriptures. We receive, then, as inspired what He set His seal upon, although others are used, as St. Jerome says, for moral teaching.

We receive the Hebrew Scriptures only, because they alone are the Scripture which our Lord guaranteed to us, and of which St. Paul spoke, " All scripture is given by inspiration of God." We receive the Revelation because the Church (though some once doubted) has attested from the first that it is the writing of an inspired Apostle.

God bless and keep you always.

LETTER IX.

THE SAME.

September 9, 1853.

It was indeed presumption to read that book in that spirit. Almighty God left you to yourself that you might feel the fruits of that presumption, and so not presume in yourself again, but trust in Him.

The case of Pharaoh is easily answered. He hardened his own heart; where God is said to have hardened, it was only that He left him to himself, when he would harden himself.

The other specific question is also easily answered. Almighty God has said that He will judge every man according to his work. How He will judge, whom He will condemn, we know not. He does not judge as man judges. He says it shall be more tolerable for Sodom and Gomorrha than for some who were outwardly exempt from their sin. Every one will be judged according to his own light.

The question, 'Whence is evil?' cannot be answered. We see that there is evil. Whence it came into the world of the Good God, we cannot tell. We who cannot understand the very least things, how should we understand the greatest? We understand not our own souls, what life is, what sleep, what is called 'instinct' in brutes, what our own free-will is, how we can be free and yet not wholly free, without the grace of God; how we can have any free-will at all, in the very least things, since Almighty God knows perfectly all things to us future. Everything around is full of mystery; we ourselves are a mystery to ourselves. How should we in our little corner of the universe understand the Ways and the Mind of the Infinite God?

But turn which way we will we have no better solution. Men do not remove their difficulties by becoming infidels: they only change them and aggravate them. Infidels are obliged to believe absurd things; we only believe what we do not understand, and which God will explain to us by-and-by. Socinianism, Rationalism, Atheism, Pantheism, all have their difficulties. The soul which loses its faith must, if it is consistent, sink down to Pantheism, and then the difficulties of Pantheism drive it upward again.

God leaves some things unexplained to us, which He will explain to us in Heaven if we come thither; and we shall attain if we use His grace. Meanwhile we have our Lord to believe in. He must have been, He is, true. We cannot but believe in Him. His Divine Truth is transparent in Him, in His words, His works. "Lord, to whom shall we go?" "Shall not the Judge of the whole earth do right?"

This is but a short answer, but your note was urgent. Butler's *Analogy*, or 'St. Augustine on the benefit of believing,' are useful books. But the great Source of faith is our loving Lord. He will increase your faith, if you seek Him. He has promised. He will do it. Tell Him that you have sinned in this reading and presumption. Ask Him to give you back your faith as a little child. He will show His Divine power by giving it back, if you ask earnestly.

LETTER X.

THE SAME.

September 26, 1853.

The book is sadly ignorant or dishonest. You ask two questions: (1) How it was just to place Pharaoh in temptation and *not to aid him*, and then to condemn him? (2) How it was just to plague a whole nation for the sins of its ruler?

I would ask first, How do you know either? Why was Pharaoh different from the other Pharaoh who acted religiously towards Joseph? Through his own free will. Else he would not be blamed. In whatever way *that* other king of Egypt who acted well became such as so to act, *this* Pharaoh might also. Doubtless God does help the heathen through their consciences, "Not having the law, they are a law unto themselves." There is a difference between good and bad heathen, people acting up to their light and those who do not. And God, no doubt, for Christ's sake, Who died for the whole world, accepts those who act up to the light which He gives them.

Pharaoh is but a picture of many Christians. God's dealings harden some, soften others, according as they receive them. We see every day how one person frets and rebels and accuses God for the very same thing which bows down others before Him. But the special character of Pharaoh's trial is that which goes on with every one who yields to some special deadly sin. God visits them by some chastisement: they profess repentance. He withdraws it. They return to their sin. He punishes again. They stop. He closes that punishment. They go back to their sin. And so it continues, until life ends. They harden their hearts continually, and God lets them be hardened.

2. There is a dreadful chapter, which I do not recommend you to read, but which begins, "After the doings of the land of Egypt, wherein ye dwelt, shall ye not do." And then follows a list of abominations. It is very ignorant then, when the book speaks of the Egyptians being plagued for their ruler. A bad king is often the punishment of the nation's sin, and it is most likely that Holy Scripture, when it says "A king arose," meant that he was raised by some revolution to the throne, probably through sin.

For the whole question, 'Whence is evil?' there is, as I said, no solution. But this is a question of great difficulty to every one. An Atheist has the same difficulty: he cannot account for it; he cannot reconcile the evident marks of design with things coming together by chance. Chance is a mere name by which to veil his ignorance. The pantheist is worse still; his god sins, since, according to him, all are part of his god.

There is no more difficulty as to the Old Testament than as to the New, if people believe it. Eternity of punishment will be understood only in heaven. We must believe here, and shall understand there.

I do not know 'the story of Hypatia.' God will not punish 'involuntary ignorance.'

You ask me about myself. I never questioned any histories in the Old Testament. Our Lord has set His seal upon the Old Testament. He tells us it is from God. I believed Him.

I do not know ———. He would have more love than our Lord Who died for us. Our good Lord tells us that punishment shall be eternal that we may be the more diligent to escape it. Our Lord promises us Everlasting Life, if we believe and obey Him. He warns of everlasting punishment, if we disbelieve and disobey. It is to set at nought our Lord's own words, if we will not believe that He means by "everlasting" in the one place, the same which He means in the other.

The way to recover faith, . . . is to pray for it. Do not despair about it, but pray. Then meditate on our Lord's Goodness, Perfectness, Truth, Love, and say to Him, 'Good Lord, I am poor and weak, ignorant and miserable; Thou art All-wise, All-good, All-loving. I trust all to Thee. Enlighten my blindness, perfect my faith, kindle my love, that I may love Thee and believe in Thee, and hope in Thee, with my whole heart.'

God bless and keep you.

LETTER XI.

ABOUT AN UNBELIEVER.

My daughter has shown me the letter about poor ———. It is a case to make one's heart bleed. Such a soul can never be lost. I do not remember what I wrote before, and so I might be writing the same thing again.

These things strike me in your report of her conversation. They are fundamental.

(1) She does not seem to have any idea of God. She and her husband are not, I suppose, consciously Atheists, but she does not seem to have the slightest idea of the relation of a creature to its Creator. Her whole idea seems to be, 'If I were God I should do so and so.' 'I should not bid my creatures love me, whom they had never seen, and I should not make myself the great object of love to my creatures, so that they could not find happiness out of me; nor would I so prize their free love as not to force them to love me whether they would or no. In fact I would make only stocks or stones, not beings who could freely love me. There should be no Angels or Archangels, nor any of the heavenly hosts, Cherubim or Seraphim. Indeed, on second thoughts, I do not think that I would create at all. For to what end to create inanimate things? They would only be as a child makes things to play with.' One may venture sometimes to

unveil the blasphemy of the thought which comes over people's minds, to scare them from it.

(2) Her only idea seems to be how to avoid some pains inseparable from one doctrine, the pain to those who will not love God, and to pass through this life as comfortably as she can; and to have what is to her the most comfortable theory, that we all should be annihilated like the beasts which perish.

But what if it be not so? The convictions of mankind are against her, all through the heathen as well as the Christian and Mohammedan world. To what end to make to herself a false peace for this world, by imagining a world for herself; when she must think it *possible*, at all events, that mankind may be right, and that she may wake up, when she closes her eyes, to find that God is a very different God from what she imagined Him, and that she has lost the opportunities of growing in His Love, and so having more of His Love? All Christians believe that this life is the time of growth in the love of God. God has told us that we shall be judged for all "the things done in the body, whether they be good or bad." To speak of the terrors of judgement might perhaps, in her present state of mind, scare her back. I only speak of loss, that she is losing day by day the degree of love which she might have had.

(3) To some of her difficulties the answer would be, 'How do you know?' 'If heaven is true, it would be no happiness to most of those I know.' But what do we know of almost any soul except our own? Our Lord says, "Judge not." St. Paul says, "Judge nothing before the time when God shall bring to light the hidden things of darkness and make known the counsels of the heart, and then shall every man have praise of God." We are very ignorant and so cannot judge; and if we attempt to judge, shall judge wrong.

These things are certainly true.

(1) God the Holy Ghost visits every soul born into this world, and speaks to them in their conscience. It is a wondrous saying of a heathen, 'To all mankind conscience is God.' The judgement of each will be how he listened to that voice.

(2) God will part with none to whom He has not disclosed His full Love, and the soul deliberately will not have Him. He will part with none whom He can help.

(3) There are almost infinite variety of capacities of love of Him. All will be full who attain. But as you could conceive a vessel which should contain the ocean, and every variety down to the tiniest acorn-cup, so there could be almost infinite varieties of love and joy.

(4) I would add as probable, but almost certain, that God does a great deal for the soul in the hour of death. The poor guess rightly from the beauty of the body which the soul has left. Even Lord Byron knew of it:

> 'He who hath bent him o'er the dead ...
> And mark'd the mild angelic air,
> The rapture of repose that's there[1].'

In some cases it is plainly supernatural beauty, which can come from nothing but the presence of God the Holy Ghost, ere the soul parted from it.

As for the lesser difficulties, e.g. (1) that she cannot love one out of sight; I wonder whether she has not yet lost one whom she loved, father or mother, or whether she thinks that she should not love a child if God took him. Her heart would yearn after her child, and despite of what she thinks probable, she cannot, I think, so have hardened her heart as not to hope her child was happy, somehow or somewhere, in the great Bosom of Love.

She thinks (2) that she 'cannot love one who had lived so long ago.' You can tell her our creed is, that He went

[1] Lord Byron, *The Giaour*.

away for our good; that He ever liveth at the Right Hand of God to make intercession for us; that He loves every one of us, her husband, herself, her four children, with an infinite individual love; that He has sent His Holy Spirit to replace Himself; that every check of conscience, if she were inclined to do anything amiss, every drawing to anything good, is from Him. We can love an unseen Benefactor, and should long to see Him, if we knew Him to be such. She does not love Jesus because she does not know Him. Why will she not read about Him? I think that if she were to read the Gospel of St. John, with prayer, some sparks of her old love would be rekindled.

In one thing she is right, not to try to get up excited feelings she was 'taught in her youth to have, or to try to have towards Jesus.' Faith is the gift of God; love also is a great grace of God poured into the heart by God. The less we meddle with our feelings the better. But let her ask of God, and He has pledged Himself to hear. "Ask and ye shall receive, that your joy may be full." Poor thing! she cannot be happy now, for instead of bringing her husband to the full faith in God, she has herself fallen away from that which God gave her.

(3) She 'can't believe in the Incarnation.' I fear that she must be very proud towards God. I am frightened at some of her expressions. They look as if she were afraid of recovering her former faith, and were steeling herself against it. One expression as to Him, Who is at this moment loving her and pleading for her, and trying to win her, sounds even contemptuous;—'this absent Person.'

Her saying, translated into plain words, would be, 'O God (I wish she could say O my God), Thou lovest me so, that I cannot believe it; Thou didst so humble Thyself for love of me too, that I cannot believe in One Who so humbled Himself for love of me.'

Alas! it looks like a hard fight against the pleading of God within her. God grant that she may yield to Him Who loves her and gave Himself for her.

I will ask the 'Society of the Love of Jesus,' which prays God in one unbroken succession of prayer night and day for the conversion of sinners, to pray for her and him. It is a very sad case. She has loved her husband more than God, and so has for the time, I fear, parted with God.

I wonder whether she prays still anyhow. Even a dry heathen philosopher believed that the gods loved those who love them. He inverted the order that "we love God because He first loved us"; still he believed in a mutual love of God and the creature.

It is a terrible prospect for ———. She thinks herself repelled from the Truth by the lives of persons who in a measure have not parted with faith. If they fail inconsistently with their belief, how must it be with those who have none?

I have remembered her; but if you could induce her to say even such a sceptic prayer as, 'O God, if the faith I once had was from Thee, give it me again,' she would be in the way to gain from the prayers of others.

God so loves us that He hears even sceptic prayers if they are the best any one can offer.

God bless you and all your efforts for Him.

LETTER XII.

To an Unbeliever.

August 5, 1882[1].

I did *not* refer to Paley. When I read him as a young man I felt if that is all what he has to say, I was better off before. His result would only be a degree of probability; what the soul needs is to have certainty. The value of Butler is, I thought, that he showed that there is no middle standing ground between entire faith and Atheism. I do not understand what your 'Deity' is. Is it One Who created us, and Who can reveal Himself and His Will? I think that you will find that you prescribe to Almighty God that He should not reveal, what you, ——, do not like to believe or think that He ought to reveal. This was much the condition of the heathen in the first centuries of the Gospel. They called the Gospel obstinacy, folly, old wives' fables, &c. Indeed even St. Paul says that 'Christ crucified was to the heathen foolishness.' Do you really think yourself wiser than St. Paul, or more loving than St. John? Do you not believe that St. Paul was converted as he says that he was? I ask these questions not as a mere appeal to humility, but that you may bring home to yourself what your real position is.

I do not think that you have made clear to yourself what free-will is. You do not believe that a free agent *can*

---

[1] From the date of this letter, it is very probable that it was the last letter of the kind that Dr. Pusey wrote.

choose amiss. But then, are not all those around you who choose what you too think amiss, free? They do indeed become, by sinning, less and less free. For "he who committeth sin is the servant of sin." But when he or she committed against his or her conscience the first grievous deadly sin, was not he or she free? Drunkenness is, I suppose, one of the most prevailing sins. Yet even those rough efforts of the 'Salvation Army' show that persons may be freed from it. It is by the grace of God alone that they are freed. Still they, using that grace, are freed. They are still free to remain in their evil habits. Many do resist the checks of conscience which the heathen too knew to be the voice of God within them, as a heathen said, 'To all mankind conscience is God.' They can persevere in evil to the end of life. You too must feel hatred to be a sin. Yet people have died in malignant hatred. No one has told us that death changes persons. I have often thought that to Satan heaven would be the worse hell of the two. For to see all the blessed loving one another and God, and happy in that love, while he himself could not share it, being what he is, would be intolerable to him. But how do we know that there is one being in hell who would leave it on God's terms? Who has told us, that one who died with all the energy of hatred, saying 'I hate you,' would love simply because he died?

I would just say that neither the Gospel nor the Church has laid down that the greatest part of mankind are lost.

Of course no evidence can force free-will. God Himself so reverences that likeness of Himself in which He made us —our free-will—that He will not force it. He will draw us mightily; He tells us, 'I love you,' and says, 'Will you not love Me?' He tells us of the bliss of the blessed; He speaks to us in our souls, or by the peace which they have who love Him, and Whom we too love. At times

Intellectual Difficulties. 163

He all but wins the souls which rebel against Him. The soul has still the terrible power to say 'I will not.' O that terrible 'I will not'! Our Redeemer said so tenderly to the Jerusalem which He "would have gathered as a hen gathereth her chickens under her wings," and "ye would not." They would not! Those of them who believed in Him escaped the temporal judgement of which He warned them; I do not know whether you ever read the horrible wickedness of the rest and how they perished. It is a Jew, not a Christian, who tells us.

As long as you say, 'I *will* not believe that Christ died for us;' 'I *will* not believe that God showed such great love for us,' God will not force your will. He has not created you like a stock or a stone. He knows what a bliss it is freely to love Him. If I fail to induce you to wish to believe Him and to love Him, I hope that He may employ some one else, who may gain an access to your heart, which I have failed to do. I can but pray for you, if you will not pray for yourself.

Yet human nature prompts us to pray. It is one of the truths which the heathen still held. God wrote it and writes it on the heart, which does not deaden itself to His voice. There is scarce a heathen nation, however degraded, which does not pray at times. Does it not strike you at times, 'Is it not a little presumptuous (I will not say conceited) in me to think that I am right and the whole world besides wrong? I, an unit among all the millions of millions and billions of billions who prayed and believed that they were heard!' You ask, 'What is the good that the Deity should bid us ask, since He knows already what we want?' God teaches us through our children. Is it not a happiness to a child to look up into a father's or mother's face, and ask them for what it wants and have it given them? Is it not nature to hold up its little arms and ask for what it wants?

Painters have loved to draw it. I do not think that you would count it a loving child which sat in the dumps and would not ask. But more, Do you think yourself wiser than Jesus, Who said, "Ask and ye shall receive"? Millions of millions have asked, and know that they have received. If you have not asked, you cannot know that those who did ask did not receive. But after all, does it not startle you, that with no ground except your own idea of what is fitting for Almighty God, you give the lie to Jesus, and say that He said what was not true?

I hope that you have been showing your worser self. Somehow your pugnaciousness seems to have been awakened. You seem to have been thinking how to answer me, rather than to inquire whether there must not be something which you do not yet know. To 'inquire,' I say, not to believe. God only can give you faith.

You will be halfway to faith whenever you come to know what God is.

But you see that there is evil in the world. It is the old crux of philosophers, 'Unde malum'? I have told you what is the explanation of Christians, that it is the result of our evil choice; of our being endowed by God with the power of choosing either way, and with grace to choose aright. Free choice, by the force of the term, involves the power of choosing either way. If you do not accept this, you must say, 'I do not know.' If you do not know the explanation of this terrible mystery, which encircles us on all sides, which thwarts us in what we would do for the good of our fellow-beings, how are you entitled to assume that such and such are not fit ways to remedy it, since you own at the outset that you know nothing about it, except that it *is*?

You too, I suppose, believe in a Creator. If you did not, you would be thrown back into a fresh set of difficulties. How came we into being at all? How is it that all creation exists in such wonderful order and beauty and harmony, and that those who study Nature with all the new appliances which we have, discover the most wondrous magnificence of beauty? How came it into being, and nothing is out of order, except what depends upon evil?

If you believe in a Creator, it is a contradiction that a Creator should have no power to make Himself known to the intelligent creatures which He has made; that He should turn them adrift, see them fall into all sort of evil, and have no remedy for them. He would then be a Being of very limited intelligence and benevolence, and we should be ashamed to be like Him, ourselves.

But you worship this 'deity' whom you have made for yourself. I wonder 'what for,' or 'how.' Do you praise him? I should be glad to know that you did, now too, morning and evening praise him. It would be something left in common, between your relations to your 'deity' and ours, Christians, to Almighty God. Can you praise him for your weak health and troubles? We Christians can with our whole heart, knowing that our Father sends them us, in love for our good. You will not mind my putting all these questions. You seem to me self-satisfied with the 'deity' whom you have made. I think that you are very easily satisfied; and if you really believed in Almighty God you would be halfway to be a Christian again. I cannot think that you have any idea what Baal was supposed to be, that you can write to me, 'To accuse me of disrespect to God is to my mind similar to accusing Elijah of disrespect when ridiculing the priests of Baal and their god.' I am so sorry for you.

I have been reading over your letter again, to see whether there was anything which I had missed. I see that you put the question about free-will thus: 'My question is, What is the justice of giving to a created being this great power [of free-will] and not endowing him with a sufficient safeguard so that he should not wrest it to his eternal destruction?' It is the Christian belief that 'God *did* endow His creatures with a sufficient safeguard.' God knew that it would be such a bliss to His creatures freely to love Him that He created them with the power to choose Him and love Him, and endowed them with grace to choose Him and love Him, even though it should involve an eternal loss, eternally to refuse to love Him. Satan, it is believed, could not endure that One in our human nature should be above himself, who was one of the highest orders of created intelligences, and so he rebelled. It is the belief of Christians that the 'pain of loss,' the pain of the obstinate will of continually rejecting God, having been formed for God, is the great suffering of the lost. Their wilful, ever-present, ever-continued rejection of God, Who formed them for Himself, to have their bliss in Him, is their greatest suffering.

What I meant to say with regard to evidence was (1) that it is now absolutely certain that the Gospels were written while the events recorded in them, the Life and the Words of Jesus, His Death and Resurrection, were still recent. Since it is so, they must be true. Do you read the words of Jesus still? The Samaritan woman heard but a few of them. When He had abode with her countrymen two days, many more believed, because of His own words, and said, "We have heard Him ourselves, and know of a truth that this is indeed the Christ, the Saviour of the world." I hope that if you read them you would come to love Him. The proof that they are His words is incomparably greater than it was in Paley's time; indeed, his proofs I thought half a century ago very poor. Renan, with all his power of description, tried to make a plausible story, apart from our Lord's being true, and the French unbelievers were angry with him for exposing the weakness of their case.

But is it indeed so, that you do not believe that Jesus came from God? The belief that Jesus came from God is one thing; the question whether we in the Church of England believe aright what He taught, is another.

To me you seem to have been very hasty. In the immaturity of some eighteen or nineteen years you took upon yourself to decide that Jesus did not come from God, and was not, as He said, 'the Truth,' on the ground of a single doctrine which you imperfectly understood. You copy some sentences which you wrote, you say, when first surrounded by new influences: there is not a sentence which is accurate. 'Faith is not an honest unhesitating willingness to believe.' This, when it exists, is a good preparation for belief; but a willingness to believe is of course not belief. You said, 'We ought to believe what is told unless the fact narrated is one wholly improbable,' &c. The improbability of a thing has nothing to do with its credibility. A clever person wrote 'historic doubts' of the history of Napoleon. He wrote it in the style of the Old Testament. Certainly it did look 'utterly improbable.' Nothing, it has been said, is so improbable as history. Walter Scott said that the only thing in his novels which had been laid down to be 'utterly improbable' was fact. So as to science, what has been proposed to us is stupendously improbable. So in mathematics, it is 'utterly improbable' that two lines should continually approximate and never meet. It is, as you know, demonstrated, but is beyond all imagination.

Your application of the principle to Christianity would make every man's mind the judge whether to embrace a Revelation from God or no. 'Quot homines, tot sententiae.' He who became St. Augustine was, for nine years, held back from the Gospel by the question 'Unde malum?' Was he right before he was converted or afterwards? Most of the philosophers of Mars' Hill mocked at the doctrine of the Resurrection. You would not doubt that those who did not scoff were right. Yet it is a difficulty in itself. Eternal punishment was no difficulty to many of the heathen: 'Sedet aeternumque sedebit Infelix Theseus.' On the contrary, the atheist Lucretius found the belief in it the great obstacle to the overthrow of religion: 'aeternas quoniam poenas in morte timendum est.' Dr. Farrar, whom you thought of perhaps as among those who disbelieve the doctrine, only excepts against the supposed number: he thinks that he agrees with me. But those who disbelieve it have not necessarily thrown off all faith in Jesus. So, on your principle, there would be all sorts of objections, which would be, in the opinion of each, a ground for *his* rejecting the Gospel, which none besides himself would think so.

You say that you woke up to the fact that a reason was required for one's faith. Certainly. To millions upon millions our Lord's promise that He would be always with the Church would be that ground. And such a sufficient ground 'securus judicat orbis terrarum.' But I suppose, still more, the personal love and trust in Jesus. When St. Polycarp was bidden to deny our Lord, he said, ' For fourscore and six years I served Him and He has never done me any harm: why should I deny Him now?' I have become acquainted with every form of unbelief for fifty-nine years, and none of them touched me, because they all ran up against my Lord and so fell back. Had you trusted Jesus more, and your own understanding less, it would have been so with you.

You say that 'men wishing to believe such and such things true have not the courage to face difficulties, are therefore angry with those who pull them up thus sharply.' What could you know at nineteen or twenty of the mind of Christians that you should have written thus broadly and positively of their motives? Nor are we angry, but grieved for those who have lost faith. How should we not be, since they have lost what is priceless? ...

Pray do not use such terrible language as, 'I do rail at God.' We would not rail on our fellow-creatures, "not rendering railing for railing"; and pray do not challenge God to His Face. We sinners must cast ourselves on His mercy. You say, 'I have inquired and I reject Christianity.' Your inquiring has been, according to your own account, to read one superficial book, to open another in the midst of examination, since 'the whole subject has been shelved, save when in conversation with one or two friends I have made during the three last years'; and on this you say, 'If for such rejection I must suffer, so be it.' But apart from that suffering (whatever it be) there is the loss of all the Love of God, which we might have gained as a Christian. There are, I suppose, countless degrees of the Love of God and of nearness to God. Each has his own place; each can, by God's grace, acquire according to their diligence a greater or less capacity of love.... But now is the time of growth. We Christians have a source of love, which you, according to your account, have not. "God is Love." His beloved disciple tells us: "In this was manifested the love of God toward us, that God sent His Only-Begotten into the world, that we might live through Him" (1 St. John iv. 8, 9). "We love Him because He first loved us." "In this is love, not that we loved God, but that He loved us, and sent His Son as a propitiation for our sins." All this is strange language to you.

"God is Love; and he that loveth dwelleth in God, and God in him." Your 'deity' does not seem to be an object of love. Even the heathen philosopher, although he strangely inverted the truth, knew that the gods love those who love them. But ask yourself, 'Do I love my deity?' Does he make you happy? Are your outward circumstances what you would wish? If not, does he make you happy notwithstanding? Our God does make us happy under every conceivable outward or inward lot, because ask what we will, as children, and we know that whatever we ask He will give us, if it is good for us; only He is wiser than we, and would not give us straw for bread. We can speak to Him, heart to Heart, and tell Him that we love Him; and He speaks to our hearts and tells us, 'I love *you*.'

I do not make out what your 'deity' is, or what your relations to him are. I have asked you, here and there, what you believe as to him. Do you believe that he created us? that he takes care of us? Whence then this existence of evil? If Reason is enough, why does not Reason give the same answer everywhere, even in the simplest matter of morality? Why are we to assume that our individual reason is right? for even we Englishmen are not agreed among ourselves. I thought when I first wrote to you, that there had been some definite points in which I could be of use to you. Now the God Whom I worship and Whose I am, does not seem to be the same as your 'deity.' If you would use even a doubting prayer, 'O God, if Thou listenest to Thy creatures and carest for them, hear me,' we should have some common ground. It could do you no harm, if, as you think, we have no authority to think that He wishes us to pray to Him. You would be but where you were. It could not displease Him. But God is so unwilling to part with any of His creatures, whom He made to love Him, that I am sure that He would listen. He is so good that He will listen to any one who does not shut out His Love. He made you His own once, and listened to your prayers those eighteen or nineteen years. Do try Him.

Your original mistake was that you took a 'reasonable

belief' to be a belief in things of which our reason is a judge, instead of a belief resting on adequate ground. Nicodemus had a reasonable belief, when he said to Jesus, "Rabbi, we know that Thou art a teacher come from God; for no man can do these miracles which Thou doest, except God be with him" (St. John iii. 2). Philip had a reasonable belief when he said to Nathanael, 'We have found Him of Whom Moses in the law, and the prophets, did write, Jesus of Nazareth."

The most salient points in Prophecy for us are (1) that when Judaea was a country no larger than Yorkshire, the prophets foretold that the God, Who was at that time worshipped in Judaea, should be worshipped throughout the world, by a Revelation which should go forth from Jerusalem. To man this was incredible. The Jews were carried captive; a few of them returned. The prophets ceased; the Jews waited. At last, Jesus came and it was fulfilled. All those millions of millions who became Christians are the fruits of a teaching which went forth from Jerusalem. (2) It was foretold that He Who should come should die for our sins and yet reign for ever. The very doctrine to which you take exception is contained in Isaiah liii. The Acts of the Apostles and St. Paul say that it was taught.

I have dwelt upon this in University Sermons, and tried to condense the evidence in a single sermon: 'The prophecy of Jesus the certain prediction of the [to man] impossible.'

But I cannot pretend to demonstrate the Faith to an unwilling mind. If you will pray, God will hear you.

God grant that you may.

III

*LETTERS ON THEOLOGICAL AND
ECCLESIASTICAL SUBJECTS*

LETTER I.

DIFFICULTIES OF THE PSALTER.

MY memory may fail me, but I do not remember an ancient writer, except the writer of the title in the Peshito, who interpreted Ps. cix otherwise than St. Chrysostom, whom you quote, does, 'a prophecy in the form of a curse.' It is of an entirely different mind from that which he showed as to Doeg or Cush, Shimei or Ahitophel. Nor had any of them any office, which another could take, as he who was ὁδηγός to them who took Jesus. On the other hand so much was fulfilled in those who repeated his imprecation on themselves, " His blood be upon us and upon our children," an imprecation which was fulfilled 'in the next generation,' in that awful destruction of Jerusalem, when "their name was clean put out." However, I cannot expect you to agree with this mode of interpretation any more than I with yours. But I could not but say to my pupils, 'When any of us can say truly with the Psalmist, "I am [all] prayer," and we are so wrapt in prayer, that our whole being should be prayer—not till then should we criticize the Psalmist, and then we shall have no mind to do it.' I wonder what idea of inspiration those have who so criticize him? For protection from what is wrong is the lowest idea of inspiration. " Thou shalt love thy neighbour and hate thine enemy," which you quote as illustrating to some extent the Jewish Creed of even the

Davidian period, is as contrary to the Old Testament as to the New. See Exod. xxiii, Job xxxi. 29, 30, Prov. xvii. 5.

The passage of Tertullian's *De Spectaculis* has done duty ever since Gibbon's declamation. I do not myself think that it represents even Tertullian's mind. Tertullian is apt to write to make an impression, and I think that in this place he wished to make an impression upon those for whom he wrote. Of course he was wrong; but a writer, whom his own hardness drove into heresy and who separated himself from the Church, as too lax, should not, in an exceptional passage, which is not paralleled by any other in his writings, be quoted as a specimen of the Church. St. Hilary says of his Treatise upon the Lord's Prayer: 'quamquam et Tertullianus hinc volumen aptissimum scripserit, sed consequens error hominis detraxit scriptis probabilibus auctoritatem.'

We are, I fear, of more different schools than I thought. For I see that you do not shrink from the language, 'the pseudo citations,' in the New Testament. We, in my day, approached the New Testament as learners, what God meant to teach us, as in other things, so in the quotations of the Old Testament. A younger generation seem to approach to teach the writers, how they should have written, if God had taught them.

LETTER II.

THE LECTURES ON DANIEL.

March 27, 1879.

I am very sorry that anything in my lectures on Daniel seemed to you unsympathizing. They were written at a time of much boastful German criticism, when people were singing in triumph over the Book of Daniel, and Bunsen appealed to the proof of its spuriousness as the greatest triumph of modern criticism. I did not then know of one who was in 'perplexity' about Daniel. In Germany disbelief in it was only the result of what in Rationalism was already an axiom, that there was neither prophecy nor miracle. Disbelief in the supernatural preceded long any attack upon the Book of Daniel. I had only to do with books, and my problem was to show our young men how baseless such boastful criticism was. I was writing about a past. In my Preface to the second edition, I did, in answer to Perowne, say that I had not lost my sympathy with any in perplexity. My life has been spent in helping them, as far as God has given me ability. When I delivered my lectures on Daniel there was (as far as I knew) no one to sympathize with. At least I had not heard of any one *perplexed* about it, though I knew of those who triumphed over the old prophet.

There is of course a responsibility about attacking a book of Holy Scripture, above what there is in defending one. Belief unravels so terribly. All German unbelief began in an attack on the reality of the 'possessions' in the Gospel. I have seen all faith melt away little by little. It is such a terrible thing to unsettle one's faith; and faith so hangs together, that one does not know what one is doing, if one touches even the skirts of the robe. . . .

And now I have shown sympathy (though in a way which you will not value) at the cost of this letter. You would only value the sympathy of those who would agree with you. At least your words imply no sorrow at having to go forth through the broken walls. Your only interest is, apparently, to persuade others that they are hopelessly broken. *Vae victis*! Victors do not court sympathy, but submission.

I sorrow for you, not with you, seeing that you are embarking on a stormy sea without a rudder, not knowing whither winds and waves will carry you. You go forth as a conqueror, when every conquest (as you deem it) is irretrievable loss. But I can be of no use to you, so I bid you in the best sense of the word, 'Farewell,' which in my own meaning is, 'May God bring you back to the haven which you are seemingly leaving.'

I say nothing more about our Lord's authority, because, flushed by your supposed victory over the defenders of the Book of Daniel, you might rather be occasioned to go on. Man cannot persuade you. I pray that God the Holy Ghost may.

LETTER III.

THE DATE OF THE GOSPELS.

February 16, 1880.

I hope that I shall not seem presuming in writing to you on a subject upon which you may very likely have read more than myself, but I have taken my chance that you have been otherwise engaged. The subject is the date of our Gospels. I believe myself that their date has been solidly ascertained. What follows from this is a subject of theology. I write only on a subject of history.

You read doubtless the *Contemporary Review*? But the Articles on this subject may have seemed to you dry, and the evidence given in them is of its own nature cumulative, and may have been unattractive, and you may have passed them by. So I will put them down on p. 3 of this note. You used, I think, to attach weight to any matter of historical evidence. The Gospels have changed the history and faith of the world. You will not think anything solidly written unworthy of attention. The theological question, 'What does the early date of the Gospels involve?' is, of course, that which interests me; but this comes later. As a Theist you must believe that God acts upon the soul, and will pray Him to set you free from all prejudices. All then which I wish, is that you would ask God (anyhow if He does interfere with our minds) to keep your mind like a sheet of white paper, on which the results of the inquiry might be fairly written.

The papers of Prof. Lightfoot in the *Contemporary Review* are on Supernatural Religion. . . .

The following books are said to be solid:—Sanday's *Gospel in the Second Century*, and *On the Authorship and Historical Character of the Fourth Gospel*.

Tischendorf, *When were the Gospels written?* would interest you, from the great scholarship of its author.

Luthardt, *Der Johanneische Ursprung des vierten Evangeliums* (Leipzig, 1874), is said to be solid. I do not myself know it.

LETTER IV.

ON THE WORD 'EVERLASTING.'

March 12, 1881.

You will excuse me for not entering at length into the subject which you open. To me it all lies in a few words, 'Our Redeemer has said it.' My whole faith is bound up in what He has said. If He *could* have been deceived, or have misled in one thing, if He could have used the same word in ambiguous senses, suggesting one belief and meaning another, I should have had nothing whatever on which to rest my soul. Forgive me, but I think that you have adopted a current phraseology without remembering at the moment on Whose words they bore. These times are days of large material knowledge; they are not days of any deep thought of God, or even of our human nature. It is the knowledge of physical nature, not of man's moral nature, much less of God, which engrosses people's thoughts.

But the doctrine of a fixed state hereafter of weal or woe is the direct revelation of Jesus. He has revealed it in every way in which it could be expressed.

> 'Christ on Himself, considerate Master, took
> The utterance of that doctrine's fearful sound.
> The Fount of Love His servants sent to tell
> Love's deeds; Himself reveals the sinner's Hell[1].'

May God in His Love guide you into all truth.

[1] 'Lyra Apostolica,' lxxxiii.

LETTER V.

AFTER DEATH.

Thursday in Passion Week.

The Faith, as believed by the English Church and the Roman alike, is, that there is no change from bad to good or from good to bad after this life. "As the tree falls, so it lies." "There is a great gulf fixed," &c. Also there is no growth in grace after this life[1]. We are "to receive the things done in the body." But it is nowhere said, that the Day of Judgement shall not produce very great effects on the soul in removing the dross which clung to it in this life. Every one must believe alike that we must be changed. We carry our infirmities to the end of life; and those, infirmities not of the body chiefly, but of the soul. We cannot have those infirmities in Heaven. It would be miserable. When then so likely as in that Day, when we shall see our sins and our sinful selves as a whole, and all our Lord's Love, and all our ingratitude? I suppose that you are afraid of contradicting Article XXII, about the Romish doctrine of Purgatory. I believe what is there said to relate to the popular doctrine, but anyhow it can have nothing to do with the Day of Judgement, which all alike must believe.

[1] On this subject, see ' What is of Faith as to Everlasting Punishment,' pp. 112 and 113 (first edition).

LETTER VI.

EVANGELICALISM.

March 30, 1881.

Thank you for your loving lines. I wish your friends would treat us with the same love. Do you remember in your boyhood, a story of two knights, who fought because one said a shield was silver, the other that it was gold? Each was right, for it was gold on one side, silver on the other. I used in my young days to study 'Evangelicalism,' because I wanted to win the Evangelicals. I used as my formula, 'I believe all which you believe; we only part where you deny.' I said to my friend, H. V. Elliott, of Brighton, 'I don't think that you can put your belief in any way which I could not accept.' I am sorry to say that he did at last; but it was not by any statement about the great central doctrines. As for language, there is no end of its confusions; but if, with ordinary understanding, one is certain that one holds what another holds, the likelihood is that one is right. Now this is what I want you to think, that having sought intimacy with Evangelicals for many years, and heard formerly a good many Evangelical sermons, and having for a long time read carefully everything which was written against me and my friends, I know what the so-called 'Evangelicals' believe, and that when I say that I believe the same, I know what I am speaking of.

Your friends, some forty years ago, used, on platforms with the Dissenters, to say (in effect), 'We will drop the things about which we do not agree and dwell upon those on which we *do* agree.' Your position may make it impossible to exercise this charity of silence towards us. But at all events, if you are persuaded that I do agree with you in all which you hold of Faith, it will be much gained. It may interest you to know that when I had to write a controversial Tract on Baptism, about 1833 (it was written to save a Hebrew pupil from becoming a Dissenter because he did not believe Baptismal Regeneration), I was careful to avoid illustrations from English writers, and so undertook a large study of the old Continental Calvinistic school for fear of alienating any among us.

I know that I hold much which you do not hold. I only mean that I hold all which you do, though it would be matter of faith to you to believe it.

LETTER VII.

THE ATHANASIAN CREED.—UNBAPTIZED INFANTS.

April 16, 1879.

It did not occur to me to think that the objections which you mentioned against the Athanasian Creed were your own. What I meant to except against was (forgive me) the one-sided way in which you put them. They are, too, not people's real objections, and they are untrue. But you, for the time, threw yourself into the mind of the objectors, and gave them a strength which they have not, with nothing on the other side. It was as if some one had given you a brief against the Creed. I think that it is a very cruel thing to revive the attack. It is scarcely seven years since some of us had to stake not our homes only, but what is much dearer, our offices and officiating in the Church of England, upon the retention of that Creed. A great enthusiasm was excited then, and the attack was dropped. I hoped that (as with Israel of old) "the land" might have "rest." But now the attack is opened in another way. The present plan seems to be to throw a slur upon the Creed, to minimize the use of it, and thus to prepare the way for those who would urge 'Why not lay aside altogether what is used only once in the year?' As to the 'may,' it is (as you know) un-exampled in the history of the Church, to leave the use or non-use of a Creed to the caprice of an individual Minister. We, the quiet people, have been always those to suffer. Newman suffered quietly until he thought his position made untenable. Now he is regretted and praised. So is Wesley. Over us Juggernaut's car may drive. And you, in putting out this one-sided attack on the Athanasian Creed, are driving it against your will. This is always the character of compromises. The unresisting are always crushed.

I do not say anything yet. But you may as well walk over a shaking bog as put your foot on the Athanasian Creed, or guide other people's. It is ever, 'they will bear this,' 'they will bear that,' until the camel's back is broken.

Having said this, I will add that I have written to the Bishop of Lincoln saying that if that Declaration about the Athanasian Creed satisfied anybody, and if no apology is made for the Athanasian Creed, I have no objection to it, though it seems to me surplusage and wordy. We shall next have to apologize for our Lord (St. Mark xvi. 16, St. John viii. 24, &c., and St. Paul, &c., &c.).

I did not send my letter of Easter Eve, because I thought that I had seemed ready to concede too much about the Service for unbaptized children. I did not mean that this Service in itself would revive the controversy about Baptismal Regeneration. This I said of your alleging 1 Cor. vii. 14, in behalf of it. This (if I remember right) is a text which Zwinglians used against Baptism, as if grace were inherited as well as nature. If the children of Christian parents are actually holy, they would not need Baptism to make them so.

I do not doubt, myself, that the children who die unbaptized are happy in their degree, for Christ's sake, as well as all heathen children, although not members of Christ, and not admitted to the Beatific Vision, which yet they do not miss because God did not create them for it. But before Convocation is urged to legislate in this 'hot haste' about this question, do try to ascertain what is the effect of this little remnant of discipline, in not saying a [Burial] Service over the unbaptized, before you propose to Convocation to abolish it. My own conviction is that any change would, under the plea of charity, be a very grave want of charity to tens or hundreds of thousands of children, who would in consequence not be made members of Christ, and so, although happy in their way, would lose the Vision of God.

What I gather from others is, that a very great mass of our poor are so ignorant of the gifts in Baptism, or what it is to be 'made a member of Christ and a child of God,' that their great or one inducement to have their children baptized is, that they may have Christian Burial. This they feel, though they submit quietly to their unbaptized children being excluded from it, because it is their own doing.

You must know how small a fraction of children in the East of London are baptized. I saw some statistics of several parishes. This may be the result of the state of heathenism in which it is left. The fewness of the baptized is startling. It would be a matter which you could ascertain : ' To what is the excessive neglect of Baptism among the poor of the Metropolis owing?' and 'Who buries them?' If they are buried by the Chaplain of the cemetery, he would hold it no business of his to ascertain whether they have been baptized or no, and they would be buried, as a matter of course, with the Service, and the little remnant of discipline would be gone. Of course it may be otherwise. The parish clergy may bury their dead. But if they do not, this burial of the unbaptized' with the Service may account for the frightful fewness of baptisms in East London. You would have also to provide a Service, not for the unbaptized children of Christian parents, but for the children of heathen parents, living in that great heathen city whom (to judge from secular newspapers) the contumacious Ritualists are most diligent in converting. Everything may be allowed to flourish so that what is the bugbear of the day does not. While there has been this declamation against Confession, what has been done for the *conversion* of that populous

East of London, swarming like a beehive with neglected souls, for whom Christ died? People are afraid of Missions, lest *some* sin-laden souls should confess; and meanwhile the reign of sin is undisturbed.

But I must not run on thus. I did not suppose that you would open the Churchyards to Dissenters. But I feel morally certain that they will be opened in the next Parliament, as nothing is done to meet the difficulty, and then your proposal for a supplementary Service in church would open the churches too.

I do not remember how long you would continue the Service for the unbaptized. The rubric lays stress on 'dying before they commit actual sin.' You would open the question, 'When does such responsibility begin?' The young person would remain unbaptized, not through any fault of his own, at all events till sixteen, perhaps till twenty-one, as long as he has not arrived at years when he can judge for himself, or is under authority of parents. Can then a young Arab, who has been educated to lie, steal, swear, commit not these sins only, but every abomination with impunity? If you fix an age up to which the Burial Service may be used, then, consistently with the Rubric, you would lay down that, *up to that age* they cannot commit such persevering sin for which they might be cast into hell, and that *at that age* they could: both of which seem to me alike intruding into the judgements of God.

I should myself think the wisest way would be, (1) if Convocation did anything about the Athanasian Creed, to enact simply that somewhat wordy Resolution. It is in itself innocent, though there would be danger that something bad might be engrafted.

(2) As to details, I should think that it would allay the panic of some, if that very moderate Resolution on Ritual to which the hundred Bishops gave their adhesion were enacted. The panic, I suppose, is, lest Ritual should be

introduced anywhere without any restriction, against the wishes of the congregation. This would not touch the question as to the cases already existing, where clergy and people are already unanimous about Ritual which they believe the Church of England to sanction, else it should have run, 'Such Ornaments, &c., shall *not* be retained and be in use,' as Lord Selborne interpreted it.

I trust that people are getting weary of this strife and that it will die out by God's mercy. They framed a good sharp guillotine, to make short work of Ritualists and Ritualism, and find that they cannot direct it, and that it excites sympathy without exterminating.

To judge by the *Rock*, Bishops and Ritualists are coming to a good understanding, as they might long ago if the Bishops would have stood to their clergy in the relation of fathers, instead of repeating the dry 'Obey the law,' which (like most of the Privy Council judgements) we knew to be misinterpretation of law, made under a bias. You will not appease the wolves by a regulation about a cope. God alone can " make men to be of one mind in a house."

I trust that you would not, if you tried, carry a Resolution about having a Service over the unbaptized. I feel sure that if you did you would terribly augment our heathen population. If children are not baptized in infancy, they are seldom baptized afterwards. In Scotland, where the Presbyterians do not baptize any (I think) except the children of parents whom they suppose to be converted, the number of adults who live unbaptized was (Bishop Forbes used to tell me) very sadly large. He knew this, as on general knowledge, so especially from the state of Dundee in which he lived and worked.

LETTER VIII.

THE CATHOLICITY OF THE ENGLISH CHURCH.

Epiphany, 1848.

It is difficult to answer in brief space your question. All will probably turn in any case upon whether one asks, 'Why should I doubt?' or 'Why should I not doubt?' 'Why should I be certain?' In the one case a person feels himself in the position of one prepared to *stay*, unless he see grounds to the contrary; in the other to go, unless he *see* the *full* grounds to the contrary. I think this is of very great moment, and is the cause of much which has gone wrong. People have put requisitions to the English Church to prove her claims, which if they had put to the Gospel they would have been infidels. Belief in what we have received is an implanted principle. In order to part with it there must be a something which, when full Divine Light is poured upon it, stands out as immoral, as in Heathenism, Mahometanism, &c., &c., or some plain want of foundation for it, or absence of authority (whereas the opposed system does contain that authority), as is the case in Dissenters over against the Church (see Article on 'Private Judgement' in the *British Critic*). And so as to Judaism; the authority it once had is clearly withdrawn from it. And so Nestorianism and the Eastern heretical bodies have the voice of the whole Church against them. But ordinarily it is a duty to hold fast that we have. The office of reasons and proof is not so much to establish it as to disprove objections to it. This has been objected to 'Evidences' generally, and I think with reason if employed to build up. They imply that one is in a state of doubt. People have, as it were, to put themselves in the state of mind of one unconvinced. I trace the feeling of being unhinged in reading Evidences to being in an unnatural state.

And I feel sure that very many in reading Evidences would have lost their faith altogether, had there not been some deeper bond within which held it together while they were looking about for those outward proofs.

This then, I think, has been the cause of a good deal of the mischief of late. People have not been satisfied with answering objections; but, being unqualified, have been analyzing the ground on which they stand; and then, if this or that, or the other ground, do not seem sufficient, they think they have none to stand on—i. e. that they have not sufficient reason for remaining where they are placed unless it is demonstrated to them: whereas the deepest foundation of all faith is that which people cannot bring out into words in its full force. I think people have begun in a sceptical spirit requiring full satisfaction, whereas it is of the very nature of religion to have to face difficulties. . . . It is of the utmost importance that every one should feel, not 'I must go unless it is proved to me that I ought to stay,' but 'I must stay unless it is forced upon me that I ought to go.' The *onus probandi* lies upon leaving the pastures where God has folded one. The grounds which to me are so strong individually, are (1) the Providence of Almighty God, of which I gave some few instances in that Letter reprinted at Leeds. (2) The life which He has continued among us, as it is never so continued in any body really rent from the Body of Christ. (3) God's marvellous workings with the whole Church of England now, awing one to be still and see the salvation of God.

One cannot think of an instrument so formed, sharpened, guarded, drawn forth, that all this pains has been bestowed upon it to no end but that it should be broken in pieces.

Of course this presupposes that we have (1) the Apostolic Succession, and therewith the Sacraments and the Power of the Keys; (2) the Faith delivered from the first; and are in nothing heretical; (3) that the Papal authority was not in primitive times what it now is; and so in rejecting it we have rejected nothing *de jure divino*, and are not in schism.

Inward grounds presuppose outward, yet the real strength of conviction lies in the inward. One believes because one lives. Outward grounds are to fence off attacks, bulwarks against battering-rams, but they are not the foundation upon which the city is built.

The question, I suppose, after all, is, 'Why do not the statements of Roman Catholics about us affect me?' (1) Because they speak of us not really knowing what we *hold*. "Doth our law condemn any man before it hear him?" They are accustomed to foreign Protestants, and do not understand us, have not been at the pains to do so, are prejudiced against us.

(2) They know not what we *have*. Controversialists speak of our not having the Power of the Keys or the Sacraments. "A stranger (and they estrange themselves from us) doth not intermeddle with his joy." We know what we receive. Our Lord makes known His power and grace to those who wait for Him—not to those who stand aloof and say, "or even as this publican."

(3) They know not what we *are*. One cannot think that fruits which one has seen are not the fruits of the Church.

(4) They are judges in their own cause, and the quarrel began in ill conduct and ambition on their side and claims unknown to antiquity. They inquire not as to soundness

of health, but require a submission which was not shown to the Popes for many centuries. Surely this is not the way to reconcile Christendom, to put prominently forward an outward authority unknown to primitive times.

(5) Of that which is peculiar to them—the Papal authority, e. g., and the Intercession of the Blessed Virgin were originally rested on great names which are now acknowledged to be spurious. I cannot see how a Church can be required to acknowledge the practical system as to the Blessed Virgin (being wholly unknown to Catholic antiquity) as a condition of Catholic unity; nor how we dare admit what sounds so very dissonant from the Epistle to the Hebrews, and has not one word of Holy Scripture to be alleged in its favour.

But people say, 'Where then is unity in the Church?' We answer, 'impaired but not lost—impaired by loss of intercommunion, maintained by one Faith in our Lord, our common Sacraments, Succession from Him.' We hold the whole Faith received in the first centuries: they hold it too (though they require of us Articles not then received). We have then the one Faith of Nicaea. But we may ask, 'Where then *on your* view is catholicity?' Surely we who hold with good Bishop Andrewes, and pray for 'the Holy Catholic Church throughout the world, Eastern, Western, our own,' repeat the Te Deum more in the sense of St. Ambrose and St. Augustine than they who hold that this Church is not where the 60,000,000 of the Russian Church are. I think the article, 'On the Catholicity of the English Church,' in the *British Critic* one of the most satisfactory in a brief space.

LETTER IX.

ROMAN CONTROVERSY.
[1851.]

I am thankful that you did not mean those fearful words 'grace-hindering schism' in the sense in which they would obviously be taken, but only that there had not been among us evidently the higher degrees of sanctity such as in St. Francis Borgia. God only knows. But this must be borne in mind. Those cases of holiness of which the world knows most were the fruits of the monastic life, and the monastic life was destroyed not by the Reformation, but by a secular Prince. Civil rapacity has been as busy of late in France, Spain, Portugal, as it was under Henry VIII. A Roman Catholic says of Fisher, who was beheaded for opposing the Supremacy: 'His accusers are Catholics, his judges are Catholics, his jury are Catholics, his executioner is a Catholic, and the bells are ringing for High Mass in the steeple of St. Paul, as the aged Bishop ascends the scaffold.'

Undoubtedly the monastic system is a loss: but a loss antecedent to the Reformation, and with which the Reformation had nothing to do. But it is as widely wanted in Spain and France. France had nominally its religious houses and its undiminished hierarchy, when the Revolution burst out through those who had been its [i.e. the Church's] children once. There must have been some sore inward decay in both (whether of luxury or wealth, or whatever else it was) that Almighty God allowed them to fall at once.

Again, you contrast the produce of all parts of the Church in communion with Rome, and of all ages—St. Francis of Assisi at the beginning of the thirteenth century, and St. Francis Borgia in Spain of the sixteenth—and contrast them with our little island. And yet, even so contrasting them, I know not where are either the saints

O

or the books of South Germany (far larger than England), which is still in the Roman Communion. Those of Spain again are of one period. Portugal has but one celebrated devotional book. But people heap all these together, forgetting the difference of countries and of centuries, that the 'Spiritual Combat' is from Italy, and Rodriguez and others from the one brilliant period of Spain, and F. Thomas from Portugal: and yet I know not that F. Thomas has more fervent devotion than some of our own writers.

The grace of which I thought that you spoke was the grace of the Sacraments. This is the 'grace' which real schism prevents. And I thought that you spoke of this grace, because schism interferes with this and this only. The monastic system is favourable to higher devotion: but it [is] through the virtues exercised in it. Sacramental grace is common to all: more is given, as there is greater longing, greater denial of self, greater use of what is given. But this is all personal. It does not belong to the system. The same individual would receive the same grace, whether he were in the English or the French Church. Our Lord is present in both in His Sacraments. He imparts Himself *in* His Sacraments to all according to their capacities. What peculiarly belongs to the Church, what other bodies have not, is 'the Power of the Keys' and our Lord's Real Presence in the Sacrament. Of both of these, we have abundant proof by His mercy. But, having these, everything beyond depends upon ourselves and our diligence in asking for and using His grace. "Ask, and ye shall receive."

You say that many know not of this. Far more, I believe, know and have known than you think. The belief of pious minds is far deeper than their words. But allowing that we are in a state of confusion, (1) it is quite certain that God by His Holy Spirit is infusing fresh light, fresh knowledge, fresh degrees of love. So that we have every comfort in His Presence. (2) No one can judge that this confusion is more displeasing to Almighty God, than, amid outward order, the inward unbelief in France before the Revolution, or Spain and Italy now, or the decay which produced the Revolution. Zealous, earnest Roman Catholics speak of the Church in France as 'the small minority of the nation.' They speak of the 'enormous unbelieving mass,' that the 'great mass of the nation is unbelieving,' that the priests are 'missionaries among unbelievers.' Yet these were once the children of the Church, and the Church through negligence and sin lost them. There is nothing worse to be said of us, than of them: no tokens that they are part of the Church, we not. You ask where [are] our saints, such as St. Francis Borgia. I ask, where are they in France? Where have they been in Roman Catholic Ireland these 300 years?

With regard to the other illustration, all depends upon the one question, which you assume, that our Lord left one Visible Head. This contradicts all early history of the Church. But unless the Papacy had been Divine, there is no question of 'sedition.' Rome acquired that power by human means: it lost it by human means. God in His Providence allowed of both. Illustrations can easily be turned back. What if a detachment of a great army under its own generals, and co-operating with another but not under its commanders, were given to maintain a certain position against its portion of the common enemy, and the soldiers in this detachment were of their own accord, and contrary to the commands of their officers, to leave their posts, and go off to some other, thereby embarrassing and disheartening their companions in their conflict with the enemy?

I must close in haste to-night. God bless you.

LETTER X.

THE SAME.

[1851.]

Intellectual answers cannot in themselves affect the heart. You sent the intellectual difficulties, and I said something, though but a very little, on them.

The way to which you are inclined, of balancing which way has most suffering, is a mistake. All suffering is not the Cross. We shall have crosses wherever we are. Reverse the case. Suppose a person to be in the Roman Church, and strongly perplexed about doctrines or practices in it, it would not be right for her to be balancing in which way she would have most of the Cross.

We cannot be mistaken about that which concerns our souls, that we have forgiveness of our sins through the Power of the Keys, and that we have His Presence in the Holy Eucharist. This is too well attested. This is quite certain to all who would receive it anywhere. We have all which we need for our salvation. Everything which is the fruit of God's grace, every degree of it, is open to us, if we will. You may not, indeed cannot, be able to solve points which depend upon learning. This is the way in which our Lord speaks to His simple ones.

As you say, none but the one Holy Catholic Apostolic Church can arbitrate between the Church of England and the Church of Rome. To it we appeal. But the Roman Church does not *make* herself *the* Church, by calling herself so. She is a part, an important part, but not the whole. I fear that if all be subtracted, which do not really belong to her, she would be much contracted. I suppose in these numerical statements, France is counted

e. g. as belonging to her, and Spain and Portugal and Italy. Alas! what devastations there are everywhere!

It is true that she is part of the Body of Christ. The Church of England allows it and prays for her Bishops as well as for the Eastern Bishops. But the question is not about those whom God has by His Providence placed in her, but about those who cannot belong to her without rejecting what Christ has not rejected. The right is not always with majorities. Israel was larger than Judah. Our Lord seems to imply that there will be very few faithful when He comes. "When the Son of Man cometh, shall He find faith on the earth?" ...

Our present duty is to pray to God, as our Church does, that 'He would inspire the Universal Church with the spirit of unity, peace, and concord.' He will heal the breaches when He has been prayed to earnestly. (I was told the other day of a remarkable Roman Catholic commentary on the Revelation, which spoke of a General Council as the means of reuniting Rome, Greece, and England.) We have begun to seek each other more. Meanwhile, neither party has formally judged the other, as neither is competent so to judge. The whole Church alone can judge. They say that in the East people's minds are being turned, not to submission to Rome, which they do not own, but to reunion. This we too should pray for. But, meanwhile, the English Church too has her sacred deposit: she has her office in the designs of God's Providence. And they whose hearts God has stirred, have their duty; remaining in obedience to her, to work out their own salvation, and win others to Him, thanking Him for His blessings to them in her.

To say that the Roman Church has remained the same from the first, is to assume the very point at issue. It is palpable that there have been additions to the primitive Faith.

LETTER XI.

THE SAME.

[1851.]

Those words of —— are words which some Roman Catholics often use, in order to hurry persons, and carry them by storm, as it were; but in using them so broadly, they must often use them, even according to their own showing, untruly. I have known them very miserably abused. If a person who is *really* out of the Church, or a heretic, were convinced of his heresy and remained in it, out of secular motives, for some worldly end—or, again, out of pride, or any sinful feeling—this would be resisting the grace of God. *You* need have no fear of this. You gave up all to follow Him. You, if you followed feeling only, would go to join the largest body in Christendom. But feeling is not conviction. It is not 'want of' religious 'courage' which holds you back. It is doubt whether you would be right. Whether this which holds you be an instinctive feeling underneath, against those which make themselves felt vividly, or whether it be the dread of the responsibility of such an act on your own judgement, or whether it be that you would not go against the judgement of myself whom God has these many years given you as a guide—whatever the ground be, it is clearly no motive which God would disown or disapprove.

On the contrary, you seem to have forgotten what you have told me, of having acted upon your own mind, in sympathizing with others, so that your present feelings are, in part, owing to your own working upon your own mind.

I forget the words which you used, but you conveyed this to me, and therefore I thought the less of the feelings, because you owned that they had been in part so produced.

Those words 'which He may never repeat, if now neglected,' are cruel words, and contrary to the dealings of God. They are not true even of sinners. They do go on long against the grace of God, and their own convictions, in deadly sin; and God converts them at last. Of course, they often do gradually harden their hearts. Yet even to such an one, one should be very unwilling to say, 'God may never give you His grace again,' for fear the person should be plunged into despair. God is so long-suffering and does endure with persons so patiently, that it would be in the last degree improbable that the person should have arrived at his last trial. We do not know that He has withdrawn His grace finally from any human being.

I say this generally. But in your case it is preposterous to speak of this. You are not withheld by any earthly or worldly motive: and you are not withheld from anything right, but from what would be presumption and sin.

It would indeed be very presumptuous to say, as you seem to say, that you have 'convictions of the heart that the Church you have been baptized in is in a state of grace-hindering schism.' This is not a matter for the heart to judge in. You may not mean what you seem to say. You cannot mean that grace does not flow through the Sacraments. It would be, ignorantly, to deny the Truth of God, and the work of God the Holy Ghost. You cannot mean this, or it must have been a hasty strong expression which you would retract. His grace through the Power of the Keys is too evident, too attested, too manifold, for any one to doubt it. One might as well question the blind man's having been healed, as that Absolution among us is a means of grace, loosing the bonds of sin, cleansing the soul, and a channel of grace. I could as soon doubt my existence. So also as to the Holy Eucharist. Our Lord's Presence there is as certain as anything can be. It has been attested in awe to those who sinned against it, not discerning the Lord's Body, in signal punishment; and it has been attested in love, often by sensible grace, but also more largely by the increase of grace in the soul.

But God does not work through a lie. When the Dissenters gain good from prayer, from reading Holy Scripture, from acts of faith and love, and trust in our Lord, this is all according to God's promise. He has promised His blessing to those who do seek Him. And if they seek Him in sincerity, not knowing more, He is with them, by virtue of the Baptism by which they were made members of Him. But in like way, in the Church of England, He blesses through what is real and true, through true Absolutions, true Sacraments.

This is the appeal to the little ones of Christ. You cannot judge as to the question whether there is Schism or no, or how the evil which exists is to be repaired. As far as human sight goes the secessions have done much harm to Truth among us, and rather delayed than aided in the restoration of more perfect unity. It is not in this way that unity is to be restored, as far as one can see, but by a General Council which shall unite East, West, and ourselves. To this people among us are looking more and more. This would be, in God's hands, a solid healing of the evils of Christendom.

Meanwhile, God shows that He has not forsaken the Church of England, and where He is, there it is safe for us to be; and it is not safe or right to leave, where He is working. It does seem that, in the order of His Providence, He has a great work in store for the Church of England. He has guided and guarded it by His Providence, watched over it, recalled it, awakened it when sleeping, infused fresh life into it, as He has into other branches of the true Vine, and as He does not do to any which are not true branches. When they decay, they decay altogether. It is His own likeness [1]. Branches cut off from Him are fresh for a while with the freshness of the Vine, but after a time 'wither.' The Church of England yields more good fruit than ever.

The Church of Rome, although a large body of churches, has no authority to call herself *the* Church. Why should she be *the* Church, to the exclusion of all the millions of Russia and the Greek Church? What have these done that they should be counted no portion of the Church of Christ? But since there is no reason to say that they are no part of the Church of Christ, then intercommunion with Rome is not essential to being a portion of the one Body of Christ. We should pray, as we do, for increased unity, but not as if unity were altogether gone, when we have the same Sacraments, the same Apostolic Succession, the same Faith in the Creeds (although Rome has added articles of Faith which were not of Faith in the early Church). Thus we are knit to our one Lord, by our one Faith in Him, by the same Sacraments, the grace whereof flows from Him, being administered by those who hold their office in succession from Him.

Rome would not accept from us the acknowledgement of her Patriarchate. You might as well speak of the Queen as Prince of Wales. But they are these very claims of the Pope, unknown to primitive antiquity, which keep up the misunderstanding between the East and West.

I have no time for more now. Give yourself more and more, as you have been doing, to our Lord to be what He wills, and rest tranquilly in His grace.

May He bless and keep you.

[1] i.e. illustration.

LETTER XII.

THE SAME.

[1851.]

I will take briefly the points which you mention in your letter, although I have dwelt upon some of them more fully in my Letter to the Bishop of London. I would have it sent you, if you cannot easily procure it; I have published it at 1s. on purpose. You must have read our Prayer Book somehow with a bias, for it cannot be contrary to St. John vi. 53, which it quotes for our comfort in the Exhortation, 'Then we spiritually eat the Flesh of the Son of Man.'

The doctrine of the Real Presence could not be more fully expressed than it is there in the Exhortation, in the Prayer 'We do not presume,' and in the Catechism. Our Divines have said, 'We believe the words "This is My Body"; we inquire not into the mode,' i.e. how it is His Body.

But I see that you say 'it is literally admitted by our Catechism.' Then it cannot be rejected. The fault must be in any mode of interpreting, which would set any other language at variance with the Catechism.

Neither is there anything in our Formularies against the true doctrine of the Eucharistic Sacrifice. What the Article objects to is only a popular error, then increasing. A body of our Divines have always handed down the true doctrine, as was shown in the *Tracts for the Times*. But on both these subjects I have written so much more fully in my 'Letter' that I should only be writing to you less fully what you could read there.

The division of the Church.—We must own that the Church is not what it was, nor what it ought to be. So must the Roman Catholics. They too acknowledge that it has not the same fervour of love, cannot bear the same discipline as at first. Love is the bond of unity. With impaired love it is likely that unity should be impaired. The Church is 'One, Holy, Catholic, Apostolic.' Alas! all admit that holiness is impaired. They gain no stricter doctrine of unity by impairing catholicity. According to them, not we only, but all the ancient Greek Church, including the 60,000,000 of Russia, are no part of the Church. Why? On what ground are they to abridge our Lord's inheritance? It is allowed by most thoughtful men of the Roman Catholics too, that their belief on the Procession of God the Holy Ghost differs only in words from ours. Nor does Rome require for union that they should alter the ancient Creed. Why then are they to be shut out? Because they do not acknowledge an authority of the Roman see which the ancient Church never acknowledged. They remain under their ancient Patriarchates. But since there is no reason to exclude these 60,000,000 from the one Church of Christ, then it follows that intercommunion may be interrupted for a long time and yet the body remain one. We have common descent through the Bishops to the Apostles, from our Lord; we have the two great Sacraments which flowed from His Side (the two which the ancient Church spoke of as specially the great Sacraments), the Sacraments, in the one of which we are made members of the Body of Christ, in the other we are fed by Him and united by Him to Himself; we have one Faith, the Faith once delivered to the Saints, as embodied in the Creeds. Holding this one Faith, united by the same Sacraments, administered by the successors of the Apostles, to the One Head of the Church, the Eastern, Western, our own Church, is one, although it has not that intercommunion which it ought to have. A family is one, although it have misunderstandings or grievances. A limb is a part of the body, although it be mangled. The Roman Catholics, on their theory of unity, cannot recite the words of the Te Deum, 'The Holy Church throughout all the world doth acknowledge Thee,' in the same full sense as we.

Thus then we do acknowledge one kingdom, although the unity is not so perfect as it was, under the One Head, Christ, Who never said that He should leave one representative on earth, nor did the ancient Church so think.

Union of Church and State, as it is called.—The question is not what power the State has (for the State, where it is nominally Christian, has generally an oppressive power), but whether the Church of England gave it any power which it ought not. English Roman Catholics have said that England is the only country where Catholics are free; they protest against any precedent from Roman Catholic States. But they admit thereby that the State has a power which it ought not to have. The State has before this nominated the Pope; and now three Great Powers have each a veto upon his election. Disorders there always have been, always will be. The only question is, Has the Church of England given to the State powers which were essential to her as part of the Church of Christ? For she might have made mistakes, been overtrustful, yet not have given up anything essential to her being. And this is quite clear, that she never meant to give up the decision of matters of Faith to the civil power. Nor is the doctrine of the Church at all altered by the Gorham decision. We are Catholic, in the same way as the Church of France is Catholic, by being a portion of the one Catholic Church, notwithstanding the interruption of communion. We could not claim to be *the* Catholic Church, because a part is not a whole. But neither does the Roman Church claiming this make them so. The Donatists were schismatics, because being a small body they claimed to be the whole. We do not so. We pray, in all the most solemn times, for the Bishops of the whole Church.

The surest sign of being a part of *the* Church, having as we have, a true succession from the Apostles, and the true Faith, is life; the continuance of God's Holy Spirit among us. This we have had and have remarkably. We have had God's good Providence watching over us and guarding us. He has brought us through every variety of trial. We have been tried in every way, by persecution or outward prosperity, by violent interference or attempt to corrupt us, and the Church has remained unchanged. He has brought us out of even the lukewarmness which prevailed among us, as well as the Roman Catholics of France, &c., during the last century. And to individuals He gives this life through Sacraments. He gives large grace through the Absolution pronounced in His Name. He gives it through the Holy Eucharist, wherein the Church of England teaches us that we receive 'the Body and Blood of Christ.' God does not bless through a lie, but a truth. But He does bless us through the Power of the Keys and through the Holy Eucharist. They must be then what we believe them to be, what persons have known them to be. Absolution must be, ' by His authority committed' to us, by 'our Lord Jesus Christ, Who hath left power with His Church to forgive sins.' For He owns it, and forgives the sins, and gives grace. And this power belongs to the Church. And if what our Church (in the Office of the Visitation of the Sick) bids us say were not true, it would be blasphemy; nor could God bless it, as He has done in thousands of cases.

The history of the Anointing the Sick is very obscure. In the Greek Church it is still used for the recovery of health. In the West it had come to be delayed until recovery was, humanly speaking, impossible. This is what the Article means by 'the corrupt following of the Apostles,' that it was not used as they intended. The simple Anointing of the Sick was retained at first in

Edward VIth's time, and was never blamed by the Church of England. The later Roman Church ascribes a spiritual benefit to it, 'the remission of the remains of sins.' But it does not appear what these can be, i.e. what the 'remains of sins' which are not removed by Absolution. The words, 'and if he have committed sins, they shall be forgiven him,' were understood, of old, of the Absolution, in which the guilt of all sins is remitted. We cannot undergo the loss of anything essential, since we may have the special forgiveness of sins, through the Power of the Keys, and we have the Body and Blood of our Lord. Nor is it at all clear that it has been used ever since the Apostles.

On the other hand, the disuse of the Cup on the Roman side is very serious; for there is a special grace through the Cup, as some Roman Catholic Divines themselves acknowledge (see further in my Letter to the Bishop of London).

Miracles have not been vouchsafed on any settled law. They were, from early times, given in one part of the Church and withheld in another, given on great occasions as God saw needful. But God has given to us, and that through the Holy Eucharist, bodily cures which were above nature. There are miracles in the Russian Church too. In France there is open avowed unbelief, and so there may be a reason why God may vouchsafe evident miracles, as He says 'signs are for unbelievers.' The sort of miracle which is vouchsafed as a direct evidence is where a miracle is worked directly in proof of what is questioned. Thus it was in St. Augustine's time; it is not now.

It would be childish to say that 'the Anglican Church was only founded 300 years ago by Luther.' Luther did teach several doctrines peculiar to himself, and we did not receive any of them; on the contrary, carefully avoided them, as the belief that to Justification it is necessary that one should believe that he is justified. But, indeed, our Church at the Reformation did not lay down anything new, and declared against nothing which had been matter of Faith from the first.

There is no question that there had been changes going on in the centuries immediately preceding the Reformation as to the doctrines of Purgatory, Indulgences (neither of which the Greek Church receives), and the cultus of Saints and especially the Blessed Virgin. But although they were changes which the Church of England had a right to reform, they were not such as should constitute a 'prevailing of the gates of hell against the Church.' Our Lord did not promise an exemption from all things amiss, whether as to faith or practice. Only we believe that the Church will not become heretical, i.e. that she will never deny any part of the Faith. There has been confessedly much amiss in the Church oftentimes; but we believe that the whole Church will never be permitted to decree and to receive anything which is contrary to the Faith, or to part with any part of it.

I have written as little as I could, on a great many subjects. This may enable you to see more clearly what you wish to know more fully.

Meanwhile, study especially to keep near our Lord, in repentance for anything amiss in the past life, in humility, in prayer, in studying to please Him, and to grow in His love, and He will not leave you. You may write to me as to a father.

God bless you.

You might find some help also in a sermon which I have just published, the Rule of Faith[1]. I suppose that you are not within reach of expensive books.

---

[1] Preached fifth Sunday after Epiphany (Feb. 9), 1851. Univ. Sermons, vol. i. serm. vi.

LETTER XIII.

Roman Claims.

Shrove Tuesday, March 5, 1878.

I understood (I hope rightly) that the mind, about which you wrote to me, is 'perfectly satisfied' at present, but that you wish for books to recommend to it to read. I know very little of controversial books, but the first question is, on what points it is disturbed. To myself, that vast system as to the Blessed Virgin has been, from the beginning, the great crux, so unlike anything in Christian antiquity that if you see a Father quoted, you may be sure that the passage is not his, if it relates to [the] cultus. The passages in Dr. Newman's Letter to myself relate to her as the being whom God chose to be the mother of our Lord Who redeemed us. The unhappiness of later writers has been that they applied to the present influence of the Blessed Virgin personally, what the older genuine writers apply to the Incarnation. But with this exception, almost every passage which writers on the Glories of Mary quote from the Fathers, has been pronounced by the Benedictines not to be genuine. The Redemptorists published an edition of the *Glories of Mary*, in which (after verifying the quotations) they marked with a † passages which 'could not be found'; as the editor says, i.e. which were spurious. They include all quoted from the Fathers except one or two of a Germanus, who is probably a writer of a later date.

Now this is a great sadness, in the present popular Roman system, how much is founded upon what must ultimately have been fraud, attaching great names to writings of a later date, to make them more valuable.

The most terrible forgery was that of the false Decretals. No one now, I believe, maintains their genuineness. They were forged, as a protection against oppression: but both Hincmar of Rheims who first quoted them, and Nicolas I who accepted them and used them against Hincmar, must have known them to be forgeries; for the originals, if at all, must have been in the Vatican. It was a terrible instance of doing evil, that good might come. They used a sinful weapon, to avert evil, instead of going to God. But this forgery has had an influence on the whole system of the Western Church ever since. Their immediate effects were pointed out by Fleury (though a Roman Catholic) in his *Quatrième discours sur l'histoire ecclésiastique* prefixed to the sixteenth volume of the 18mo edition. They culminated in the decree of the Vatican Council, which was carried by the Pope's will. 'To obey,' said Monseigneur Darboy to one who repeated it to me, 'is not to believe.' 'Aliud est obedire, aliud credere.' The Vatican Council was more like a debate in a House of Commons, than a Council of the Church met to bear witness as to the Faith. The Council of Nicaea (as St. Athanasius impresses upon us) bore witness to the Truth which each and all had received from the first. In the Vatican Council, a considerable minority said, 'There is no evidence that this was part of the deposit of Faith committed by the Apostles to the Church'—'This never can be matter of faith.'

This is in two ways a defence of us.

1. Since it is acknowledged by all, everywhere, that the Faith cannot be added to, that which is of Faith must have always been of Faith. Then there is no room for their

taunts of us about the divisions among us. The divisions, for centuries, of those who affirmed or denied the Immaculate Conception, were fiercer than any divisions among us. The Infallibility of the Pope was denied on very solid grounds, among them e. g. by Monseigneur Maret, who was a very able writer of the Sorbonne.

2. The new doctrines directly contradict the belief of old. Fathers, Bishops, Doctors, Saints denied, one after the other, the Immaculate Conception of the Blessed Virgin. General Councils and Popes acted as if the Infallibility of the Pope were untrue. One of the greatest Popes (Gregory I) said, 'I venerate the four General Councils as I do the four Gospels,' whereas according to this theory, he might have written them himself. The Article of the Creed would have to be changed. Instead of, 'I believe one Holy Catholic Apostolic Church,' it must run 'I believe the Lord Pope,' since he is the one authentic channel of Revelation; what he declares to be true is true.

Our Church, being left by herself, reformed by herself. The need of reformation was loudly repeated on all sides by Councils and individuals. Our Church took as her standard those 'ages which are most uncorrupt and pure,' the 'quod semper, quod ubique, quod ab omnibus': Holy Scripture, as interpreted by Councils and by those who were approved by all men. No heresy has been proved against her. The Council of Trent when convened at length, did not condemn anything which she affirmed to be true. It was directed against the foreign reformers: nor were her Articles directed against the Council of Trent....

We have then a place in the Church, as witnesses to the ancient Truth. And God has prospered us. We have been tried in every way, but have survived all. We have been rather like a tree, violently shaken, but which, after three centuries, has struck deeper roots than before, and is spreading in all lands. Abiding life is a great test of the Presence of God, since it is the Presence of God's Spirit.

Perhaps my own Eirenicon, Part I, although the immediate occasion of it is passed, might be of use, as touching upon a variety of subjects. Or I might write more definitely if you told me what touched the mind most. We have everything which we could have anywhere, and our laity have the Blood of Christ, as a special Gift. Our restoration has been eminently through Sacraments, which are God's gifts in His Church, and God has set His seal upon them.

LETTER XIV.

ROMAN CATHOLICISM.

July 25, 1880.

It is very sad; but the young man will probably not write to me, or if he did, would only show it to the Roman Catholic priest, whose advice he has sought. It is part of the disease of the present day, that the young are their own advisers, read things out of their depth, and because *they* do not see the answer, suppose that there is none. Possibly, in another case, this brief answer might save from precipitancy.

The Church of England is no way more independent of Rome than the whole Church was in St. Augustine's time.

1. Every part of the Church made laws for itself. (Thus you have the Apostolic Canons, the African, Spanish, Gallican Canons.) These were authoritative within each province: only the Canons of the Council of Nicaea, as being Canons of a General Council, were paramount.

2. Every province made its own Bishops, who, according to the Council of Nicaea, were confirmed by the Metropolitan without any reference to the Bishop of Rome.

3. In single cases Bishops of Rome sought to receive appeals not on their own inherent authority, but on that of a supposed Canon of Nicaea. In the remarkable case of Apiarius, the African Bishops, of whom St. Augustine was one, sent to the East for a copy of the Nicene Canons; and since they gave no such authority, the African Council sent a letter to the then Bishop of Rome in strong terms censuring him and asking him to desist. This case was ended by the voluntary confession of his

crimes by Apiarius, whom the Bishop of Rome had wished to restore. The other remarkable case of interference was in St. Cyprian's time. Basilides and Martialis, Spanish Bishops, had for their crimes been deposed by the Spanish Bishops. One of them went to Rome to get restored, and was acknowledged by Pope Stephen. The Spanish Bishops wrote to St. Cyprian to ask what they should do. St. Cyprian (as his wont was in any question of moment) assembled an African council, and wrote back in their name—that Basilides and Martialis had been rightly deposed for their crimes; that their successors had been canonically elected by the Bishops of the province in the presence of the people, and that therefore they were the rightful Bishops; and that Basilides (I think it was) had only made his case worse by imposing upon 'our brother Stephen' (the then Bishop of Rome). The Bishops so elected by the Spanish Bishops remained *the* Bishops. One of their names appears in a subsequent Synod.

But there is no other way in which a Bishop could interfere in another province than by (1) confirming its Bishops; (2) confirming its canons (legislation); (3) hearing appeals.

If we were back in the times of St. Augustine, i.e. in the close of the fourth century, there could absolutely be no ground of schism between us and Rome.

The modern system is owing in great measure to the forged Decretals, which Fleury too asserts to have in many things changed the discipline of the Church.

When I consulted Archbishop Darboy about my first Eirenicon, I said, in answer to a question, 'We acknowledge the primacy of the Bishop of Rome, not the supremacy[1].' He was quite satisfied, and said, 'Supremacy is no ecclesiastical term.'

[1] See Life of E. B. Pusey, D.D. vol. iv. p. 129.

LETTER XV.

THE UNITY OF THE CHURCH.
[1880.]

I believe the Unity of the Church, which we confess when we say 'I believe in One Holy Catholic Church,' to be real and numerical. I believe that unity to be organic, inwrought by God's Holy Spirit, and by the communication of the Body of Christ. We are all baptized into one Body. Partaking of One, we become one in Him. But then, whether individuals or bodies, those who part with the one Faith, do no longer believe in the One Lord. Rejection of the true Faith or of God's commandments separates from Christ. Hence wicked individuals, and heretics, whether individuals or bodies, cease to be members of Christ. Heretics do not believe in the same Lord.

This unity involves the duty of love and of unity of will, of which the highest expression is inter-communion. But inter-communion does not make union; it is an act of love. It is that in the Church which mutual communication is in a family. A family, in which there is dissension, is one, although not 'at one.' This is, of course, an imperfect analogy of things natural and spiritual. But it remarkably illustrates the unity of the Church, in that the real unity of the Church and of the family is one of nature; the harmony is a duty flowing from it; its loss injures the well-being of either, but does not destroy that unity which comes, in the one case by natural, in the other by spiritual descent.

The statement that the unity, of which our Lord speaks, is one of nature, not of will, is not mine, but that of St. Hilary and St. Cyril.

You say 'the Jewish Church, the type of the Christian Church, was undivided.' In what way, more than the Church now? Holy Scripture does not give us authority to say the ten tribes were no part of the Jewish Church.

God Himself says, "Yet have I left *Me* 7,000 in Israel, all the knees which have not bowed to Baal." More prophets were raised up in Israel than in Judah. Jeremiah speaks more severely of Judah than of Israel. Again, after the Captivity, the Jews in Egypt set up a temple, which was wrong. It broke the type of unity, although not so grievously as the Calves. They had been forbidden to go to Egypt by Jeremiah; they were to be punished for it; they left the Promised Land, through worldly considerations. Yet even after building the temple, they did not cease to be part of the Jewish Church. Again, there seems no doubt that the ten tribes did not go up to the temple at Jerusalem, nor did the prophets exhort them to do so. The very object of the sin of Jeroboam and his policy was to deter them. It appears from 2 Chron. xxx that they had not gone up to eat the Passover, which was sin. I do not mean to parallel the ten tribes. To assume that there is a visible centre of unity under the Gospel, is to assume the whole question, and is contrary to early antiquity. I mean it in answer to your question. The case was the stronger, because the full service of God could not be performed except at Jerusalem, which our Lord says is done away.

You say the prophecy of the mountain of the Lord's House, the figures of the True Vine and the Body, are all of numerical unity.

This I have answered. The English Church believes a numerical unity. Holy Scripture speaks both of 'Churches' and 'the Church.' Roman Catholics ask sometimes, 'If the Churches are "branches," where is the trunk?' Our Lord says, "I am the Vine, ye are the branches." The Church was founded at Jerusalem; believers were added to it. The Apostles preached the Gospel among all nations, and founded Churches everywhere, and these were held in one by the common Sacraments and by common descent from the Apostles. The Heavenly City in the Revelation has twelve Foundations; all of which rest on the One Foundation, Christ.

You ask 'how can a parallel be drawn between the prophecies of individual sanctity and *unity* and the institutions of God which are Divinely preserved?'

The unity of the Church we believe to be preserved on the part of God; as you say, 'her unity is, *on God's part*, perfect.' This is precisely the line which I drew myself, that what was on God's part was perfect, what on man's, imperfect. It would be well if you were to ask yourself what you meant by unity, and on what this was grounded. We (as I have said) believe that there is one Body, with one Faith (that 'delivered at the first'), united in our Lord by one Baptism, and His one Body given to all; and all the functions which He has left in His Church discharged by the successors of those whom He has appointed. He has said nothing of living under any Head except Himself. There are no traces of a monarchy in the Acts, or the Epistles, or the primitive Church; i.e. none in actual life to bear out a certain exposition of our Lord's words to St. Peter, which do not contain it in themselves. Our Lord is so often called 'the Head of the Church,' and no other is called the Head, that we are not justified in assuming that there must be an earthly Head. The *à priori* grounds which Roman Catholics use are not safe.

The parallel which I meant to draw was not between God's doings and man's, but strictly as to man's. I said that man continually falls short of what God intended for him. I do not mean that the promises fail altogether, but that we are obliged to take up with inferior fulfilment of them. Our Lord prophesies in the same way of the love of Christians generally, and of the love of the whole Church: " By this shall all men know that ye are My disciples, if ye have love one [towards another]."

LETTER XVI.

ROMAN QUESTIONS.

Passion Week, 1882.

... I have also lost my hearing, so that if you were to come I should have to ask you to write any important questions which you have to ask me, or any important answer which you would have to give to any question which I should have to ask you.

I need not say how sorry I am for you. I shall have to ask you, (1) How did your doubts arise? (2) Did you read controversial books? (I should think them out of your depth.) If so, what? (3) What points made an impression upon you? or, (4) Has it only been a general impression, arising from the extent of the Roman Communion, and the relative smallness of ours? (5) Have you used all the spiritual helps which the English Church would give you (as Confession)? (6) Have you been careful about your Communions, preparing diligently for the coming of our Lord beforehand, thanking Him for His great love to *you* individually in them, in that (by a miracle greater than the raising of Lazarus) He sends His Holy Spirit to make that particle which you are to receive, sacramentally and ineffably, His Body?

I have often felt the gift of His Sacraments to be one great proof of our being a part of His Church. He blesses through Truth. Those of the Kirk and other devout persons believe in a spiritual Communion, that the soul, on occasion of the outward symbols, ascends up to Heaven to feed on our Lord. This is a truth as far as it goes; but we might do so with every breath. Again, what the Wesleyans teach is a very naked Gospel: 'Jesus died for sinners; He bids all sinners come to Him. We are sinners; come to Him.' It is true, as far as it goes, and God blesses through it those who know no more. But we believe more. We believe that God forgives sins upon confession through Absolution by His priest. We believe, as I said, that God consecrates by us His priests mere elements of the world to be sacramentally, spiritually, supernaturally, His Body and Blood. I have accepted the saying, 'The Church alone has the Sacraments' (except that the Sacrament of Baptism is valid by our Lord's ordinance, by whomsoever given). But then I reverse the argument. God has attested His Sacraments among us. Therefore we are in the Church. This is not the judgement of individuals. He has judged their profanation terribly. . . . The graces which have followed upon good Communions have been marvellous. So have the fruits of individual Confession and Absolution. . . .

I have dwelt upon these, rather than upon points negatively against the Church of Rome, because it is more healthful and happier. If there be a test which has been verified again and again, it is that given by our Lord: "If a man abide not in Me, he is cast forth like a branch and withereth." 'Withering' has been the lot of every body really cut off from the Church. So it was in every heresy. After a time they withered. So it has been with those who were cut off by the German schism. Lutherans became rationalists. So did the Danes and Hollanders. Geneva became Socinian. The French became semi-Arians, a large body is rationalizing.

The English Church has been tried in every way. It has seemed like a tree, rudely shaken, but striking ever anew. In the United States it wins from every sect. It quadrupled while the whole population doubled. About one-eighth of its clergy only were born in the Church, and so on of its people. It has no external support there. There is nothing but the power of the Truth, which has drawn them. The Irish Roman Catholics who migrated there became lax. In the next generation they became lost to the Church. I have heard only lately that in Ireland a good many of the Roman Catholics have left off going to Confession. It is well that they have, for for them to confess murder would be horrible. A Roman Catholic Bishop said that he could not but think that they had thrown three of the Commandments out of window. The sixth and eighth were, of course, two. Yet another Roman Catholic Bishop seems to justify things. It is a terrible scandal.

To me the crux has always been the excessive cultus of the Blessed Virgin, and I accumulated together a great deal of the evidence in my first Eirenicon. I thought, as I quoted one startling expression after another, 'they have but to disown it.' An eminent priest wrote to me, 'I cannot think that the Blessed Virgin likes it.' The Abbé Gratry, when I mentioned the devotional books, said, 'Oh! ces livres de piété!' And yet they go on. Bishops prohibit them. Some others crop up. It seems as if there were something amiss in the Roman system that it throws out these things continually, and with all the discipline they have they cannot restrain them.

These were my hopes when I wrote my first Eirenicon; that they would see what we wanted, and since they were not formally committed to it by any decree of the Roman Communion, we could be in communion with them, and yet be guarded against them. Instead of remitting anything, they have under Pius IX added two articles to their Faith, both in opposition to Catholic antiquity, the Immaculate Conception of the Blessed Virgin Mary and the Personal Infallibility of the Bishop of Rome, although so many Popes have spoken in error. Roman Catholics have owned some of these. But it is, besides confounding everything which came from the first, contrary to the old belief,—that the Faith was from the first, that there could be no new Articles of Faith. Pope St. Gregory said that he 'reverenced the first four General Councils as he did the four Gospels.' According to the Vatican Decree the Popes of the day might have settled the matters of Faith themselves. The Councils were useless. . . . And yet what Popes there have been, as in that miserable tenth century, when Popes were intruded by their mistresses; and Popes were, Baronius says, of no use except to carry on the succession. Happily for the Church, they thought of nothing less than theology. But one of the most striking books, I thought, written beforehand against the Papal Infallibility was by Monseigneur Maret on the connexion of the perception of truth with holiness. The instances which I collected in my third Eirenicon, I collected at the instance of persons within the Roman Communion, who thought that it might have some weight with the Council, to know how the declaration of the Personal Infallibility of the Pope would affect us. A Jesuit told me that we had brought it about by disputing it, for if it had not been made matter of Faith then, it never could have been. And yet it was at one time opposed by as many Bishops as formed the Second General Council. . . .

The Vatican Council was the greatest sorrow I ever had in a long life.

God bless you.

LETTER XVII.

THE SAME.
Easter Monday, 1882.

I will just mention to you two or three things which do not seem to have occurred to you. (1) That there is often real agreement where there is verbal disagreement. (Bishop Daniel Wilson, on his way to Calcutta, said that 'people in England were divided by the meaning which they attached to a word' [regeneration], i.e. Bishop Daniel Wilson and his friends had attached to it the meaning of conversion, which it has not in the Prayer Book and never had. A pious Evangelical clergyman asked me, soon after I wrote my Tracts on Baptism, 'If you call the grace of Baptism, "regeneration," what do you call that grace from which a man never falls?' He differed from us about the meaning which he attached wrongly to a word.) . . .

This was your first mistake. Some people were disturbed some time ago at Dr. Hampden being made a Bishop. He had said rash things. What he really believed, I forget. But when they spoke about leaving the Church on that ground some eminent Roman Catholic said, 'I have no patience with these men, there always have been such things in the Church and always will.' He was afraid that if this person were driven out of the Church of England on this ground, he would be driven away again by some scandal in the Roman Communion.

So as to contradictions of Truth. It became a sacred duty to me lately, to finish a preface which my son had written about Nestorianism in the fifth century. I could not but congratulate myself that I did not live in that century. Here was an eminent writer, now much valued, Theodoret, trying with all his might to obtain the condemnation of another, now esteemed a Saint, St. Cyril, and the General Council of which St. Cyril was the centre.

And in so doing he used language which the fifth General Council rightly condemned as heterodox. Yet he had the whole large Patriarchate of Antioch (including a large portion of the East) with him. And he had no term for St. Cyril but 'heretic,' or for his writings but 'heretical.' It required a good deal of time and patience to obtain the recognition of the fifth General Council itself. Two of the chief founders of Nestorianism were eminent teachers in the Church; one of them had the title 'the Interpreter.' But Nestorians call them their 'fathers.' A Council, now called the 'Robber Council,' maintained the opposite heresy of Eutyches. It was assembled legitimately, but went wrong. There is a long list of these distresses.

(2) What is of Faith, must always have been of Faith. The Faith may be expressed in different terms at different times, but the Faith itself must have always been the same. 'Development' cannot be from a contradictory. For centuries the Western Church was distracted by the contradiction of two large schools, the Scotists and the Thomists; the Thomists (which was the most popular school) denying the Immaculate Conception of the Blessed Virgin, the Scotists affirming it. Pope Pius IX, against the advice of a large proportion of the Bishops whom he consulted, declared it to be matter of Faith. If he rightly declared it matter of Faith, it was matter of Faith (although not declared to be so) all along. The Faith (if it were so now) would have been denied all along. If it had come to a decision at the time of the Council of Basle, before which the question was formally laid, it would have probably been decided the other way; the evidence prepared for the Council by an Ultramontane theologian (Card. de Turrecremata) was so solid. Those who investigated the question for the late Pope only had a very slovenly book before them (De Bandelis), and gave him bad advice, he himself being fanatically eager on the same

side, and expecting that the Blessed Virgin would do great good to the Church in requital of the honour done to her. . . . It was said by eminent Bishops in that Council, that it was not matter of Faith, nor ever could become such. It is not thus that matters of Faith are framed.

(3) The Church teaches through her Creeds and her prayers. . . . There is no way in which the Faith can be so taught as by being put into our mouths in our prayers and in our Creeds. It may be a harass to the mind to hear the truths which we have confessed in them contradicted in the sermon. It often happened to me in my young days, or my children told me the preacher contradicted the Prayer Book. I taught them (as I would teach you) to understand his words in the best sense they could. But they saw, as you have, that the preacher was wrong; only they bore it patiently.

And I rather suspect that your first fault was impatience, not at the contradiction of what you rightly held and knew to be the Truth, but that one who seemed for the time to have the office of teacher contradicted it. We pray three times a week, that God would 'bring into the way of truth all such as have erred and are deceived.' I often cannot but think that if we had *all* said that prayer more devoutly and more earnestly we should be in a better state than we are now. There may be something unbefitting that God should hear prayer which was not said very earnestly to Him. People say such prayers rather to satisfy themselves that they have 'said their prayers' (as they call it), than that they really want Almighty God to give them what they ask for.

But I am rambling on, rather having a misgiving of the effect of reading any book. I will only then add, that should you have difficulties after reading the Eirenicon, I think that I could remove them *if* you were to come to see me.

God bless you.

LETTER XVIII.

ON OBJECTIONS TO ENGLISH ORDERS.

August 5, 1882.

I began the enclosed in a letter to ——, but as it grew I thought that there would be risk of further delay, so I have had the answer copied for you myself. I dwelt on the successive cavils, because they help to show the animus of this last. Negligence there will be everywhere. Cardinal Newman mentioned to one who told me, the case of an Archbishop of Paris who had never been baptized. Everything was done from the beginning. But what became of all his previous priestly or archiepiscopal acts? I do not believe that God so ties down His unfathomable depths of mercies, that an accident or carelessness should vitiate His gift, or that He would send empty away for no fault of theirs little ones brought to Him, whom when on earth He received so lovingly, took them up in His arms and blessed them. St. Dionysius the Great refused to baptize one who had been inadvertently to Holy Communion without due Baptism; on the ground that he could not baptize one who had so often been partaker of the Body and Blood of Christ. People may think St. Dionysius mistaken, but they would hardly believe that he whom he refused to baptize died unregenerate.

God bless you.

(*The Enclosure.*)

August 5, 1882.

With regard to ——'s question, the supposed carelessness of our Baptisms is but a myth which grew out of a story of some clergyman's having a number of Baptisms at once in some large town. The attack upon our Orders has been most persevering. Knowing that our Sacraments depended upon them, the Roman Catholics have taken up first one stone, then another, to distress our people. First, there was the Nag's Head fable; though invented forty years afterwards, it was taken up too soon. For one was still living who had seen the Consecration (it was some nobleman, I think). Lingard got into bad odour with the Roman Catholics for giving it up as a fable.

(2) Then it was said, that Barlow the chief Consecrator was not a Bishop. His Consecration, upon investigation, was proved to be true. But after all it came out that nothing turned upon it. It was taken for granted on both sides, that he alone had said the words, so that if he had not been a Bishop, the whole would have been invalid. It was ascertained from the Lambeth register, that all four Bishops had imposed hands, and all four said the words.

(3) The Lambeth registers were denounced as a forgery. Besides another record in Trinity College, Cambridge, it was clear from the names which appeared, which were attested by other sources, that it could not be questioned except in a way which would throw doubt on all historical evidence. I myself had occasion to examine the Lambeth records, in order to ascertain whether the process of Confirmation was a mere form. I found that it was formed most carefully upon one in Archbishop Chichele's time, when the English Church, not recognizing either of the two or (I forget) three Anti-popes, revived the old form of Confirmation. Du Pin (a Roman Catholic) praised it as formed carefully on ancient models.

(4) The form of Consecration was taken from an Exeter Pontifical of Lacy. Our first form of Consecration only had the words of Lacy's Pontifical, 'Receive the Holy Ghost'; afterwards, 'for the Office of a Bishop or Priest' was

added. Then it was objected that it was of no use to have the office expressed there, unless it was named in some other part of the Consecration Service. This was an obvious cavil. However, the office was expressed in the Litany, so the cavil fell through.

(5) Then Cardinal Wiseman put all this aside and rested the objection on the one point, that we had no jurisdiction. But jurisdiction from the earliest times was in the chief See, the Metropolitan. But it was the Metropolitan See which was vacant. And the jurisdiction is inherent in the See itself. Parker's possession of the See was not disputed. Hoping for the reconciliation of England, it was never filled up. Down to the 'Papal Aggression' in your memory, they did not attempt to fill up our Sees, and even then they avoided our names.

And now, after all these attempts, comes, limping, this about our Baptisms, which has not been thought of these more than 300 years. I may as well put in the first instance that an eminent Gallican theologian said to this effect, 'Take care what you are about, you may wound yourselves. How do you know that amid uninstructed priests in such a district the right forms were all used?' (And this when midwives were allowed to baptize and even Popes rose from the ranks! You remember how Sixtus V's mother was a washerwoman.) 'Trust God that He in some way supplied any defect, so that none of His people should be deprived of the Bread of Life.' I forget where I have quoted this. I think that it must have been in my first Eirenicon. I have sent for it. Amongst us the objection is childish. Of the supposed miscellaneous babies, boy-babies and girl-babies, who were alleged to have been baptized carelessly in some great town, what likelihood would there be that any (as they are supposed to be of the poorest class) should be a priest? God, we may be sure, will protect His own ordinances; He will not give us ashes for bread. The objection only shows the animus of the objectors. As for the special cases in which A or B said that C or D were not baptized, I am very sceptical about them. Infant Baptism by affusion is prescribed by the English ritual, but Baptism by sprinkling would still be valid.

The use of water and the words is alone necessary.

LETTER XIX[1].

ROMAN DIFFICULTIES.

August 4, 1877.

The questions put in the letter to your friend require a book, not a letter, to answer them satisfactorily.

(1) As to visible unity, the writer ignores the fact of the Eastern Church, and puts the question as if it lay simply between the Roman Church and ourselves. Yet whatever he may say of us, Roman controversialists, until of late, acknowledged that the Eastern Churches were simply schismatic, not heretical. Yet they cover a large portion of the face of the earth, and if they were denied to be a portion of the Body of Christ, our Lord would be deprived of a large portion of His inheritance. But the Eastern Churches are out of communion with Rome, because they remain under the same form of government which they had in the earliest ages, and do not accept the modern accretions which have grown up since, and to which the forged Decretals gave such an impulse. If things could be restored, such as they were in the time of the great Greek and Latin Fathers, whom all look up to as Fathers, there could be no schism between East and West. However the doctrine of the Procession of the Holy Ghost may have been put forward, intelligent and remarkable writers have seen and said that the real ground of disunion is 'the Sees.' If East were to submit to the West, the whole Patriarchal system would have to

---

[1] In this letter, several passages which have already appeared in substance in other letters have been retained for the sake of the completeness of the argument.

be given up, and whatever titles they might be allowed to retain, Patriarchs, Archbishops, and Bishops, could only be curates of the Bishop of Rome. Yet the great Eastern Church has been doing the work of the Church and carrying on our Lord's commission, "Go and baptize all nations." It has been converting and is converting its tens of thousands where the Roman Church is not. No sooner had Schamyl been driven out of the Caucasus than he was replaced by monasteries for the conversion of the people. Apostolic Bishops have been labouring beyond the bounds of the great Russian Empire. They had lately Apostolic Bishops who were converting the north of China and the isles between Kamchatka and America. The two provinces, which were conquered a few years ago, were converted in great measure, although unequally, from Lamaism. And this altogether independently of the State.

I have written about the Eastern Churches because it is an advantage to write apart from self-defence. But then, since they are acknowledged by the Romans not to be heretics, to have all the gifts of the Church and to do the work of the Church, it follows that there may be suspensions of communion, which do not destroy organic or supernatural unity. Consent of human wills cannot produce a supernatural unity. Supernatural unity is that which is wrought by God the Holy Ghost through the Sacraments, whereby, by Baptism millions are continually added to the Church, and by our Lord's Body and Blood that unity is preserved. Inter-communion is ordinarily a duty, yet it has been suspended many times without either part being cut off from the Body of Christ, as about the keeping of Easter with the Asiatic Churches (which was healed by the Council of Nicaea), the wrongful consecration of a Patriarch of Antioch over against the great St. Meletius, who yet became President of the Second

General Council; the rejection of St. Cyprian in which a subsequent Bishop of Rome gave way; the East and West; the Anti-popes, &c.

There may, then, be suspensions of communion, which do not cut off from the Body of Christ. Real schisms always run into heresy.

(2) The writer says that in Roman countries 'there are not two opinions on the articles of the Faith *defined by the Church.*' This is an inadequate statement. A doctrine *may* become certainly or more widely known to be an article of the Faith through its being defined by the Church. But what is the Faith must always have been the Faith. The Fathers of Nicaea and of the other General Councils met to reject those who denied the Faith. The Faith which the Councils of Nicaea and Constantinople embodied in creeds was equally the Faith and known to be the Faith before. A heretic was mostly rejected by a local Council, as Arius, Pelagius, Eutyches, before this was confirmed by a General Council. The Fathers of Nicaea declared as to the Faith (as St. Athanasius pointed out), 'thus have we received from our fathers,' whereas in a matter not of Faith they said, 'it hath seemed good.' They decreed it; the Faith they only attested. If then the new dogmas of 'the Immaculate Conception of the Blessed Virgin Mary,' or of 'the Infallibility of the Pope,' were articles of Faith now, they must have been matters of Faith from the first, part of that body of truth, that 'good deposit,' which our Lord committed to the Apostles, and they to those whom they left as their successors. But the Immaculate Conception was matter of hot controversy for centuries between the Scotists and Thomists: doctors, saints, besides the common current of writers, spoke against it. Just before it was defined by Pope Pius, eminent persons said it could not be made an article of Faith, because there was not evidence enough for it: there were not the tests

of the 'quod ubique, quod semper, quod ab omnibus.' The eminent Ultramontane writer, de Turrecremata, was commissioned by the Papal legates at the Council of Basle to draw up the case against it. He drew up a very strong case. There is no disputing about it now, because such disputing is not tolerated. But it is the authority of the Church, not the Faith (according to them), which must not be disputed. They must hold now, that the Immaculate Conception was always matter of Faith ; but that the Church, for fear of worse evil, may allow the Faith to be denied. You too will remember how vehemently Papal Infallibility was denied at the Vatican Council itself: how bishops declared that it could not be made matter of Faith ; how it was carried by what resembled a parliamentary majority rather than a decree of a Council. It has been accepted by men unconvinced. 'What use is there in struggling against one who is stronger than one's self?' the murdered Archbishop of Paris[1] said to one who told me. The ablest writing which I came across, against the dogma, was that of Monseigneur Maret of the Sorbonne (Bishop of Jura in partibus). Again, the Roman Church allowed what the Vatican Council declared to be the Faith to be contradicted. Time was when it was only taught by a small school and by certain 'Doctorculi' as they were contemptuously called. St. Leo and St. Gregory knew nothing of it. St. Leo allowed his famous 'Tome' to be discussed by the Council of Chalcedon. Their objections to it were met by the argument that the same language had been used by St. Cyril of Alexandria ; it was accepted, because it agreed with the three previous General Councils before Chalcedon, and notably with the Epistles of St. Cyril of Alexandria, received by the Council of Ephesus. St. Leo, who excepted against the alterations of the order of the Patriarchates at the Council, did not except against

[1] Archbishop Darboy.

this. He spoke of his letter being 'confirmed by the Council'; St. Gregory the Great said that he venerated the four General Councils, like the Gospels; when, according to the Vatican decree, he could have written them himself: and henceforth the Church of Rome is to depend not on General Councils, but upon the pronouncements of the Pope.

The Church of England then, in bearing with the present confusion, does no more than the whole Church, according to the Romans, has done before upon matters which it now declares to be *de fide*. Who knows what would have become of those who have since become defenders of the Faith? They were first won to the faith of the Church, and then defended it. I do not know how much Dr. Newman meant, when he said, that 'when he was ordained he believed neither in his Baptism nor his Ordination.' But apart from him, the most numerous recruits of those who taught most energetically Sacramental truth, were from the Evangelical, i.e. an unsacramental school.

But amid all this disputing, there is no doubt what the teaching of the Church of England is. It, above individuals, is the teacher of its people, by giving them a Prayer Book in their own language. It is a remarkable instance of Pope St. Celestine's great saying that 'lex supplicandi, lex credendi.' You cannot have a more impressive way of teaching the Faith, than by putting it into the mouths of the people in their prayers to Almighty God. It becomes part of them. If any one contradicts it, he condemns himself. It would indeed have been a miserable thing, if any one sought the Faith, and could not find it. But this is not so. People knowingly reject the Faith, as in Rome they reject it altogether, and become infidels. 'We have lost the middle classes,' the late Archbishop of Paris said to me. I never knew any one who had any difficulty in finding out what the Faith of the Church of England is. At this moment, in all this wild rebellion against Confession, no one who wishes to know the truth doubts about it. Nay, the rebellion teaches it, and increases Confession. People who dislike the Truth explain it away for themselves, if they do not set themselves directly against it ; no one who felt e.g. the burden of his sins, ever had any doubt how to be absolved from them. So as to the Sacrament of Baptism. Some twenty-seven years ago, people who had taken for instructors the Nonconformist divines disbelieved the plain teaching of the Church. There was no doubt as to the plain meaning of the thanksgiving to God in the Baptismal Service that it had 'pleased Him to regenerate this child.' The shift that this was 'the judgement of charity' only shows how plain the teaching is. So as to the Holy Eucharist. Its Catechism and the Liturgy alike teach unmistakably the doctrine of the Real Presence.

I should then simply deny, 'That the Anglican branch is a Church of compromise 'twixt heresy and truth.' And I should ask 'wherein ?'

There is then no occasion to write to the Bishop of —— as to what lies on the surface of the Prayer Book. I have heard this objection made during many years : but I never heard of any one, who made it, having any difficulty or doubt as to his own belief. What they are really impatient about is, that discipline is not used as to their opponents. But if the Immaculate Conception and Papal Infallibility had been matters of Faith, as the Roman Catholics believe now, the Roman Church would have done far more. It gave absolutely no teaching about those two, which it now declares to be articles of Faith. It allowed it to be declared currently that they were matters of opinion. The Immaculate Conception was called 'a pious opinion,' which is the very opposite of Faith.

The Church of England taught the Truth, although it allowed it to be contradicted for fear of worse evil.

But indeed there is not so much difference of belief among us as one might infer from the language of some. There is often more difference in language than in belief. The diligent preparation which Evangelicals used to make for Holy Communion, showed that they believed more than they definitely expressed. People do not make a week's preparation to say their prayers.

(3) I do not myself worship in Roman Catholic churches, as being so painful: I should think it wrong to worship in them in preference to our English churches. But I do not hold their *public* worship corrupt. . . . I think then that the Church of England had a very definite object to restore primitive antiquity,— the 'quod ubique, quod semper, quod ab omnibus.' There is nothing in Holy Scripture to support this cultus of the Blessed Virgin, nor in early antiquity. I wrote once to one inclined to Rome, 'I am very happy in the Fathers; what they believe, I believe; what they disbelieve, I disbelieve. I reverence them as fathers: I hope they would own me as a son.' And I gave him as an instance, We have printed forty volumes of sermons from the Fathers. The ground of our selection was to bring their interpretations side by side with Holy Scripture. It would occupy three years to preach their sermons, preaching two sermons a Sunday. We could preach them consecutively: the Roman Catholics could not, for it would be asked, 'where are the special Roman doctrines?' My question was forwarded to an eminent Roman theologian. His only answer was, 'No: they would only say that the preacher's religion was more of the head than of the heart, and that he was not devout to the Blessed Virgin.' Conceive the religion of St. Chrysostom, St. Augustine, St. Gregory the Great being 'more of the head than of the heart'! Such an answer concedes the

force of the objection. The system of the Blessed Virgin has been all along my great grief, apart from the love of the mother, in whom and through whom I have received whatever God has given me for my spiritual life.

(4) With regard to the Bishop of Rome being the centre of Christendom, this is modern Roman doctrine. The Church of England is not more independent of the Bishop of Rome than were the African Churches in the time of St. Augustine. All provinces elected their own Bishops under their own metropolitan. The Bishops of the province chose a Bishop in presence of the people. St. Cyprian calls this an apostolic mode of election. The Bishops were confirmed by their own metropolitan, not by Rome. Each province framed their own canons for themselves. Hence we have collections of African, Spanish, Gallican, Oriental canons, in which the Bishop of Rome did not interfere. They settled judicial causes among themselves. No one appealed to Rome except bad men. These appealed where they were not known, as the Western heretic Pelagius appealed to the Bishop of Jerusalem, when he was condemned by the African Bishops. A bad priest, Apiarius, appealed to Rome, which would have restored him. But the Bishop of Rome rested his claim to do so, not on any authority as a successor of St. Peter, but on a supposed canon of Nicaea. The African Fathers professed themselves bound by a General Council, but said that the alleged canon was not in their list of canons of the Council of Nicaea. They sent to the East for an authentic set of the canons; and the alleged canon not being there, they sent a monitory letter to the Bishop of Rome, against mixing up the pride of the world with the affairs of the Church. This is remarkable, that successive Bishops of Rome do not rest their claim on their own inherent power, but on a supposed canon of a Council. The African Bishops were ready at once to submit to the

General Council. Among those Bishops was St. Augustine, whose vote is preserved. Equally remarkable was the failure of an attempt to restore two bad Spanish Bishops. The other Spanish Bishops consulted St. Cyprian. St. Cyprian, with an African council, gave judgement that the two Spanish Bishops had been rightly deposed for their crimes; that their successors had been rightly and canonically elected; and that Basilides and Martialis (the two deposed Bishops) had only made their case worse by imposing on 'our brother Stephen' (the Bishop of Rome). Conceive this now.

I wonder how they think that, whereas St. Peter exercised no authority over the other Apostles, Bishops of Rome should exercise authority, by virtue of words said to him, which conveyed none to himself. He was the only Apostle of whom we are told that he was resisted. . . .

One word more about unity. Inter-communion does not make it, and so the absence of inter-communion does not *itself* break it. It is broken to the individual or individuals, when want of 'charity' cuts them off from the Body of Christ.

(5) It is not true that any one in the Church of England has only just discovered its Catholicity. There were always 'two manner of people' in her as there are now. The Puritans were always opposed to the Catholic teaching of the Prayer Book. Archbishop Laud was a martyr for his Faith. Had the Church of England been Protestant there would have been no Dissenters. The Dissenters correspond with the foreign Protestants. . . . We learned all we taught from the Church of England and its doctors.

(6) The Roman Church does not deny our Orders and Sacraments on the ground of our want of communion with itself. For it allows them in regard to the Eastern Churches which are equally out of communion with it. Its controversialists knew that because of our Catholic

Faith the validity of our Orders was essential to us, else we should have had no Sacraments; and so they took up first one stone, then another, not caring much what they took, so that they had something to fling. . . .

I write this because it is not an abstract question or matter of interpretation of Holy Scripture, but simple matter of fact. I heard that a Roman Catholic Bishop at the Vatican Council was much impressed with the last book on our Orders.

In St. Luke xxii. 32, on which the letter-writer lays stress, he forgets that St. Peter was the Apostle who thrice denied his Lord, the only Apostle who needed conversion, who was the first of the 'lapsed' who in after-times were restored to Communion with so much difficulty, whom our Lord restored to his Apostolate, after a threefold confession to undo his threefold denial, but who alone needed restoration, and who, as a great example of penitence, all his life through, wept his fall at every cock-crowing. But further, 'strengthen' is not 'rule,' 'govern.'

I have now answered your questions as well as I could in a letter.

On the Infallibility I wrote, at the wish of Roman Catholics who were afraid of its being made an article of Faith, in my last Eirenicon; on the want of evidence as to the Immaculate Conception, in the other two. My hope in writing was that Roman authorities might accept the Faith as we hold it, as an adequate statement of Faith. The English Church has, on controverted points with the Roman Church, denied the maximum, but has not laid down any minimum. The Roman Church has often (e. g. as to the Invocation of Saints) laid down a minimum, but has not limited any maximum; and it has no maximum whatever. But something very extreme is practically their Faith. They allow converts, who are so minded, to be received into their Communion, professing a minimum (they admitted one who told me she denied articles of Pope Pius' Creed); but it would be unreal to enter the Roman Church without mentally receiving its extreme teaching.

The writer speaks of the 'glaring absurdities of Anglicanism.' I can hardly imagine anything in more glaring contradiction to all Christian antiquity and history than the Papal Infallibility. If this were true, General Councils were an absurdity, since, according to the Vatican decree, the Pope is infallible apart from the consent of the Church. He could have written creeds and decrees with the same authority, according to them.

I have written all this because you wished it.

For myself, your friend's grounds are very satisfactory. (1) I am where I am, by the Providence of God. I could not reject the Church of England without denying the work of God the Holy Ghost in her. I used to say, when people asked me, 'Where God the Holy Ghost is, and works, there it is safe to be.' Life is the most remarkable test of anybody. It is a wonderful analogy between physical and spiritual nature, which our Lord points out, "If any abide not in Me, he is cut off as a branch and withered." The branch seems for a time to have the freshness of the tree, but being severed from the sap which maintained the life of the tree, it withereth. So also bodies really severed from the Church have a certain freshness for the time, which they carry with them, but they fade. This has been observed since St. Cyprian's time downwards. . . . The English Church, on the contrary, is like a vigorous tree which had been rudely shaken, but after three centuries was putting out fresh roots and branches and filling the earth. It is carrying on the Lord's work beyond the bounds of the Empire. Africans, neglected or unknown heretofore, are being won to it. The discoveries of geography become pioneers to the kingdom of

Christ. The last century was 'saeculum tepidum' everywhere. In France it prepared for the French Revolution and the reign of the goddess of Reason; after the churches were reopened (I was told by a French authority) there were only fifty communicants at Easter in Paris. The unsatisfactory state of South Germany at that time is admitted. I inquired for religious books of the last century, like St. Francis de Sales, or the 'Spiritual Combat,' or F. Thomas, or Rodriguez, and could hear of none. (F. Thomas was the one Portuguese work.) Italy had all its conventual orders, monks and nuns, its superfluity of clergy, and it became what it became. All went to sleep together, all have revived together, but the revival has been in the *Churches*. The French Revolution was like a thunderclap of God's anger, and woke *us*. Roman Catholics themselves, although they have only observed the later stages, have been struck by the fact that our revival was wholly from within ourselves and without any aid from *them*. They were as sound asleep as we were under the Georges. I remember a popular book which spoke simply of the Roman Catholic controversy as a thing of the past.

When we were awakened the Revival (as I have said publicly) was wholly from within. We did not open a Roman book. We did not think of them. Rome was quiet at that time in itself. It was only, for political ends, assimilating itself as much as it could to us. 'We must own,' Cardinal Wiseman said, 'that we have been a little ashamed of our special doctrines.' However, we had all which we wanted within our own Church. We had the whole range of Christian doctrine, and did not look beyond, except to the Fathers, to whom our Church sent us. One, of whom I thought far more than myself, said, 'We have range enough in those before us, to whatever we pigmies may grow.'

This is what is unexampled anywhere out of the Church;—that a Church, not alive, for the time, to the Truth contained in her, in a state of lukewarmness like that of Laodicea, should be revived by our Lord to the whole range of Christian truth, without any agency from without.

I have, in a preface, reprinted in the *Daily Express* (which you have probably seen), dwelt on the additional fact that the Revival has been through what are the gifts of the Church alone, that God has blessed them, and yet that God blesses through Truth.

I shall be glad to answer you any other questions.

If anything of moment in this is illegible, I would gladly correct it.

I have said next to nothing on that which has been my great crux, the elaborate system as to the Blessed Virgin. The Greeks, too, use a good deal of invocation, but they have not the Latin dogmatizing. You might find a good deal in my old controversial books and in my first Eirenicon, barring what I have quoted from Oswald, who has been repudiated. The practical teaching comes to this, that it is safer to go to the Blessed Virgin than to our Lord. This is taught explicitly in the vision of the two ladders, at the head of the one of which was the Blessed Virgin; at the head of the other, our Lord. Many of those who went up the ladder to our Lord fell back; of those who went up the Blessed Virgin's ladder, none fell back.

This seems to have been your friend's frame of mind when he asked St. Peter to teach him about the authority of the Pope, not our Blessed Lord, or God the Holy Ghost.

But this would need a fresh Revelation, and it would practically come to this; that either the Church of Rome knows now more than was revealed to the Apostles, to whom our Lord promised that the Holy Ghost should lead them into the *whole* Truth (εἰς πᾶσαν τὴν ἀλήθειαν), or that they did not declare it to the Church. I hoped when I wrote my Eirenicon that we might, if re-united, remain under our own Bishops, elected under any of the old canonical modes of election, and might remain free from that vast practical system which goes so immeasurably beyond the Council of Trent. The Vatican Council dashed to the ground all Bishop Forbes' and my hopes.

I did not change my ground when I wrote my Eirenicon. The *Times*, in an elaborate article, told me that it was a dream. I went and consulted eminent French Bishops, and they said it was a reality: the Vatican Council has shown that The *Times* was right.

LETTER XX.

THE HEALTHY CONDITIONS OF RETURNING TO THE CHURCH OF ENGLAND.

July 1, 1871.

I do not see how one can recommend one to express his belief in what one cannot believe one's self. I trust that —— might safely return, as having made a mistake. In some cases, one dreads a person losing all Faith, leaving one Church criticizing it, and then the other, criticizing it. This is my anxiety about people returning, lest they lose all faith. But —— does not return, criticizing the Roman Church, but, as being required to believe as of Faith, what he was not required to believe when he joined it; and that, contradictory to all history, and carried as nothing was ever carried in Councils before against an orthodox protesting minority. He is, in fact, expelled the Roman Communion, and does not leave it.

I think then that you might safely receive his Confession and admit him to Communion; but he should confess whatever there was amiss which led him to leave our Communion.

God be with you.

LETTER XXI.

THE SAME.

February 24, 1879.

I have always had much anxiety about those who propose to return to our Communion, for fear that they should return in a wrong way, as they left it. The only way in which a person ordinarily can with safety return to our Communion is by acknowledging a fault in leaving it. I should fear lest all faith might be jeoparded, if a person left our Communion, criticizing it, and then the Roman criticizing it. The case, in which a person might be startled back by the Vatican decree, is a case *per se*, for in that case the Roman Communion has undergone a radical change and proposes to him a condition of Communion which she did not when he entered it.

Your friend's ostensible difficulties are easily met. The question to me is whether he would not return with a doubting conscience, which, of course, he ought not to do.

His difficulty about contradictory teaching is met partly by the fact that it is only the effect of a weak discipline, partly that there has been the like contradiction in the Roman Communion. It is acknowledged in it too that there can be no new Article of Faith, that the Church cannot make one. The doctrine of the Immaculate Conception of the Blessed Virgin and the personal Infallibility of the Pope, apart from the Church, must, according to them, have always been matters of Faith. But the Immaculate Conception of the Blessed Virgin was denied for centuries by Fathers, Doctors, Saints, Popes. There is no evading the fact that it was so denied. I have put together the evidence in my first Letter to Dr. Newman out of De Turrecremata, who was commissioned by the Legates at the Council of Basle to collect the evidence on that side. Had the Jesuits who advised Pius IX about it, studied De Turrecremata, instead of the slovenly work of De Bandelis (which a Jesuit, De Buck, told me was used), I do not think that they could have pronounced in favour of the decree. The Infallibility of the Pope was, as you know, disputed at the Vatican Council itself, and the minority at one time amounted to 200. The decree was carried by the personal influence of Pius IX.

The difference then is one of discipline. The Roman Communion is very strict about external obedience to the Church. But the principle remains the same; that the Church of Rome also allows what it holds to be *de fide* to be disputed, so that no disrespect is shown to its authority, as it would if what it has formally decreed be denied.

But any one in the Church of England may know the Faith in her if he will. According to the long received rule (it occurs in a letter of Pope St. Celestine, A.D. 423), 'The law of prayer is the law of Faith' (*lex supplicandi, lex credendi*). You cannot put the Faith more energetically into people's minds than by putting it into their mouths in prayer. God the Holy Ghost Who gives them the grace of prayer, works it into their minds through their prayers. Prayers in our own language teach Faith and make it part of ourselves, i.e. God does it through them. I suppose that the first four petitions of the Litany make the belief in the Holy Trinity part of ourselves, more than anything else could. I remember the impression made upon myself when, soon after the Supreme Court of Appeal had decided that the Church of England did not teach distinctly that children were regenerate in Baptism, I had the office of baptizing a child. Not having any cure of souls, the office very seldom came to me. Let people explain away the Articles as they might, I felt that the Church of England was teaching Baptismal Regeneration in the most touching way that it could. So as to the Holy Eucharist. This is the teaching of the Church, which all Bishops and every individual Clergyman are bound to acknowledge. If any contradict it, he condemns himself. And in matter of fact, I never knew any one in perplexity what to believe. Whenever I have asked any one, who complained of the contradictory teaching, I have always found that he himself had very clear knowledge of the truth; and that what he meant to complain of, was that others were allowed to contradict it. Having the Prayer Book in our own language, any one, who does not set himself against the Truth, may know it. Everything amiss involves its own trial. An eminent living Roman Catholic has said, 'I would rather have the open infidelity of the nineteenth century, than the hidden scepticism of the Middle Ages.' What must have been the state of the Gallican Church, when Massillon had (for fear, he must have supposed, of worse evils) to consecrate as a Bishop a notoriously bad priest, and when Talleyrand, Sieyes, and other Bishops were unbelievers. When Talleyrand was French Ambassador at our Court, the ex-Bishop was told that an honorary degree would be disputed if asked for at Oxford, and it was, on this intimation, not asked for.

With regard to a visible head, the Church of England has no independence which the Churches of Africa, Egypt, Spain, France, Asia Minor, had not in the early centuries. The only way in which a Bishop could interfere in another diocese would be in the executive (by appointing its Bishops), or legislative (in confirming or revising its Canons), or judicial (in hearing appeals). But none of these powers were exercised. The African Church had received the

Gospel from Italy; but when a right of appeal was claimed by the Bishop of Rome, on the ground of a supposed Canon of Nicaea, it was ascertained that there was no such Canon, and the claim was formally refused by a full African council. St. Augustine (who died before the answer came) was one who counselled that things should abide as they were until they should ascertain whether the Canon alleged was really a Canon of Nicaea, since the African Church had no such Canon. The Bishop of Rome alleged, not his own inherent authority, but the supposed authority of a Canon. The Bishops of Africa were ready to obey a General Council, there was no question of obeying the Bishop of Rome, otherwise. It was not even mooted.

The acts of Henry VIII could not have any bearing upon our Orders. The Bishops who submitted to his supremacy, were in communion with the Church of Rome. Every sort of question has been raised about our Orders by Roman controversialists, who were eager to find stones to throw and careless what stones they threw: but all have been answered, so that Bossuet in his day had no doubt about our Orders, and other Roman Catholics since, who have examined the question, have been satisfied as to them. There is no doubt about them.

The threefold commission " Feed My sheep," " Feed My lambs," is regarded by Fathers as a cancelling of the threefold denial, by which St. Peter had forfeited his office, to which our Lord's threefold question " Lovest thou Me " points. In the sense in which the other Apostles were sheep, St. Peter was also a sheep. As St. Peter was a shepherd, so were the other Apostles. St. Peter had no authority over them. They were [as] infallible as he. The Bishops received everywhere their authority from the Apostles, not from St. Peter specially.

Much of this you will have answered your friend already. He must not come back except on the ground that he was wrong in going, and with a full conviction, that, by virtue of the succession from the Apostles, we have, in the Church of England, the Power of the Keys and of consecrating the Body and Blood of Christ.

He is in a sad position, but temporal circumstances and his treatment by individual Roman Catholics seem to have had much to do with it. And, if he believes that Communion to be alone the Church of Christ, he has only to return to its full Communion. He must do nothing which concerns his soul with a doubting conscience.

LETTER XXII.

THE ADMISSION OF IRVINGITES TO COMMUNION.

September 3, 1874.

I should think that you might say to the Irvingites that they must make their choice to communicate in their body *or* in this Church. It is a strange delusion of Satan, rested by its founders upon supposed miracles, 'the gift of tongues' (which they mistook), and prophecies which were falsified, supposing that [their] apostles (most of whom are now dead) were called by the Holy Ghost to meet our Lord Whom they expected presently.

I do not think their being bewildered with this fanaticism a ground for refusing them Communion.

I should say that I could not communicate them, if they communicated with the Irvingites; but it would be for them to complain to the Bishop, not being a case contemplated by the rubric. I should say nothing in public, if they came, but simply pass them by.

I should hope that the Bishop could not sanction their *communicating* in both.

LETTER XXIII.

THE SAME.

December 14, 1874.

There is, as you say, a difference between you and me (and I suppose between the new school and the old) about the relation of Priests to their Bishops. I am very sorry for it, and for the whole attitude of the new school to their Bishops. If they had prayed earnestly, instead of despising them, speaking against them, ridiculing them, as the so-called High Church organs have done (and when I have read the *Church Times*, the correspondence of the clergy has pained me more than the editor's articles which pained me), things would not have been as they are.

I certainly did not contemplate that the Bishop would support the Irvingites in communicating in their own body and in the Church. As he insists on this, if I had been a Priest under him, and he had commanded me to communicate them, I should have obeyed him, and have thrown the responsibility on him. . . .

In the matter of ritual, such Bishops as have required compliance with the Purchas Judgement (as far as I have understood) have not required such compliance as obedience to them, but as obedience to a law, which we believe to be non-law.

I recommended to you to advise the Irvingites to make their choice, not because I thought that communicating them was a sinful act, but because it would be confusing to them, to be, at one time, receiving bread and wine, at another the Body and Blood of Christ, as the same act of Communion.

I have no doubt that as the Courts always favour laxity, if the Bishop were to prosecute you, you would be cast, and so the further evil would result that it would be established that the law permitted that Communion should be given to those who received schismatical Communion elsewhere. It has however another side, that they acknowledge our Communion, and so may be more readily won altogether to us than if they were severed off altogether.

I should have obeyed, but my own impression is so strong that the Courts would give it against you that, if I felt that it was my duty not to obey my Bishop in this, I should have resigned my cure. But I should have obeyed, not in view of these consequences, but as considering that he superseded my authority, and that he, not I, communicated them, though he communicated them through my hands.

The question is a wide one. It is, of course, a great evil that more or fewer of our aristocracy should attend the Presbyterian Communion in Scotland. But a wide evil is not to be corrected, I think, by individual priests disobeying their Bishops.

God guide you.

LETTER XXIV.

Good Works.

[*About* 1850–1.]

I think that you must wait with patience. Have you been able to show your father the places of my writings which I named to you? I am sure that I believe nothing as to the value of 'Works' which any Christian must not believe who believes the words of Holy Scripture, "He shall reward every man according to his works." They are Christ's works in us, not ours, if they are good, or in whatever degree they are good. There must be such things as "good works," however little any of us may feel our works to be good. For Holy Scripture speaks of being "zealous to maintain good works." But any goodness which any of the best works of the Apostles had, came solely from the grace of Christ; as St. Paul says, "not I, but the grace of God which was with me." I think, if people thought more of this, they would not be so much afraid of good works. Those who speak so against good works, must think that people think of them as their own. It is by the grace of God that we have the wish to do anything which pleases God. It is by the grace of God enabling us, that we do it, if we do it. It is by the grace of God that any persevere to the end. And in the end, those who are placed at the Right Hand shall be accepted only for the merits of Jesus, and (as St. Augustine says) 'God will crown His own gifts in us,' 'Deus in nobis dona coronat sua.'

Perhaps, if you were to read this to your father, and it did not satisfy him, he might suggest any question which would enable me to satisfy him.

God bless you.

LETTER XXV.

NOVEL TEACHING.

August 30 [1879].

I am truly sorry for the unwisdom which you tell me of. The Assumption of the Blessed Virgin originally meant the taking of her soul into heaven. I forget when it began to be taught that the body too was taken. Some of the clergy seem to me to be vying with one another, who should puzzle their people most. Faith will have a hard struggle to maintain its ground. It has already. The heresy of Universalism is, I fear, making progress. Our Blessed Lord says, "When the Son of Man cometh, shall He find *the* Faith on the earth?" i.e. not faith in Him, as a virtue in individuals, but the Catholic Faith which He left as a deposit with His Church. Our duty surely is then to impress on our people the great truths of the Faith, so that by God's grace they may sink deep in their hearts. This we did some forty-five years ago. And God prospered it. One of dear John Keble's simple earnest sermons would do more good to the soul than any sermon about the Assumption of the Blessed Virgin. The great truth which His Apostles, as commissioned by Him, set before people's eyes was our Lord, God and Man, crucified for us, and at the Right Hand of God, in that ineffable Glory, making Intercession for us. Of course this spread out into all the glorious truths of the Athanasian Creed. He Himself was the Centre of their thoughts, their faith, their devotion, their practice. Now people's minds are taken off from those glorious truths, to be taught about these lesser things, or worse still about birettas; and the people are alienated from us by things about which there is a good deal of pedantry. Why should people say 'Mass' instead of the Holy Eucharist? I do not say that your clergyman does, but very many do. They might have gone far to Catholicize England, if they would have taught as dear John Keble did, without whom they very probably would not have taught at all. Now they only strengthen a party.

Practically there is nothing to be done but by prayer. You would do best to tell your clergyman, how these novelties puzzle you, and if you like, you could show him this letter.

God bless you.

LETTER XXVI.

'ANTI-DISSENTERS.'

1848.

I think I collect that it is chiefly, if not only —— who has a strong negative way of teaching about Dissenters. My own way of teaching has, I believe. been mostly positive; it is very easy to unteach, very difficult to teach. We had, two years ago, anti-Dissenters more than enough, who had yet no idea what the Church is. A dislike of schism has nothing necessarily good in it, such as sorrow for schism has. I do not think that were I called upon practically to teach or speak on these subjects, I could speak negatively at all.

In the past Dissenters have been filling up our deficiencies. Dissent, indeed, must in the end all return to the Church or go to some form of Deism or Atheism, but it is mixed yet. As it retains its religious element it is winning some to the knowledge and the love of Christ, many of whom would not otherwise have heard of it. It is an imperfect form of Religion, but as far as it is such, and possesses life and fervour, it is good. It is, alas! more and more decaying, certainly in most of its divisions. And this is a sorrow to those who love souls. But the Church cannot afford to part with it until it can replace what is good in it. In time God may give us clergy to go to all our mines, ports, manufactories, and reclaim our heathen population, and He will the sooner the more people pray that He will send forth labourers into

His vineyard. But in the meantime what there is good in Dissent seems a sort of dispensation by which God supplies to souls something that does not reach them through the Church.

Of course it has an evil side as well as a good one. And as time goes on the evil will more and more predominate in bodies separated from the Church. And as bodies around become more and more secularized, they will more and more oppose what is good in the Church, not what is amiss in her members. Still, our feelings should be that of compassion for individuals who are under these systems as under a loss; and I should think the way to win them is not by speaking against Dissent, which involves them in abstract questions, apart from their own consciences, but in teaching them something which they have not. Such as are Dissenters, if conscientious, are so because it is the form under which they have learned the Truth or to care for their souls.

To speak to them broadly against Dissent would be to speak against God's Truth. A person who is so speaking means to speak against the evils of Dissent, whereas the other (if so be) only knows that, through that which is spoken against in the mass, he came to know that he had a soul to be saved and a Redeemer Who died to save it.

As far then as I spoke about the Church at all I should speak of what it possesses and Dissent has not, not *against* Dissent at all.

But I fear lest among those you have to do with are very many with whom (as you have to teach it all) there are questions antecedent to those of Church and Dissent— as to their being Christians at all—about Righteousness, Temperance, and Judgement to come.

In like manner I could not speak sweepingly about religious tracts, Dissenting or other Evangelical tracts, when they teach positively. Most tracts teach nakedly one or two truths, as the corruption of Human Nature—the Redemption of our Lord. If any one make use of this teaching to go on to deny the use of the Sacraments, or the Church, or of good works, the evil begins then, but it does not mostly lie in the tracts themselves. We have only to acknowledge and enforce the Truth, and supply what remains.

This is of the more moment because Satan is certainly employing, and very successfully, much of the controversy and even of the religious activity of the present day in throwing people off from their own souls, and Judgement to come. And to the poor who have a strong sense of reality, to speak about Church and Dissent, while they are conscious they are neglecting their own souls, seems unreal.

Of course I do not wish any of you to say anything of this. This seeming praise of Dissent would mislead as much as any vague censure of it (although indeed it is no praise of Dissent—for Dissent, as such, is simply bad—but of the good which is brought with it from the Body whence it came), but I think it may be useful to you to bear it in mind : for the more you feel yourselves the privileges of being in the Church the more anxious you may naturally be to warn others who are not of it, and yet not do it in the way which might do harm.

LETTER XXVII.

SUDDEN CONVERSION AND ASSURANCE.

In Baptism we are not merely admitted into outward covenant with God in Christ, but we are 'born again of water and of the Spirit,' we receive the Holy Ghost, and the first germs of spiritual life as Hooker says.

The spiritual life thus received, may be cherished, enlarged, or on the other hand may be neglected, stifled, or destroyed by deadly sin.

Not any deadly sin (such as a lie) estranges the soul of the child from God, or throws it out of the state of grace, so that it should need conversion, but such perseverance in sin as would, if it died, cause it to be cast into hell.

The essence of sin is to turn away from the Creator to the creature, preferring the creature to the Creator.

Whosoever has thus turned away from God, must, by the grace of God preventing, disposing, enabling him, return to God.

This return to God requires repentance and faith: repentance including the abandonment and hatred of whatever in the former life displeased God, sorrow, for the love of God, that the soul has displeased God, a purpose and commencement to lead a new life; and faith in our Lord Jesus Christ Who died for us and has promised forgiveness of sins to all who with hearty repentance and true faith turn unto Him.

If a person, after having been thus turned to God, relapses or becomes lukewarm or falls into deadly sin, this does not show the former turning to God was not sincere, else David would not be supposed to have been sincere before his fall.

Although this turning to God often takes place through some outward event, either a visitation of God, or some outward or inward warning whereby the soul, through God's grace, is arrested and converted at once, it may take place by degrees and almost unperceived by the soul itself.

Grace, if lost, may be restored and re-established in the soul through a series of Godly motions from above, which the soul obeys even amid other partial disobedience, and this change may be so slow, that the soul may not be able to distinguish sensibly the latter from the former. So again, after a first restoration, there may be one or more relapses, breaking the course of a true conversion. But although the period of the change may not be known, the soul *should* know, if it has been the servant of sin, that now by the grace of God it no longer serves sin.

The tests of being in a state of grace are, power over deadly sin and continued struggle through the grace of God against sins of infirmity, or in the words of the Article, ' the working of the Spirit of Christ, mortifying the works of the flesh and their earthly members, and drawing up their minds to high and heavenly things.'

Peace being one of the fruits of the Spirit, it is to be expected that those who are in a state of grace, will be in a state of peace.

This peace is an inward habitual gift, rather than any result of intellectual reflection upon the spiritual state, so that it may be possessed equally by persons who would express themselves differently about their spiritual state.

It is certain as matter of faith, that Christ died for all, and that He will receive all true penitent sinners who truly believe in Him; but it is nowhere taught that one who has been plunged in deadly sin, or been far away from God, shall know at once with the certainty of faith that he has true repentance; and the more vividly he feels his sin, the more he will often doubt whether his repentance is what it ought to be; so he may often be in considerable doubt about his conversion whether God has forgiven his sins or no: and this very doubt is often a means of deepening humility and repentance and hatred of sin. Such a one will have evidences by which he might if he understood himself discern that he was in a state of grace, but a " broken and a contrite spirit" does not reflect on itself: and he may very often throw himself more entirely on the mercy of Christ because he does not find any confidence in his own faith or works or repentance.

Again, persons who have needed no *marked* change at all, may be disquieted because they see in themselves no great increase in their victory over their spiritual sins of infirmity. Another, who knows them, may see that sins of infirmity (e. g. temper) are lessened in their degree or frequency. To themselves they seem to be making little or no progress or they even think they are going back, because they are more keenly alive to their own failings, and so may doubt their faithfulness to grace and their whole spiritual state.

A direct supernatural assurance is sometimes given, whether in conversion or as the result of a continual spiritual life, but such assurance has not been promised in Holy Scripture. It is not therefore to be expected, nor is the absence of it any reason for any anxiety whatever about our spiritual state.

The feeling of assurance may exist and be strong, apart from any real Divine gifts, and must be tested by evidence and especially by that of power against wilful sin and striving against sins of infirmity. If a person seriously doubts his being in a state of grace he should be directed to look into himself whence this doubt arises, whether from some unsubdued sin, or from lukewarmness, or from want of full reliance on his Redeemer. Each may require different remedies according as the case is different. If it arises from want of full reliance on his Redeemer, he should be led to prayers and acts of devotion and trust in Him, or else, as the case may be, to a more diligent watchfulness against sin, or more careful cultivation of those graces whereby God will strengthen his hopes, as more earnest prayer, watchfulness as to sins of infirmity, humility, &c.

A person may doubt as to his state of acceptance with God, from habitual mistrust of self, or from natural temperament, or because fear predominates in his character, or from awe at God's judgements, without any defect either in faith or love, and consequently without any need for conversion. The fact that a person has no 'assurance' is no proof that a person is not in a state of grace.

That assurance which is the direct gift of God may appear to the person who receives it, in the form of simple peace of mind, he knows not how conveyed.

Justifying faith is a loving belief in Christ as the Author and Finisher of the soul's salvation, "Who loved me, and gave Himself for me."

It is not the belief that one's self has that faith and repentance through which His Redemption avails.

Faith, which is without love, does not justify (1 Cor. xiii. 2), but love exists in justifying faith in very different degrees, and sometimes is not perceived to be love by those who have it. Love often exists in what to the individual seems the proof of the absence of love—dissatisfaction at the poorness of its love, and longing to love more.

LETTER XXVIII.

QUERIES ON THE SAME SUBJECT.

1. Whether it is not distinctly written that the Peace of God passeth all understanding?

2. Whether this does not mean, as Luther says, that many who have it not, think they have it, some have it who fear they have it not?

3. Whether the Pharisee in our Lord's parable was not an instance of the first, and the prodigal son on his journey before he met his father, an instance of the second?

4. Whether it is not a presumptuous thing, a token in fact of a lurking tendency to Rationalism, so to set bounds to God's grace as to say He may not sometimes keep His servants in doubt for a while, as He did the woman of Canaan?

5. Whether it can be shown from the plain Word of God as interpreted by the Church universal, according to the analogy of faith, that this state of partial doubt always of necessity terminates before death?

6. Whether in default of such evidence it be not a very dangerous thing to reason from one's own impressions and say, it was so and so in my case, therefore I am sure it must be so in others?

7. Whether going on such reasonings to exclude those who cannot receive or preach the doctrine, as though they rejected the Gospel, be not alarmingly like the error of those to whom St. Paul said Anathema, because they preached another gospel, i.e. they added unauthorized conditions to our Lord's covenant of grace and so in spirit broke the second Commandment?

LETTER XXIX.

Prayers to God the Father.

April 28, 1877.

We cannot, plainly, pray to Jesus too much. He is our Lord and our God, the Author of our salvation. What I was afraid of was not that you should pray to Him too much, but that you should pray to the Father too little, and so might be guilty of negligence, through which you might injure your faith, as poor —— lost his. Our Lord Himself taught us to say, 'Our Father.' When we say it, we pray to the Father as the First Person of the Blessed Trinity; yet not so, as if we could separate Him from the Son and the Holy Ghost, with Whom He is One God.

When the Church prays, 'Almighty and Everlasting God,' she speaks primarily to God the Father, as the Source of Being of the whole Holy Trinity; but since the Three Divine Persons mutually indwell One Another, you do address All, since They are not three Gods, but One God.

But generally, the more you can go to God, as a little child, asking no questions, the better. If you were to ask a child, 'To Whom have you been praying?' he would say, 'God.' If you were to ask him, 'Who is God?' perhaps he would say, 'Father, Son, and Holy Ghost', but make no more questions. If you were to ask him to whom he prayed when he prayed to Jesus, perhaps he would say, 'To my Saviour, God and Man.'

So do, and do not speculate.

LETTER XXX.

THE SCOTCH COMMUNION OFFICE.

I have, now as heretofore, had Articles sent me written for the 'English Churchman,' recommending proposed alterations in the Scotch Communion Office. I believe that I am writing to a clergyman. I am myself perfectly satisfied with the English Office. In the place occupied by the words of Consecration it intellectually recommends itself to me more than the Scotch. But the change recommended by Bishop Wordsworth relates to words which have expressed the Faith of the Church from the first. It is one thing not to have them; another to abolish them, having them. It does not follow that the words recommended by Bishop Wordsworth because they are Scriptural express the whole truth. I believe that the word 'become' expresses what our Blessed Lord means by the words 'This is My Body,' and that by rejecting the word 'become' the Church of Scotland would, in fact, be rejecting our Lord's words.

Of course, you do not think so. I write only as one of a class who ought to be considered, as we consider others. You are on the aggressive, promoting change. If I were a presbyter in the Scotch Church, and it made such a change, I should renounce its Communion; if I were a Bishop, I should part communion with those Bishops who altered it. I have thought these many years that the maintenance of our actual state is the only safety of the Church of England. You promote change in the Church of Scotland; others promote it in the Church of England. If either party succeeds, I believe that that Church will go to pieces.

LETTER XXXI.

THE NUMBER OF COMMUNICANTS.

April 1, 1874.

The third rubric after the Communion Service must be so far dependent upon the first before the Communion, that now that the notice of intention to communicate is universally disused (so that it would be thought intrusion to enforce it) the celebrant cannot be bound to know who or how many are going to communicate. Yet in order to keep to the spirit of the rubric, I think that it would be best if your communicants would fix different days for themselves on which they would communicate, so that there should always be some communicants. This clearly was the intention of the Church, that there should always be communicants. The Council of Trent also regretted the solitary Masses, saying that they were owing to the indevotion of the people; so that if any among us encourage them, they go against the Council of Trent, as well as against the Prayer Book, and are more Roman than the Romans.

I should then tell my people, that if there should not be more Communicants I should be obliged to diminish the Communions, in order that there might be Communicants at every Communion; that they should get rid of this lazy way of going to Holy Communion and not being fit to receive.

Such a case as that of there being no Communicants among thirty present might be excused exceptionally, but it cannot be the rule. If they will not be more in earnest they must lose the Celebration.

You are quite right not to increase Ritual. It would be spreading and crowding every sail, when no small storm is upon us. The Ultra-ritualists are risking the whole work of the last forty years, are putting all England in a fever from which no good can come, and are selfish towards the quieter members of the congregation, whose devotional habits a simpler service suits better.

LETTER XXXII.

Confession.

January 20, 1870.

I was unable to answer your question at the time, and perhaps now too it were best answered by another: 'If our Lord were to come to judge to-morrow, should you be glad to have heard His Absolving Voice to-day?' For all which is done in His Name is done by Him. It is true that Confession at first was only that open penance for great sins which our Church gravely regrets cannot be restored. But its use in lesser cases too was learned by experience. The best way probably for you will be to review your past life as a whole. This is of great moment to all, whether they use Confession or no. People think of their single sins in the evening, but unless they look over their past [life] carefully, they have no idea of themselves as a whole. They think perhaps that they had better not have repeated this ill of their neighbour, or sought praise for that thing, or have coloured a story to make it look better: but they do not see that exaggeration was a form of vanity that ran through their life; or that love of human praise has forfeited for them God's praise for much, humanly speaking, well done; or that they have habitually injured love and humility by looking on the wrong side of their neighbours; or that they have lived in an habitual robbery of God by taking His gifts, as if they were their own.

If you wish it I could send you a tract which might help you in that review, at the end of this month. Perhaps after this review you might look on Confession and Absolution as it is, as a gift of God, for which to be thankful. For if Confession is sincere, Absolution is God's forgiveness.

LETTER XXXIII.

THE SAME.

Jan. 12 [*about* 1874].

Confession in the earliest Church was only for those few deadly sins which slay the soul, such as sins against the sixth or seventh commandment, or apostasy. The first instance of [confession of] venial sins was [in the case of] St. Basil's monks, who used it as a discipline.

The Church of England does leave it free, believing that true sorrow, for the love of God, for having displeased God, does obtain forgiveness from Him for Jesus' sake.

Practically, it is found that Confession is a means of grace, and is not a snare to people's consciences. It is not necessary to the validity of a Confession that a person should enumerate all sins, but only that he should not wilfully keep back any because he is ashamed to own them.

I have known it to be a great means of grace. It is our Lord's Absolving Voice saying, " Thy sins be forgiven thee " by virtue of His own words, " Whose sins ye do forgive, they are forgiven." Though not absolutely necessary, it has been found a great help on our way to God.

I have delayed writing, having been working against time.

God bless you.

LETTER XXXIV.

Fasting Communion[1].

December 4, 1873.

Fasting Communion has a twofold aspect; (1) with regard to the well and strong, (2) with regard to the delicate and sickly. There is no doubt that, in itself, the practice of Fasting Communion has been from the time of those irreverences among the Corinthians a universal custom and rule in the universal Church. It was the practice in the second century, and St. Augustine thinks that it was one of those things which St. Paul says, "I will set in order when I come." 'Whence,' St. Augustine says, 'it is given to be understood that what is varied by no diversity of custom was ordained by him.' Ep. 54 (Ad inquisitiones Januarii, 1. § 8). It is not a written law of the Church. 'It is' (I quote a living Roman Canonist) 'not written in any law except the spurious collection of fifty Canons, called the third of Carthage. This is quoted in all the books as genuine[2].'

It is also said (Devotus, t. 1, p. 433), 'There is no divine precept in this matter.'

---

[1] These three letters, although they contain many repetitions and traverse the same ground, are inserted as showing Dr. Pusey's constant and deliberate teaching on this important subject. Throughout all these letters, he recognizes Fasting Communion as a custom of the Church from the earliest ages, which ought, *as a rule*, to be observed by all members of the Church. From the nature of the correspondence however, the stress of the argument is against the 'rigorist' interpretation of this custom.

[2] The 'Roman Canonist,' whom Dr. Pusey is quoting, is most probably wrong in regarding these Canons as spurious. They are now generally accepted as the authentic decrees of that Council. In the next letter, he expresses his own view of the Conciliar authority on this subject.

'It is,' the same Canonist says, 'not a divine law. Divine laws are such as the two primary laws, and the precepts of Holy Writ about faith and morals. These are binding at all times and in all places. Human laws are positive arbitrary laws, because men may enact, change, and abolish them.'

It is then, I think, very wrong when some among us have spoken of Non-fasting Communion as a deadly sin, or even as sacrilegious.

If there had been anything irreverent in receiving the Body and Blood of our Lord after food, our Lord would not so have instituted it. If people say that it was to connect the old dispensation with the new, our Lord was the Founder of both. Again, if there were any intrinsic irreverence, the last Communion of the sick would not, by express provision, be allowed to be after food.

Again, it is allowed everywhere that the Christmas midnight Communion should be after the food taken a few hours before, without any intervening sleep; and, as lately, when Christmas Day was on the Monday, the day before was no fast. But the division of the day at midnight is only arbitrary. When the day begins at sunset it is the same day. There is no difference in principle or in the nature of the act in itself. Again, in the Roman Church also, the non-fasting Communion cannot be accounted intrinsically wrong; since it was customary, I am told on good authority, for the kings of France and Spain to be allowed to take some brodium (broth) before Holy Communion, and King James II was allowed to receive the Sacrament after slight refreshment (tenuem cibum) ' on account of his health.'

When they say it is a 'deadly sin' they must mean that it is against an express and known law of the Church. The sin is in 'the formal contempt of the law or the legislator.' But it appears that although there is a pious custom from the earliest times, there is no law the infringement of which would involve 'contempt.' I suppose that people would hardly say that the neglect of Ash Wednesday was anyhow a mortal sin. We should be very slow in multiplying mortal sins.

In reverence then for the Holy Communion, even apart from the primitive and probably Apostolic custom, I myself have for very many years communicated fasting. I wish that all Communions were early, and I cannot think that any who believed that in the Holy Communion we receive the Body and Blood of Christ, would have anything to do with those Evening Communions which have been creeping in of late.

But on the other hand, there has been, I think, a good deal of sewing new cloth upon old garments. There are many cases where from delicate health a person would be unable to go out (certainly in winter) at an early hour without having taken something, or where for months together they would be where there is only late Communion. I was myself present at one late Communion when one fainted at the altar; another vomited in the street when he left the church. In such cases I could not but think that our good Lord, if He were here, would dispense with the bindingness of the custom of the Church, and after a person had tried all expedients, the natural one of taking food late the night before and the supernatural one of prayer, I should think that such an one would show more reverence and love for our Lord's Body and Blood by receiving it at a definite time (three or four hours) after light food, or sooner after some liquid, than by excommunicating himself from It, it may be, for months together, or being, very probably, incapable of thought at the time of communicating. I should think that, being of the nature of a positive law, it comes under our Lord's rule, "I will have mercy and not sacrifice."

LETTER XXXV.

THE SAME.
March 15 [1879].

I have been in the habit of saying, 1. that there can be no intrinsic irreverence in non-fasting Communion: since (*a*) our Lord instituted it after Supper; (*b*) the Communion is given to the very sick, although not necessarily *in extremis*.

2. That there is no positive law of the Church on the subject. At one time *it was supposed* that there was, and Bishop Forbes (whose authorities were often out of the common path, but accurate) told me that, in consequence, dispensation used to be given to kings of France and Spain to receive Holy Communion non-fasting, because it was thought edifying to their subjects to see them communicate. Provincial Councils and the Council of Constance have forbidden non-fasting Communion, but no Council to which we owe obedience.

On the other hand, there is a universal custom, reaching back to the second century, of communicating before receiving any other food.

3. That the division of the twenty-four hours, so that day shall begin at midnight, is of course perfectly arbitrary. The Roman Communion has, of course, perfect right to lay down what rules it thinks right for its communicants; but the Eastern division of the day, whereby night should begin at sunset and morning at sunrise, is much more natural. We retain it still in our 'midday,' 'midnight,' 'fortnight,' 'sennight.' It is then perfectly arbitrary to

date the beginning of the fast from 12 p.m. We are not bound to it, not being under the Roman rule. This might meet the case of taking food, e.g. milk, at night before 6 a.m.

4. Though, on account of the abuses of evening Communion and their irreverence, one should be very sorry to infringe the rule, yet the case of the midnight Communion on Christmas night shows that the mere fact of having taken food is not in itself a hindrance to communicating. For if Christmas Day fall on a Monday (as it did a few years ago), then the Roman Communion also allows a person to have full meals all through the Sunday. (I have heard two different accounts; (*a*) that persons have to abstain from 6 p.m. on the Sunday, which if the dinner has been (as it may be) a full meal is no abstinence at all; or (*b*) that they are under no limitation.) But anyhow there is no difference in principle between a person's communicating at the midnight Communion after all the meals of Sunday (the midnight being a merely conventional distinction) and taking what is necessary to sustain strength to keep up attention and so to communicate devotionally, at a sufficient distance of time.

All Roman Catholics hold that the Bishop of Rome could dispense with the rule of communicating fasting; they cannot then hold it to be of Divine law.

5. The command to communicate is Divine: the rule of not communicating after food is human. If then they notably clash, the Divine command supersedes the human.

This is decisive in the case of A., in which you say that 'the priest told her that if she could not go fasting, she ought not to go at all, even if she did not communicate for years.'

But in the Church in which God has placed her, it is a command to communicate three times in the year: everywhere the Easter Communion is a law of the Church.

One who did not communicate then would be *ipso facto* excommunicate. She then, according to her adviser, is to break a law of God and of the Church and excommunicate herself.

I wish that these rigorists, who 'sew new cloth upon old garments,' would think a little what is meant by 'mortal sin.' Of course all own (though they may not bring it home to themselves) that mortal sin expels the grace of God, and slays the soul in that single act. But non-fasting Communion, according to them also, is only 'mortal sin,' as breaking a command of the Church. I wonder whether they think they commit a mortal sin and are out of the grace of God if they neglect, on any occasion, to say the Morning or Evening Service.

And then if A. did not know that it was anything wrong, her 'director' made it mortal sin to her by telling her so, for to break commandments of the Church in ignorance is not sin at all.

I see that the Conductor of the Retreat to which B. went also, said that 'God would not allow a soul to be harmed if it' broke His command to communicate 'for years and years.'

Our ladies would do well to abstain from going to Retreats, if the Clergy are so to entangle them. I wonder whether they teach as energetically against people speaking evil of authorities and of their neighbours. Church papers used to be full of it, yet God said, "Speak not evil one of another, brethren."

This would be a very one-sided zeal.

LETTER XXXVI.

The Same.
1879.

I think that the subject of fasting Communion is pressed very unduly upon people's consciences by some, so as to set an ancient custom of the Church against our Lord's command, in some cases.

No one could doubt that early and fasting Communion is the most devotional; the poor feel this. The question arises, when any do not feel themselves sick enough to ask habitually for sick Communion at an early hour, and yet it is impossible for them to go out without manifest risk of health or life; or (as is often the case in the country) Holy Communion could only be had at a very late hour, with the same risk, though they be well.

I have had letters asking me whether the rule of fasting Communion was so absolute, that a person must give up Holy Communion for months together: or from Clergy, whether if they have to celebrate late, they must give up their cure. I have been asked this even by the Chaplain of a Religious House (with which I am not connected). It has become a great practical difficulty.

Those who preach or teach the *absolute* duty of fasting Communion, generally preach or teach (as far as they are aware) to those who can communicate early, or where there is early Communion close by. They have no idea of the practical difficulty. It is sewing new cloth on old garments. Midday Communions used to be the rule among us. The early Communions of late years almost date from the revival of about 1833, except in towns on great Festivals. And it is a difficulty affecting thousands of Clergy throughout the country. I suppose it would, in very many cases, be a question between non-fasting Communion and death.

When asked, I have been wont to begin at the beginning.

(*a*) There is no irreverence in non-fasting Communion, else,

(1) Our Lord would not have instituted it after eating the Passover, for He was Lord of both Covenants, and it was of His own Will that He so connected them.

(2) The Viaticum is everywhere administered after food, but no one would make the last Sacrament an act of irreverence.

(*b*) There is no binding law. I cannot here look over books, but I remember seeing it in the hand of a learned Roman Catholic.

(*c*) It is then a very early and religious custom, originating in such abuses as those at Corinth, yet not without exceptions. Bishop Forbes, who had such varied learning, told me that it had been the custom to allow kings of France and Spain to communicate non-fasting, because it was thought edifying to their subjects to see their kings communicate. The Christmas midnight Mass at some chapel at Rome was or is celebrated (I forget for what reason) an hour before midnight.

(*d*) There is no difference in principle between communicating at the midnight Mass on Christmas night when e. g. Christmas Day is on a Monday, and on the Sunday full meals have been allowed, and taking food at an early hour on the same day. For the division of the twenty-four hours is of course wholly artificial.

(*e*) In some cases at least there would be a direct conflict between our Lord's command and the observance of the pious custom. Whether the "This do in remembrance of Me" be or be not addressed primarily to the priest, it must include the people. Frequent Communion is the life of the soul : prolonged abstinence would be starvation. The Easter Communion is accounted the very least which would fulfil our Lord's command.

The rigid rule which is laid down by some now, that non-fasting Communion is to be avoided as mortal sin, would in very many cases clash with our Lord's command to communicate.

I wish the young Clergy were less free with the words 'mortal sin.' I cannot understand why it should be 'mortal sin.' It would not, according to their own showing, be mortal sin in their people unless they made it so. For a person cannot fall unknowingly into mortal sin. I suppose they place the mortal sin in contravening a positive law of the Church. I do not believe myself that there is any such positive law of the Church. I wonder whether they themselves think that they commit mortal sin, whenever they omit saying the Daily Service. 'Mortal sin' is, as you know, what kills the soul at one blow. Do they mean that one who communicates non-fasting kills his soul? ...

I believe non-fasting Communion comes under our Blessed Lord's rule, "I will have mercy and not sacrifice," and I feel sure that if He were here, He would dispense with the custom Himself in many cases; as of the weakly. I am certain that He would rather they communicated non-fasting than were starved.

Fasting Communion is, I believe, a pious custom to be aimed at and commended, not one to be enjoined under penalty of mortal sin. This is bewildering to me, and would, I should think, confuse in people's minds the thought of sin altogether.

I need not say that we old Tractarians communicated and communicate fasting, but we cannot lay the burden on the shoulders of the weak or sickly.

LETTER XXXVII.

Non-communicating Attendance.

Advent Eve, [1879].

My reason for not putting in[1] anything about non-communicating presence at Holy Communion was, that it seemed to me a different kind of recommendation from the others in my letter. They were, in fact, 'You have forgotten your first love: you are not so earnest as at the beginning: repent and return to it.'

This seemed to me the tenor of those two earnest laymen's letters. But the rising early in order to be present at Holy Communion was not one of these. With *us*[2], not priests only, the first thought was to communicate. Our life centred in Holy Communion, past or to come. If any came into a church where there were preparations for Holy Communion, he made, on the spot, as earnest preparation as he could, and communicated. We should have thought the opportunity to be a call. To have gone away would have seemed to us to be excommunicating ourselves. If we rose early, it would have been to communicate. It was our one thought. Of course this implied a very different state of things. Our week was divided between thanksgiving for the last Communion and preparation for the next.

But again, I have been afraid of spiritual laziness in the non-communicating attendance. I hear that the actual

---

[1] He is referring to an Address which he had issued to the members of the English Church Union.   [2] i. e. the older Tractarians.

Communions are few. There is no preparation for 'hearing Mass.' Some go, are satisfied with having performed their duty, but return in a lazy state. This would not of course be if the frequency of communicating is regulated by a spiritual adviser. I used to advise earnest persons in the world to communicate on Sundays and on any other day, in which they would not be led, by the hurry of the day, to forget Whom they had received in the morning. Then the being present on any other day would be a gain. What I am afraid of is, lest they should lazily substitute presence at Holy Communion for communicating: not even feel that, if their habits of mind were better, they might communicate daily as in the Apostles' time: not trouble themselves for not being fit to communicate oftener, or even make a devout spiritual Communion as being unworthy of actual Communion. I am afraid of laziness in everything, and people being satisfied, while resting on their lees, with very little.

I suppose that all non-communicating attendance at Holy Communion should be accompanied with a real confession of unworthiness of actual Communion (as in the 'Paradise'). If this were done, I should suppose that people would return much humbler than, from the popular way of speaking, they seem to do. At least I hear it spoken of as an act of Adoration, without any reference to a person's own self.

LETTER XXXVIII.

DIFFICULTIES ABOUT THE BURIAL SERVICE.

January 4, 1864.

All blessing this year and always to you and all yours.

It has always seemed to me that the difficulties raised about the Burial Service really apply to reading any Burial Service at all. Every one knows that the 'sure and certain hope' applies to the Resurrection generally, not to the individual over whom it is read. There are only the expressions, 'Forasmuch as it hath pleased Almighty God of His great mercy to take unto Himself' and 'as our hope is this our brother doth.' But we know so very little of any other, of his light, his temptations, his resistance, his repentance, the secret relations of the soul to God, that one can have some degree of hope where one does not *know* any one to have died finally impenitent. How very few are they, even of the bad characters in Holy Scripture, of whom one should be absolutely certain that they are lost! Only those very few, of whom Holy Scripture says it. But if one is not absolutely certain that they are lost, then one must have a hope that they are saved. One knows not what God may do in that last hour, when they have no power to express themselves. One is sure that they are saved, who have not finally rejected God.

And if one has any hope at all, then one is sure that God has taken each just at that time, which He in His Eternal Wisdom and Love knew to be best for them.

He, without Whom not a sparrow falleth to the ground, how should He not order the outlet of life as is best for those whom He created and redeemed in His Infinite Love?

But neither would it do any good to alter any part of the Service. To say any part of it, even the Lord's Prayer, is to express hope. Else why say it over the individual? If it were only to express our own belief generally, we might just as well, or better, say prayers in the Church. To say any prayers over the remains of the departed is to include him as part of the Body of Christ. This is the ground why we are not to use it over the unbaptized, because they are not part of the Body of Christ. We do not mean that they are lost, but that they are not part of that Body of Christ which prays and to whom the prayers relate.

In that dreadful case of the drunken sexton at —— who, to clear himself, communicated in the morning, and committed suicide in the precincts of the church at night, dear —— consulted me, what could be done, if the jury should call it temporary insanity. I could not think that he could say any one prayer, because every prayer implies a hope. We went over each prayer. He agreed with me. The jury did bring a verdict 'Felo de se.'

You remember —— saying that he had never known a case in which he had to read the Burial Service in which he had not some, however varying, shade of hope. Except in those cases in which God visibly interferes, those words, "Judge nothing before the time," seem to apply especially to that case where judgement is to take the office of our Judge, unless He have taken it Himself unmistakably.

And in those terrible cases, men's feelings and consciences would bear out the Clergy. I remember the case of one in ——, a known infidel, who had been trying to seduce others to infidelity, who awoke from his bed of adultery, said 'I am ill,' and fell back dead into the arms of the poor being, the sharer of his sin. Strange to say, his infidel companions wished to have him buried with the Service of the Church. The clergyman said he could not, and they carried the body to [another town] where his history was not known.

But, except in such extreme cases, it would be wrong for the individual clergyman to pronounce sentence. And so, any change which should leave any choice, would be utterly wrong. Then, the only other change would be to sacrifice the friends of the good for the bad, and make the Service over the good less religious, in order to make it less unsuitable to the irreligious. And yet, if you go over the Service, the other parts which are now less prominent would only come out into greater prominency if the stronger expressions were pared off. What, for instance, would that text mean, "Blessed are the dead which die in the Lord," unless we hoped that he over whom it was read had so died? and so on. Until men should have frozen out the last ray of expressed or implied hope, it would still be unbefitting to those who are really lost. And when it was done, it would be most ghastlily unmeaning to have any Burial Service at all.

I believe that our refuge in this case, as in thinking about those departed, about whom one may have ground to be anxious, is in our own ignorance and in God's mercy.

LETTER XXXIX.

Reading in Preparation for Holy Orders.

I suppose one may take it for granted that any one who comes to ask for a course of theological study is, at least, well acquainted with the letter of Holy Scripture, such as might be acquired through the Daily Lessons, and the frequent reading of Holy Scripture in church. Otherwise, the first step would be a knowledge of the Holy Text itself, and especially a careful study of the Historical Books of the Old Testament. This presumed, the object would be to deepen the knowledge of Holy Scripture, of the substance of the Faith, and of practical wisdom, with some knowledge of the History of the Church.

In this we should begin with the Gospels as the centre; and in this, I suppose, what persons would chiefly need, would be the deeper meaning of the whole, and of the several words as drawn out by the Fathers, rather than mere verbal criticism. It would then, probably, be best to begin to study the Gospels, either with the 'Catena Aurea,' or each Gospel with some one Father who had commented on it:—St. Matthew with St. Chrysostom and St. Hilary; St. Luke with St. Ambrose; St. John with St. Augustine and St. Chrysostom.

This study would not only bring out the context, and connexion, and meanings of Holy Scripture which people are not in the habit of thinking of, but would, incidentally, bring a person acquainted with a good deal of exposition of other parts of Holy Scripture. It is like reading Holy Scripture with a new sense. St. Ambrose, especially, brings one acquainted with a great deal of Holy Scripture. Besides, in this study of the Gospels, much might be learnt by way of meditating on them.

If the 'Catena Aurea' were used, it would probably be best to take two chief Fathers only at first, that a person might not be lost in the manifoldness and fullness of exposition. Other expositions might be reserved until afterwards.

The reading of the Fathers themselves has the advantage of their being a whole, and that their mode of practical teaching, in connexion with the exposition of Holy Scripture, is so learnt.

After, or with this, might be taken the Exposition of the Psalms, by St. Augustine, both as teaching the spiritual meaning of the Psalms (which it does even amid variance of translation, but much more when the translation is the same), the relation of their meaning as to our Lord and His members, and for the great value of its moral teaching.

For a first study of St. Paul, no work would perhaps give such a general view of the scope and connexion of the Epistles as St. Chrysostom. St. Augustine, again, beautifully unfolds St. John's Epistles.

Together with this, it would be best to take some hard book, which should be the subject of real study, in order to make it your own. Butler's 'Analogy' may be presupposed. Then Hooker, Bk. V, ought to be turned '*in succum et sanguinem.*' The deep view of the connexion of the Sacraments with the Incarnation is probably hardly to be found elsewhere, save in the Schoolmen. 'Pearson on the Creed' should follow, and later 'St. Athanasius against the Arians,' with the notes in the Library of the Fathers. There is in these a very important doctrine, upon which people, if not instructed how to think, are continually thinking amiss, and even unconsciously falling into heresy. On the doctrine of Justification should be read Bishop Bull's 'Harmonia,' or Mr. Newman's work.

Bishop Bull's 'Defensio Fidei Nicenae' should be taken

later, if there is opportunity ; and, as a great repertorium on all the questions which have been raised on sacred doctrine, Petavius 'de Trinitate' and 'de Incarnatione.'

For History it might suffice, in this stage, to read Eusebius and Collier's 'English History.' Parts of Bingham's 'Christian Antiquities' might also be read. Eusebius is a very suggestive book as to further questions.

On Moral Subjects, and as to practical teaching, I suppose he could hardly do better than take Bishop Andrewes' Festival Sermons, on account of his reverent and loving way of dwelling on Divine Mysteries. Bishop Taylor's Sermons, 'Life of Christ,' 'Holy Living and Dying,' for personal practical experience. Newman's Sermons for deep moral and religious truth, and to read himself. Manning's Sermons for vivid realizing of things unseen, and the end of our being. St. Augustine's were named, and those on Select Portions of Holy Scripture (Library of the Fathers) might be added to them, as models of clear, affectionate, fatherly teaching. Perhaps on Penitential Subjects might be added the 'Sermons at St. Saviour's, Leeds.' More direct spiritual guides are à Kempis, and the 'Spiritual Combat, the Way of Eternal Life'; for Devotions one might name Bishop Andrewes, and the 'Paradise for the Christian Soul.'

In this whole course of study it is best to prevent weariness by combining at least several portions of it. Especially every day should be taken one of the harder books, upon which, for the time, the whole mind should be concentrated, if but for a short time, half an hour or an hour; and then the main extent of study be given to Holy Scripture, keeping always some time for Practical Reading, and that with a view, primarily, to the person's own soul.

Begin and end all study with at least a short prayer.

LETTER XL.

THE OBSERVANCE OF RUBRICS.

March 1, 1844.

I have some difficulty in answering your questions, because I have never had a parochial cure, and so cannot judge of the temper of people.

I should think that there should be a difference between those Rubrics which relate to yourself, and would affect those only who wish to avail themselves of the provisions so made, and those which would affect all who go to church at all. We have, in restoration, not our own duty only to perform, but to regard our people. It may be ground enough for restoring anything, that it is required of us; but, unless people have been first taught to look upon the Church as a parent, this, *alone*, is rather a dry ground for them. If we are pledged to obey every Rubric, this is ground enough for us; but for our people, it is a cold way of resting the obligation, if it seem to rest on the mere letter alone, apart from the value of the appointments themselves. There is an obvious objection in their minds, that the Church has not, for above a century, had any power of revising her Rubrics, that we do not know whether she would have retained them. It seems to be speaking of an abstraction, rather than following the directions of a living mother. And there is something in this. We ought not to be in the state in which we are. The very necessity of change implies defect and a previous acknowledgement of it. Unless we were wrong before, we should be wrong now; and until people see that we have been so, there is a rightful prejudice against changes.

Then, restoration ought to be the act of the body, so that people should feel that they were obeying not only disused laws, but a living authority. I do not, of course, mean that there are not grounds of obedience for them also, but that there is a good deal by way of set off, and reasons why we should make people's way as plain as we can, giving them grounds for what we do, and not requiring them to rest on authority, without reasons, when they can be alleged. But this in some respects takes time. I think that harm has been done, by introducing changes, without teaching people about them before, and trying to raise their mind to them. It does not seem to me right by our people, to bring all at once a practice before them, which they have to receive or reject, so unprepared. It seems to me risking the putting them in a worse condition, and a want of Christian consideration. We should not set about restoring, as if things were in our own power. We have not only acts and Services to restore, but, which is far more, habits of mind to recover in our own people. It seems to me an unpractical, inconsiderate way (I do not mean of course culpably so, we must do our best and make our way through mistakes) to restore things as matters of course or mere obligations on the minister, without preparing men's minds for them.

My own theory, then, for restoration would be, I think, to commence at once those things which did not put people decidedly in a worse position if neglected, and require them to choose at once for the better or worse. Thus, unless there were local reason to the contrary, I should at once commence Daily Service at an early hour, because attendance on that office is at all times a balance of duty, and being at an unusual hour (I believe an early hour is far the best), it is not like a deliberate refusal. It is meant, as things now are, not for all, but for those who can attend.

The restoration of Communions is far more difficult unless they also are placed at an early hour, which would in itself be far best, and which in most places is almost an absolute duty in the case of frequent, i. e. weekly Communions. For, on the one hand, that feeling which has been handed down to us of 'never turning the back' upon

It, is so valuable, that one might be risking serious injury to persons, and much inward strife and distress, by bringing them to the choice, unprepared, and might be breaking down a valuable feeling; or, on the other hand, we might lead them to diminish preparation, and the awe with which they now approach It. For there is among the uneducated a much deeper reverence often, and unwillingness to approach without full preparation founded upon that reverence, than among the rich. I should be disposed in this to lay down no rule for myself beforehand; but ascertain who were communicants, learn something of them, and then speak with them.

With regard to the Prayer for the Church Militant, I think it would be best to prepare people's minds by a sermon on intercessory prayer, which might make part of a course of sermons on prayer (including the Daily Service). For all which has been said about it of late might make people think it a mere form or badge, and so they might never come to feel the full beauty and value of it, whereas, I think, if they learnt how Apostolic and exactly prescribed by Holy Scripture it is, and how full, none of the better sort of people could object to it.

For ordinary charitable collections, that way of collecting at the door, leaving God's House, as if not to do it in His sight, is really so heathen and irreverent, and the other of offering the alms to Him with prayer for their acceptance, at His Altar, is so beautiful and fitting, just what any mind of simple piety would wish, that I can hardly think there would be any difficulty, if the subject were adequately explained, high ground taken, and withal arrangements made as to length in collecting and privacy in giving (by some sort of box or bag).

But the weekly Offertory is a high thing. It also is so clearly Scriptural, and would seem such an obvious act of grateful piety and such a manifold blessing on the week's labours, that I should hope people might be brought, without any great difficulty, to this also. Still, a habit which involves a weekly sacrifice (more or less), which acknowledges and implies a sense of our continual dependence upon God, and so contrary to the ingrained habit of mind, of thinking themselves lords of their money, requires, alas! some time to form, especially as the benefits of giving, as contained in the sentences in the Offertory, have been kept back from them. I should think people ought to be prepared for this, by long teaching, individual and otherwise, on the blessedness of Almsgiving.

Intending to carry out the Rubrics altogether, you would restore Catechizing in the Evening Service, which, if pains is taken, may be much more interesting and instructive than a sermon. With regard to Baptisms, our Church clearly never contemplated such large parishes as there now are, and it would not be meant that the Service for Baptisms should be a regular part of the Sunday Service. The plan, then, which some Clergy have adopted, of having them once a month in full Service, and others, if necessary, at other times, seems to me, in a case of almost conflicting rules, the best.

I hardly think it expedient to consult the Bishop, when the case is clear, because it makes him responsible, which they had often rather not be. I do not think that it is any compromise not doing everything at once, provided that it is your intention to do so, and you delay only until you have prepared your people's minds for it.

I hope my delay has not kept you in suspense. I began writing as soon as I received your letter, but have been so pressed that I was obliged to break it off till now, and you said you had some time.

(I have been obliged to express my opinion straightforward; but you will suppose it all written with the diffidence which one without experience ought to have.)

LETTER XLI.

TRACTARIAN REMINISCENCES.

[*February* 3, 1879.]

I heard some time ago that you really *had* set to work about the history of the early stage of the Oxford Movement. Dr. ——, who came to see me yesterday, had been moved by some early notices in some papers of ——, to wish earnestly that there was such a history. A generation, with whom he is brought into contact, is so taken up with Darwinism, that it cannot understand the interest in Theology which was the ruling passion of Oxford forty years ago. This generation is αὐτάρκης. Darwinism is enough for its head and for its faith, upon which faith it makes far more demands than the Gospel. What it does with its heart I cannot imagine. It does not even trouble itself to deny God; it forgets Him.

Of course there are better things, and a rising generation which gives good promise for the future.

On the other hand, Dr. —— talks of the 'Ritualists' of 1833!

It was a grand Movement, and if you could tell its tale, before memories have faded, it would be a good work. What a picture it gives one, to see dear Keble finding his way with a lantern through the snow to his little church at 5.30 on a winter morning to say the Litany for the Church 'in its present distress'; or again, as an American saw him, sweeping the snow off the path in the churchyard for his parishioners, that they might come with dry feet to the early Communion.

A very highly intellectual man, well known in Oxford, told me that he was emerging from unbelief by aid of Paley, when he heard dear Newman's 'thin voice' in the University pulpit. But before Newman had got through three sentences his attention was arrested (he did not know Newman by sight), and he thought—'This is worth listening to.' He said, 'Paley had moved my understanding: this sent me home to pray.'

So now I have given you an anecdote for your book.

I sent one to dear John Keble to get settled as to some Romeward unsettlement. He stayed a fortnight at Hursley. John Keble did not say a word of controversy, but lived. At the end of the time my friend told me that he was quite settled and could work heartily in the English Church.

LETTER XLII.

BAZAARS.

August 12, 1880.

I still detest Bazaars as you do. It goes against me whenever I see a large sum collected through a Bazaar. Still, it has its good side. Those whom one pities are the buyers, for fear that they should think that they were doing an act of charity, when they were buying a knick-knack. But the workers do give their time. One's instinct goes against it. But one should like to know more about them. If buyers knowingly give five shillings for what to them is only worth half a crown, then I suppose that the other half-crown might do good for their souls. But then there is the matter of fashion and notoriety, which goes into the other scale. The Roman Catholics think nothing of it. I have had Lottery tickets, which I was asked by some nuns to dispose of, in which I remember among the prizes were a pony and a gold watch, &c. I returned the tickets, saying, 'I knew of no one who would buy them'; but they are better than Indulgences! You see I don't know enough of Bazaars to have an opinion for others, as to what I should not do myself. Mrs. —— would anyhow do a good deal by all the trouble which she would take. If she fails, I will put in among requests of Companions in the Paper of the 'Company of the Love of Jesus,' 'St. Hilda, a district separated from the Parish of St. Saviour's, Leeds, that God would give —— to finish the church, which is built up to the roof-tree.' The Orphan House at Halle was built through the prayers of the Pietists in their early fervour.

LETTER XLIII.

A NATIONAL CHURCH.

[1880.]

Loving thanks for your loving letter. ——, in looking on one side, our loss of discipline, forgets the advantage of being 'a National Church,' that we claim as belonging to us all who have not formally left us. We, the Clergy, claim all who have been baptized, however unfaithfully to their baptism they may be living. 'You *are* ours, live as ours.' Faber, somewhere, says that he 'should be in despair, but for the conversion of a drunken Irishman now and then.' He claimed the 'drunken Irishman' as already his, notwithstanding his drunkenness. The Sisters of Charity found many in Bethnal Green who called themselves 'Church of England,' but went nowhere. What a hold this gives to a mission[er]! 'You say you belong to us, live accordingly.' It appeals to their affections. In my younger days, we claimed as belonging to us every man and woman who had not formally rejected us. I forget how I came first to use the words 'my sons' to the younger ones here. Of course I did it as feeling it. But I was struck with Tyrwhitt's[1] account of its effects; something of this sort—that 'every rough lad who had just come up, found himself claimed as standing in a personal relation to the preacher.' The old 'my brethren' meant the same, only it lost its power, from being so common. What an appeal our '*dearly beloved* brethren' is! What a claim!

[1] See 'Hugh Heron,' by Rev. R. St. John Tyrwhitt, p. 187, in which is a description of a sermon by Dr. Pusey. The words are, 'He did what he alone could do, for he looked round on the crowd of undergraduates and spoke to them as his sons with a fulness of feeling that was authority. For it made every rough lad there present understand, that one of the most historical persons he had ever seen claimed him, cared for him, and bade him repent and be clean, and hold fast by the Faith.'

IV

*FRAGMENTS OF
CONVERSATIONS AND LETTERS*

FRAGMENTS OF
CONVERSATIONS AND LETTERS

—•—

I AM apt to say, 'If it is in the Bible, it *must* be true, though I may not be able to explain it; it has a meaning, only we are not able to give it.'

A holy man wondered much why souls are so stunted, why there is not a more vigorous growth. He thought of all sorts of things. 'Is it the want of asceticism? Is it the want of love? or prayer?' At last he discovered that it arises from 'want of sorrow for forgiven sin.'

Satan was once a cherub, as we find in Ezekiel, and he fell! Probably from envy at us; when he heard that his high nature was to be passed by, and our poor nature united with the Godhead, he could not bear it; but though he with his knowledge fell, the Seraphim continued steadfast, because they so burn with love.

And his own face would lighten up with love, while he would pour out, 'Oh that boundless, shoreless ocean of the Divine Love! If we had not been told, we could never have imagined it, that GOD should unite Himself to us, the least of all His rational creation, and *dwell* in *our hearts.* Oh the wondrous, marvellous intensity of that Love!'

He went on—'God in His Immensity is without us: God in His minute creation is still without us: God in His Incarnation is still without us, but God within the heart, dwelling in us, here we are united to Him. Hence we may worship and adore Him.'

It is very remarkable how the telescope and microscope were invented together: one showing the greatness, the other the minuteness of God's works.

Modern Science is all on one lead—all of matter—it can rise no further—it can touch nothing of spirit or of eternity. Space is what God has made, and what He fills.

Time is nothing—if we wait it seems long: if occupied it seems short.

I have often said, 'If you will explain to me the Eternity of God I will explain to you the Trinity.'

God is everywhere, He is between you and me. God is a 'Spirit,' and therefore we have no faculties by which to understand His Being. Our only idea of a spirit is the most fine air; but that is matter, and not 'spirit.'

We cannot understand even our own souls, how much less, then, God!

I have often said, 'God is wholly everywhere, and wholly nowhere—for it is of faith that in God there are no parts.'

Wherever space is, there is God, for space is contained in God, not God in space.

Some of my children have learnt to feel the Presence of God, walking from here to there again and again. We move about in God, He is around us and within us. We are like tiny sponges immersed in the Ocean of God.

To gain the sense of this Presence is His gift, to be prayed for, and sought by continually doing little acts to please Him, so that almost unconscious prayer may grow more and more.

When asked as to his own manner of celebrating, he said that at the Consecration he always leaned over the whole time, as he thought this the most reverential way he could use, as he could not bend quickly. At Cathedral, he said, he could not do more, for 'some among us have not been accustomed to any more,' and 'at such a moment one could not grieve any.'

As to bowing to the Altar—'We have always retained that custom at Christ Church. If you think of the Altar as the Throne where our Lord vouchsafes to come, of course one must show all the respect we can. Even in human things, every one bows to the Queen's throne, even when vacant.'

CONTENT WITH CHURCH OF ENGLAND.

Your sister —— should resolutely dismiss all things which are said against the Church of England as temptations. She is obviously not fitted to engage in controversy as to the points at issue between us and Rome; and it would be unprofitable for her. She has, where she is, all things necessary for her salvation: she has the Sacraments, the Presence of her Lord, the forgiveness of sins, guidance as to her duty, His grace for the subdual of all things amiss. Her Saviour is always ready to hear her. She has all which she could have anywhere.

To one distressed, he said—
'My dear child, you are not living in heresy and schism. You believe all that the whole Church believed always and everywhere till the division of East and West. You are no more in schism than the whole Church unhappily is. It is preposterous to imagine that St. John, who leaned on our Lord's Breast, did not know all the Truth, or that he kept it back. Is it possible to conceive that if he came to this

earth again he would have to learn truths which he never knew? Your text argues all the other way. The Spirit was promised to lead them into all Truth—therefore it did. If it had not, it would not have fulfilled the promise. The promise was to the Apostles.'

Less than a month before his death he was speaking about the consecration of Archbishop Parker.

'Of course we looked into these things (the due consecration of the first Bishops after Mary's reign) in our early days, when it was life and death to us. If I were not absolutely certain of having received the power, every Absolution I pronounce would be a horrible blasphemy.'

'Parker was a very particular man, and would not have allowed anything to be done imperfectly.'

'Oh, I must read up my history.'

MEMORY.

Memory *is* an awful power, nothing is lost in it; all ready to wake up in an instant, as I have been told by one who fell overboard: all his sins which he had ever done came and stood out before him in an instant.

As they come up in this life, they give us the opportunity of saying to God, 'Would, O my God, for love of Thee, I had not done it.' And so we come to be of the same mind with God, even in those things which once were other than His Mind and Will.

How strange the change of that one moment of death! We think of people according to this or that outward peculiarity, or this or that prominent defect, whereas the real self is hidden within, rarely perhaps, or never wholly seen, but, when it has been in the grace of God, bursting out in all its beauty, when this outward mantle falls off for a while.

Reckon everything which is not heard as so much gain. God says, "Be careful (literally, anxious) for nothing: but *in everything* by prayer and supplication *with thanksgiving* let your requests be made known unto God; and the peace of God *shall* keep your hearts and minds." He bids us pray God for what we want; thank Him for what He gives; and then promises that "the peace of God *shall* keep your hearts and minds." He says, 'Do the one and God will do the other.' We do not, of course, any of us, nearly thank God enough. I fear that what will surprise us most, when we see our Lord, will be the extent of our own ingratitude. But He says, "Pray, thank, and the peace of God shall, &c."

We may sometimes learn from the heathen. Terence makes one of his characters advise another: 'On your return home, picture to yourself your house burned down, your daughter run away, your slaves gone, &c., &c., and whatever of these things has not happened, *set down as gain*.' So thank God, ——, for all the evils which have not happened.

It is awful what power Satan has to put it into a person's thoughts to do a thing instantaneously, which spoils all he has been doing. I mean the devout feelings longing to be like the Saints are so far good; then comes the quick suggestion, What do others think? acted upon as soon as thought of, and what was good was made an occasion of evil.

TALKING AMONG WOMEN.

Eve of St. Barnabas, 1847.

You must indeed set yourself more resolutely against this talking of self. Talking is one of the greatest snares of women, and has the most faults in one. You cannot expect that God will give you what you wish, while you do not set yourself resolutely to amend this. There is self often even in condemning self. This seems to be one form of excitement. An idea takes possession of you, and you follow it out, absorbed in so doing, and not regarding the way of doing, or the faults it brings.

What worldly vanity about Patricianism! I always especially admire the vocation of the lower classes. For the higher (as they are called) are fastidious, and often do not marry; but the poor [when they become Sisters] give up, what is the dearest human wish of woman's heart, some one who should love her best.

They forget that the King of heaven and earth was the Carpenter, and the princes of the heavenly court, the fishermen, the tent-maker, the tax-gatherer.

Their theory used to be, that all was misunderstanding and would come right in Paradise. I reminded them that the Day of Judgement came before Paradise.

On the Mistakes of Sensitive People.

July 16, 1877.

You must take care not to be over-sensitive or to watch manner. I remember —— thought that I disliked her coming to me, and declared that my countenance showed it. The fact was, as I told her, that she came in with a worried look and my face reflected this. A person went to the late Sir Robert Peel to ask him to do something for him. On Sir Robert Peel's silence for a few minutes, he took umbrage and began apologizing for intruding, that he ought not to have troubled Sir Robert Peel, &c. Sir Robert Peel: 'Oh, it is my unfortunate manner; I was thinking in what way I could serve you.' There is more wrong than right in the world; and so those who are apprehensive of wrong will be more commonly right. But even if there is wrong, Holy Scripture says, "Be not overcome of evil; but overcome evil with good."

TO ONE TAKING UP A DIFFICULT WORK.

It must take some time for things to settle again. Remember the counsel given by the old men who had counselled Solomon, to Rehoboam, "If thou wilt be a servant to this people this day, and wilt serve them, and answer them, and speak good words unto them, then they will be thy servants for ever." "The meek shall inherit the earth."

It is one essential qualification for an office to feel one's self unfit for it.

'And now (if one may use the language of better and simpler days), if any find profit to their souls from this little book, their prayers are asked by the unknown translator, that she may have part with them in the blessedness of knowing and loving God: and would that they, who think their brethren so need to be censured, would turn their censures into prayers for them, of which we all have so much need; so might our disturbed Church obtain peace, and the prayers turn into their bosom who offer them.'

ON DEVOTIONS DURING THE HOURS OF THE NIGHT.

With regard to waking in the night [for the purpose of prayer], I should think it best to lie down desiring that, if it be best, one should wake; and on earnest desire people do wake very wonderfully just when they wish. But sleep cannot be trifled with; it seems almost better, as humbler, not to attempt to abridge it much. One cannot abridge it long; one sleeps when one ought not. Early hours seem to be what suit us.

I should think seven hours' sleep was the average for most people. Less may do for a time, but it makes reprisals. Some may need seven and a half or eight. Others will do with six and a half or six. Less in summer than winter.

The thing to be secured is your devotions.
Bustle hurts the mind and soul and benefits nothing.
Set yourself specially to cultivate the sense of the Presence of God, i.e. that you are walking about, acting, thinking, in God. For He is nearer to us than the air which we breathe. The air enters into our bodies and is cast forth again: God enters our souls to abide there.

Remember that since God has said, "Speak not evil one of another, brethren," it is a sin to do it, unless it is a sin not to do it. Pray God to keep in your mind, when you are tempted to speak evil, to ask yourself, '*Must* I say this?'

A good watchmaker is one who makes watches and prays: a good housemaid is one who sweeps and prays.

Make acts of God's Presence, as 'What doest thou here?' 'What is thy business?' "Thou God seest me."

Take all that befalls you from God: this would be a great help—to think, 'It is God's Will for me'; and then leave it.

In acts which might be somehow to God's glory, offer them to Him.

Set apart a fixed time or fixed quantity [for] unexciting employments.

Try to do things more carefully and better, when alone.

Be watchful against excitement and occupation in outward things, so that they may not return to mind in church.

Try to do things simply, as well as you can, and do not be cast down when you do them ill. If your arm were half paralyzed, you could not lift it well: only, lift it as well as you can.

Seek to rule speech, and think how at Christmas the Eternal Word became dumb and denied Himself the saying 'Father and Mother' for your sake. (Isa. vii. 16: viii. 4.)

Collectedness is to do all as in God's presence. In its perfection, a collected person would never do anything useless or needless. Again, it is to have power over one's self: to be restrained, not to let self go.

Make a rule about little things once for all, for a while, and then think no more of them, that the mind may be fixed on something better.

The way of looking about cannot be cured by watching: it must be by occupying yourself in something else.

Do acts as well as you can, praying for help, and then rest on God's hearing your prayer and do not examine yourself till afterwards. If a man climb on rocks, he must not watch himself, but look steadily at his point, else he would slip directly. So in writing, if one thinks of it, it stops one directly.

Pray while the hand is on the handle of the door, and then do as well as you can.

Try to stop the first beginning of foolish thoughts.

Specially be earnest that the first morning thoughts be of God.

Mere workings of the imagination are not sin.

Not only commend acts to God at the beginning, but in the midst.
The mind must be in the work: but we may rise up from it to God.

Aim to respond more closely to God: to commend every act to His special grace: to seek more to be nothing: to know your own nothingness: to grow in humility and intense love of God and ardent zeal for His glory.

Thank God most heartily for any humiliation: if the under will rebel, yet thank Him, yet not in your own strength; as nothing must be done in our own strength, but in His.

Do not depend upon ordinary grace, but ask special grace in every temptation.

Seek to do every day something which may win the praise of God at the last. Dread praise *now*, which would rob of that.

As a leaf or the wing of the more delicate insects is so slight that it seems nothing but the power of reflecting the outward light, so may your soul be: yourself nothing, God all.

Better use no violence, but be as God wills.

Take every humiliation as a special gift and kindness from God, to cure pride: thank Him gratefully.
Consider contradictions, unkind words, &c., as benefactions; those who vex us as benefactors.

That another's presence should make one do things better, is not wrong. Self-consciousness is the punishment of self-love.

Ask help before each Psalm, and then throw your mind into the meaning of each verse. Falls, then, are the imperfections of prayer. If this ends in asking help at every verse I shall be glad.

We should humble ourselves before God in prayer [in] the lowest humiliation before our CREATOR. Yet if our nothingness and helplessness and want were fully felt, prayers would not be said so carelessly as they are.

Nothing makes prayer bad or good but perseverance and longing: all the rest are accidents. Sweetness is God's gift: a sort of answer He sometimes makes to prayer. To pray in dryness and heartlessness may often be the most acceptable sort of prayer.

If a person longs earnestly to pray and yet falls asleep, we hope God accepts the intention, though they lose the things they might have asked for in prayer.

Prayer may be equally with words or without: it may be 'Jesu': 'My God and my All': 'Love,' as desiring its outpouring: 'Thy Glory,' &c.

Like the Samians throwing their empty sack before the Spartans and saying the word 'Flour'; which they said was a word too much, since if they only saw the empty sack it was enough; so if we bring our emptiness only before God, He will fill it.

There is no danger in addressing Jesus alone in prayer, because in public prayer it is chiefly to God the Father, and at Terce to the Holy Spirit: and in praying to Jesus we pray to the Father through Him, and especially in the Son's own words.

We cannot tell whether the soul prays to God in our sleep.

The soul is a holy and Divine thing: sick through sin. First begun to be healed at Baptism by the Holy Spirit, Which dwells in it, and more and more largely as He is desired.

In walking, try to say some Psalm or verse as, 'My God, be Thou my All.' 'Thou art my soul's portion, O my God.' 'Knit my heart unto Thee.' Look on any other thoughts but these as impertinence and loss.

Strive to rouse yourself to prayer.

Do not make reckoning of thoughts which flash across the mind, but pray to God.

O good Jesu, I would grieve, for the love of Thee, that ever I offended Thee! Oh that I may never offend Thee any more with this tongue which Thou hast cleansed by Thy most Precious Blood!

Dust is the serpent's food and the penalty of sinful words.

Meet thoughts about food with, 'Be my meat to do Thy will, O my God.' 'Feed me with the Bread of Life.' 'Oh when shall I loathe all earthly things for love of Thee?'

When excited, pray, 'Jesus, calm me.'

It would be a very good prayer, to offer God your whole being, with a full earnest wish to do all to His honour and praise: that is, to seek to please Him in all: and to agree that every time the clock strikes you renew this with great intensity, though at the time you may not remember it, or be engaged, or unable.

To 'rest in Him,' is to rely on Him: cling to Him: resign your whole self to Him: leave the care of yourself to Him. He died for us: He made us: He sanctifies us: He gives us His Body and Blood: He absolves us: He loves us with an unchanging love: He loves us as we shall be, which He knows in the midst of all the imperfections and miseries which grieve us and ought to grieve us: yet He knows what He will make us become.

We must come to Christ, 'Just as I am'; sick and poor and naked: not wait to be anything. Not as if He were only a just Judge and we obliged to have something to say for ourselves. We must be like little children resting on His Bosom, or lambs which He gathers; if we must cry, it must be on our Father's Bosom and be hushed there.

The words we use are figures from bodily actions, but they all mean the same thing—reliance and trust in the Love and Goodness of our God.

The sight of our sinfulness must be to keep us humble, but we must not be ungrateful for or forget the grace of God, which gives the victory many times.

We must try to go on with a glad, hopeful heart. God will help you, and 'finish the work in you.'

Think of all the company of Heaven around and you as a poor penitent before Him. Or make an act of faith as, 'O Lord God, Thou art about me on all sides, and fillest everything, and art most present here: be present in my soul and fill me.' Or, 'Oh when will all self, curiosity, and earthliness be absorbed in Thy Presence!'

Try to picture our Lord on the Cross, or Rising from the tomb, or Ascending to the Right Hand of God.

When the soul has no special prayer to make it would be better to have a book to refer to. Sometimes a word is enough, or the mere taking it. Better to pass on to this or some new petition for self or others, than to be buffeted with distractions. It is best to give the soul to God, to work on it what He wills. St. Francis' 'My God and my All' must have been often repeated, and have been but a small part of his prayer.

Novelty has a certain power over the mind in prayer, and helps it. Books do but suggest prayer.

Wherever you find devotion, there pause.

Though you cannot see God, and believe, love, and speak to One you never saw, it is no 'phantom,' but faith to realize the unseen.

After Holy Communion you may pray to Christ as within you. At other devotions either to Him on the Cross, or you as the lowest and least in the heavenly courts, as described in the Revelation.

To speak of feelings is a great ill.

Say the Collect for the sixth Sunday after Trinity. Try to meditate upon it a little while—as 'Pour, pour, pour.' 'Thee, Thee, Thee.'

Let your one prayer almost, be—'O God, fill me wholly with Thyself: that all self may be absorbed in Thee.' 'Knit my soul to Thee.'

The soul may take that word, "Who is this coming up from the wilderness leaning on her Beloved?"

Speak to God as a child to One it may freely speak to.

If anything seem good, thank God.

If evil thoughts assault, pray God. If a hundred times, still pray a hundred times, and it will be a hundred victories.

Go on resisting, by praying.

Pray to Jesus for the love of Himself, that the soul may be full of Him and have grace to love Him: and do not try to rouse feelings, or look for comfort, or consolation.

The more the soul learns to be hushed to outward things, so will it be more inward.

To have 'the consciousness of God's Presence' is His blessed vouchsafement to some, His gift: to be prayed for.

To be quiet in God's Presence is mostly a gift to be prayed for. In praying this Collect (sixth Sunday after Trinity) it may be quietness to dwell on the words, as not being discursive.

Have that picture in your mind which you have seen of our Lord, as a little Babe lying with outstretched arms in a manger, as on a cross. Pray to be like Him and to be of His Spirit.

Pray to cling closer and closer to God, the more trouble you have: that trouble may bind you to Him.

Pray to be more and more humble, and that He will build you up on that sure foundation.

You must not disparage yourself, but be grateful for the grace of God.

Try to turn every trouble and anxiety into prayer to God.

Try to forget earthly things in Heavenly.

Try to be gathered up in God.
Try to judge of things as God judges of them.
Try to love all in God and for God.
Try to be more dead to the world.
Try to care less about things of earth.

The Cross of Christ bind you to Him everlastingly!

Usually it is best not to speak of God's favours: let them ripen in your heart before you speak of them.

Calmness, serenity, and peace are the best signs: as the direct fruit of God's Spirit.

Great sweetness is God's gift, to lead to thankfulness.

Dwell on the greatness of His Love.
It is of His Love if we have the least love of Him.
He loves us as He sees us when He has made us what He wills.
He loves us as He will love us unchangeably.
He loves us as members of His Son: a child of God, because a member of His own coequal Son.
Jesus loves you so as to die for you, and every desire to love Him and hate sin is of His Love.
The great evil of sin is, that it is against His Love.
Pray to Him for love; enlarged, great love.

Think of the precious stripes of Jesus which do away all sin.

Have an ejaculation constantly ready to say, 'My God and my All!'

Be very strict about the hour of Watch[1]. It may be Almighty God waits for one more prayer before the conversion of some one: it may be unfit for Him to grant

---

[1] i.e. the 'Watch of Intercession,' undertaken by members of the 'Society of the Love of Jesus.'

it unasked : the Angels may be wondering that He should do it unasked.

We may be as the Holy Angels. They ever behold the Face of God : yet also minister to us tiresome, wayward things.

God does not want our words, but our hearts to be fixed on Him. Often the best prayer is when the soul thinks it cannot pray at all. 'No sinner so great as I.'

St. Catherine of Sienna made a cell in her heart. Her parents were urging her to marriage and trying to distract her. Afterwards, in a most busy life of advising in politics and every one seeking her, she could keep quite close to God and without the least distraction.

Pray especially and earnestly for humility. Without this you are building without a foundation : God can give you no grace.

Getting on (in the spiritual life) is not by strides but by little acts. Every real act of self-denial and humility is a step.

Have some ejaculation for the day, or some Psalm.

At night say some verse till asleep again. Put all thoughts away but that of Christ's Love.

Think badly of distractions.

In praying for others' faults, recollect how long you have been correcting your own.

Desire what you pray for and pray the best you can.

When seeking any special grace, make it the subject of more frequent self-examination.

Natural failings are to be overcome. Holy men have

pleased God most by the grace opposite to their natural temper. We must never despair of God's grace not being strong enough to overcome our sin.

Let any reproof make you enter yourself to see if there be not some little drop of reason in it: if you have not in some little way deserved it.

Prayer for Humility, 1849.

O Lord Jesu Christ, Who, though God, didst take upon Thee our flesh, and didst hide Thyself, and became subject to an earthly parent, and didst call a woman Thy Mother, give me, I beseech Thee, true, deep humility. May I take the praise given to others, as if mine, and grieve for their faults as mine own: may I seek in all things to please Thee alone: cast myself into others' minds for the love of Thee: seek their salvation as mine own: long that each soul should be what Thou wouldest they should be: desire Thy glory and kingdom in the world of those hearts which Thou hast redeemed: ever remember that for them Thou didst die: ever strive to do things to serve them and so please Thee: that hereafter, under the feet of Thine elect, we may praise Thee for ever.

The Cross of Christ fill thee with His Love!

Prayer of Blessing, 1851.

The Lord bless you and keep you, the Lord lift up the light of His countenance upon you and be with you in the hour of distress and desolation, of dryness and deadness, of temptation and weariness, of sorrow and trial, the hour of death and the Day of Judgement.

To say the Psalms perfectly, is to say them to God; they need leave no impression. It is the spirit, not the understanding, which is to do the work.

The perfect way in everything is to do it heartily to God, and pray; not be absorbed too much in it.

Set yourself earnestly to receive any, the least word, which can show you any fault, however small, even the breadth of a nail in you, as caustic against self.

Do not be downcast at your continual trials and struggles. Rather take them as matters of course. Regard them as dints on a soldier's shield who has been fighting all day to maintain his ground.

Do not be discouraged at all your faults. A child who would pluck up a handful of grass by the roots, and takes as much as his tiny hands will grasp, falls back, disappointed and hurt. But if he patiently pluck one blade at a time, it will take long, but be done.

Or like the boy who was sent to his father's garden to clear it of weeds, but lay down in despair, till his father told him to clear daily as much as he had lain upon; so it was, in time, done.

In faults, it is better to say, 'What could be expected from me?' and humble yourself before God, and do not dwell on it.

Do not be discouraged. Habits of years cannot be plucked out in months, or even years.

To pray and to do single acts, is the way to gain any grace; and so collectedness.

One who was not full of self would look at things in the abstract; one who is so, looks at them personally.

There are four states which St. Augustine speaks of: (1) that of nature, in which there is no struggle against sin; (2) of the law, where there is a struggle and defeat; (3) of the Gospel, where there is victory in the main; (4) the state of the blessed, where the victory is complete and the struggle over.

The difficulty is to distinguish between the second and the third, and not to despond because we are not in the fourth. Where there is no strife, there is no crown.

Even St. Paul willed not at first to have the thorn in the flesh: he cried out, "Who shall deliver me from this body of death?"

Where evil gives pain, there is not sin. Nothing is sin which is not preferring the creature to the Creator.

Feeling a thing hard, or a trial, is not sin; if we did not feel it, it would be no trial.

The most blessed thing is instantly to consent to what vexes as being God's Will; like that good monk who was no way put out by losing all his cattle, 'I suppose God thought I had got too much.'

Try to make an instantaneous act of conformity to God's Will, at everything which vexes you. Make a minute list of these and classify them, and try to make the act directly.

If it is about the poor, for example, if you are refused anything, pray God to take care of them, to supply it to them, to bless the trial to them.

Take everything as from the Hand of God. If it is unreasonable, so much the greater the lesson of conformity to His Will.

Let humility be your chief aim. Set Jesus before you, Accused and Silent.

It is a proverb, 'Humility comes through humiliations.' To make an act of humility might cost nothing. Mortifications from others do cost.

Remember, if you have not the station you think you might have, it might be the ruin of your soul. God sees what is the best place for you.

The way to high things is through low things.

ON HOLY COMMUNION.

In Holy Communion, seek no feeling or comfort, or method or way of His Presence. Believe simply that in It He bestows Himself, and pray Him to do so. Ask in short words, unless the soul asks without words.

After Holy Communion, make acts of the mind to recall It. 'Abide with me.' 'Leave me not.' 'Cleanse me.'

Spontaneous conviction of His Presence is His gift.

Ask for special graces at Holy Communion. Seek deeper lowliness, so that He may give you more grace.

After Holy Communion, speak to our Lord as assuming He is present with you: some short word, as, 'O good Jesu, how great Thy love in coming to me!' or ask for the graces you need, and so on.

Always choose some special thing to ask for at Holy Communion, and make it your earnest aim afterwards.

Christ is present with us by His Spirit, therefore use spiritual Communion; but in Holy Communion He gives His very Body and Blood, His whole Self. Therefore every day say a prayer to thank Him for this His great condescension.

Before and after Holy Communion, thank Him, adore Him; this is better than to think of self about it, which leads to self-reflection; but to adore and thank Him is going out of self to Him, in a direct way.

By all means, do not take food before Holy Communion, if late, if you can help it. It is a custom of the Church, not an order, probably from St. Paul's time. It may be dispensed with in possible cases.

If having to go to Holy Communion late is only for a few times, undoubtedly do it fasting.

'Holy Communion' is the highest name.

In spiritual Communion you may believe that there is an increased Presence of Christ in the soul, although not in the same solemn way as in Sacramental Communion.

Be very careful not to let the thought of Holy Communion go away during the day.

After Holy Communion, take some text or word by which to recall It often.

Make acts of reminding the soul of His Presence. Never mind their being formal at first, till collectedness is gained as a thing of course.

Pray God to bless disappointments when about Holy Communion. Humble yourself, as our Blessed Lord seeing you too unfit. Pray Him to come into your soul and supply the place of what He denies.

Seek not at Holy Communion to feel anything; go, not as hoping or expecting to find comfort or pleasure, but pray Him only to come Himself to dwell in your heart and unite Himself with it.

ON CALM.

When excitement is part of the natural constitution, all that can be asked for, is to have it sanctified, as St. John's naturally warm character was wholly turned into love and zeal. Very remarkably, of the only three incidents we know of his life, two speak of his ardent zeal.

It would be like trying to make a rapid stream into a slow current; all we have to do is to hinder its overflowing, and direct its course.

So that a person need not be dispirited about it.

Strive after, cultivate a more cheerful love of God. You are His child; think of yourself then, when full of faults, as a poor, ignorant, foolish child, and try to do better, but do not be discouraged.

Tell Him you cannot do anything as you would, or be reverent, and pray Him to help you.

It would be far better, instead of many thoughts, with filial love and confidence to do everything you think would please God.

When over-activity is the temper, meddling comes from it; if not done in a proud spirit, it is not sin, but imperfection.

Hurry and over-eagerness are the roots of uncollectedness, forgetfulness of God's Presence, and uncalmness.

For gaining collectedness do acts slowly; it may excite impatience, but will at last, by God's grace, do good.

Eagerness about trifles gets beyond your own power. You set the door ajar by beginning things eagerly, instead of trying to set yourself to do them simply as to God, and then you cannot stop the flood of distracting thoughts which overwhelm you.

Pray to be calm and quiet and hushed, and that He will vouchsafe you the sense of His Blessed Presence; that you may do all things beneath His Eye: to sit with Mary calmly at His Feet and hear His Voice, and then calmly rise and minister to Him.

In Him do all, and do all to Him. Love Him alone, and intensely and all in Him.

On Thoughts.

At Holy Communion it is best to make some very short prayer, in order to avoid distraction. In such a word as 'Lord, I am not worthy,' thoughts are so many it might distract.

'Come, Lord Jesus' (is a help). So when the priest comes it is not on a sudden, or any shock, but the answer to the prayer; you say 'Come,' and HE comes.

In distraction, it is quite well to pass on directly and go on with your prayer.

So also in private prayer: only say something fervent and intense.

Take no heed whatever of thoughts, not even to turn them into prayer: only go to Jesus. Say some prayer.

Do not examine thoughts, but only if you have often gone to Jesus: 'Knit me unto Thee'; 'Be my All'; and let this be your confession.

In foolish, conceited thoughts, think 'How very silly!' If of crosses, thank God for doing what is the very best for us.

Be sure not to recall bad thoughts, or thoughts of ill towards another.

Think not so much of the past, as to do the best now. The soul will thus learn thankfulness amid other things.

Correct having given a wrong impression to your own advantage.

Be careful to correct exaggerations.

Confess faults, that so you may be more united to our Lord, and attain greater grace.

What we do not will, is not sin : not to be confessed.

Frequent confession implies a strong desire to uproot every fault.

We should feel ourselves nothing. That anything God gives is beyond and against our deserts: that we have nothing, are nothing, can do nothing, feel nothing. That He only can do anything in us, and that anything He helps us in is only through His boundless mercy.

Pray for humility, at Holy Communion, that you may feel yourself nothing, and try earnestly to act as being nothing: if things go wrong, it is better they should if you can learn by that to be 'nothing.'

One sharp word is worse than all the faults you see in others.

Remember the Pharisee.

Pray for a deep foundation of humility, built up with love, to give up your own will and way.

If thoughts of vanity are not harboured, they are not sin, not being a person's own.

Pray at every hour, or so, as an Advent prayer: 'O sweet Jesus, Who didst humble Thyself to become a little Child for me: make me humble as a little child, for love of Thee.'

Pray for humility. To count nothing too little to do for the love of Jesus; nothing too high or holy to seek after. That humility may deepen, and love rise in your heart: that love may ennoble all done for God, however low: rise up even to the contemplation of Himself.

A criticizing spirit is the direct opposite to humility and one which dries up devotion.

Never make criticizing, overt observations: if mental, turn from them.

Be very careful to follow any drawing which seems to be the Voice of God.

It is plainly wrong to lean at prayer, when it would bring sleep.

Complain to God of pestering thoughts, want of faith, &c.

Be careful not to look on in books at Service time.

To do anything in church which you know will bring sleep must be wrong.

It is no matter omitting one devotion for another: only that it be not through idle thoughts or laziness.

In dryness, have you made acts of resignation to God? In what proportion?

Do not encourage imaginations of the future.

If you cannot speak to Jesus, yet cling to His Pierced Feet.

To remember that God the Holy Ghost really dwells in your heart, well considered, would make all things on earth appear the ashes they are.

Have I ever told you of St. Augustine's story of the man who complained to Almighty God about one of his neighbours, saying, "O Lord, take away this wicked person"? And God said, "*Which?*"

ON THANKFULNESS.

Be thankful for everything: especially for what is against your will.

Take everything from the love and mercy of God, Who does all for the good of each soul.

If it is a time of thankfulness, let thankfulness be your prayer; so in other times, other prayer; but thankfulness and love are best, as going out of self. Eternity will be full of love and thanks: so it is a beginning of eternity.

Thank God for every trial, everything which is hard, every humiliation.

OF MEEKNESS.

All we hear of Moses at first is that he was so violent as to kill a man, but after he had endured all the tiresomeness of those 600,000 people, from morning till night, we hear that he was the meekest man in the world. Still he fell into a sin of hastiness.

God does not want our words. We hear of Moses that God said, "Why dost thou cry so loud to Me?" And yet we are not told that he said a single word.

On Public Prayer.

Collect yourself very earnestly, with your whole strength praying for help, at the places where you usually fail.

Pray for the Queen and Court, that it may be Christ's kingdom and to His glory. Think of how great their difficulties. If the Queen had as many minutes as you have hours for retreat, how glad she would be, and how she would improve them.

Pray for the teachers and the taught.

There is no excuse for acts of distraction in prayer.

In church try to read and fix your eyes on the book.

Pray earnestly to be able to say your prayers.

In church, if distracted, try at the first pause to gather up, in one short thought, the sense of the prayer. Of the Queen, her difficulties; of the teachers and taught, throughout the land. In the 'for all estates,' for the unconverted, converted, and in distress.

In the Thanksgiving, thank for all mercies and make a self-oblation. So, try to catch the sense of each Collect in one thought, and pray it. It may be more intense than the whole prayer.

To make confusion by one saying one thing and another another, is very bad.

Pray and strain for intense devotion.

Every prayer may be said with many degrees of devotion and meaning.

Pray for grace to pray them intensely.

Do not be satisfied with habitual grace or with praying at the beginning [of each Psalm], but go on praying for grace.

To say 'I *will* love *Thee*, O God,' with the whole heart is very different to saying it indifferently.

'O God, Thou art *my God.*' 'We *praise* Thee, O God.'

Try to say 'God, help' before each Psalm or change of posture, and try to say the first words as earnestly as possible. Make the heart ask.

Shame on saying anything ludicrous to the singing-class in church! It is God's House.

On Holy Scripture.

Read Holy Scripture with a commentary, to see its deeper meaning.

Read in a Bible at church.

Read and pray: read and pray, if no thoughts come without.

If dryness continues, and you find you cannot pray in the first five minutes, take some book, which you have chosen before; not to be tied by it, but to be led by what it suggests.

It would be plainly wrong to feel reading it 'a burden.'

You help to deaden your own mind by giving way to dislike of reading.

Read Holy Scriptures on your knees: the Gospel of St. John.

Pray God to speak to you through His Word; and that you may speak to Him on occasion of them.

Do not make it all your devotion, but listen to Him in them.

When you hear Holy Scripture, may it be as His Voice; when you read, as hearing Him.

Be very careful about not using Holy Scripture in the wrong place.

Read St. Matthew and the Revelation, and St. Chrysostom; the last to get deeper, fuller thoughts upon it.

In thoughts against Faith, fall back on faith; do not argue or even try to put them down. There is an answer, but you may not know it, or have it at hand. 'I have a way of saying, "It is in the Bible, so it *must* be true." If I do not see how, there is a way in which it is true.'

Think of any sudden thought which strikes you, for which you have no authority, that most likely it is not just.

Let Him be your All. Have Him alone: seek nothing but Him.

Dissatisfied thoughts of our Church should be a forbidden subject: if they come, pray to God.

It is wrong to speak of doubts: from their very nature they may be untrue, and they may cast disquiet into the hearer's mind.

It would be inconsideration and selfishness to disburden one's own disquiet by adding to another's.

The moment of Holy Communion is no time for weighing controversial points. To believe only 'that He gives Himself as He wills; as He would without Sacrament,' when what He promises is His very Body, is very awful! We might say the same in any branch of the Church, the Roman, or Eastern.

On this argument Dissenters were better off than we. They look for nothing in the Sacraments which they cannot receive at any other time by raising the heart in prayer: so they are not disappointed. If we go, looking for one thing and receiving another, we are disappointed. They go subjectively and look not for anything objectively: we look for a GREAT GIFT.

Talking to others may increase disquiet.

Some may be more specially liable to receive impressions and adopt them.

The meaning of 'Propitiatory Sacrifice' in the Holy Eucharist is, representing to the Eternal Father the Death of His dear Son, in praying for mercy herein believing what all allow, and what, if rightly understood, perhaps none believe any further.

Of this world, it is but an opinion that it will be again.

The redeemed will be engulfed, overstreamed, be-oned in His glory and ever near to Him.

If we had eyes to see, we should see God, here present.

God, it is of faith, is indivisible and everywhere present.

God in everything shows us His Love. His Body and Blood are pledges of His Love.

Jesus loves us for no good thing in us, but out of His boundless Love.

Every, the least thought of love, or desire to love, is from HIM.

God loves each for Jesus' sake. "Accepted in the Beloved."

Every, the least good is from God: in short, all that is not the devil's.

It is a most inverted thought to think love is on our side: the very least desire to love God springs from His boundless, unfathomable Love.

Do not think of every thought which overwhelms the mind, that it is sceptical. Adore God only the more. If He were not Infinite and utterly above our comprehension, He would not be GOD. It is our privilege to worship and believe what we cannot understand. We are surrounded with what we cannot understand. Scarcely of anything can we know the 'how.' Rather think, 'Because I cannot *understand*, therefore I believe.' We cannot understand each our own soul: how it can be everywhere in us, wholly, and yet, where is it? It can reach in thought beyond all that is finite, and stretch out to the infinite, yet what is it? If we imagine it, it is but to think of it as thin air; yet without it we do nothing: if then we cannot understand our little selves, how much less God!

Matter appears to us infinite, as it is compared with ourselves, yet we know it to be *finite*. Let this be a shadow to us of God. All the words used of Him are but shadows of the Truth; we cannot know *anything really*, till we see the Beatific Vision. The joy of the creatures for ever will be to see the Creator, and to know Him [to be] Infinite.

Here we can only "see through a glass darkly," yet every glimpse of God is His gift, to lead us to long more for that most blessed, ever-longing, ever-satisfied knowledge of Him, which will be the bliss of Eternity.

The Infinite love of God could not, perhaps, have been shown but in His taking upon Him the nature of the lowest (probably) of His rational creatures.

"Begotten before all worlds" means, not that it was an act in time, but a state of Being from all Eternity. God the Father was never without God the Son, and the Holy Ghost Proceeding from Both.

The slightest glimpse of the Incomprehensible bears down the soul: but from this adore Him all the more.

Think every day, for a month, of the unspeakable humility of God; Who would take upon Him the nature of His lowest rational creature, to teach that creature meekness and humility.

The love of Heaven will be a dependent, adoring love: so our love now must be adoring love.

Union with God—not hypostatic, as of our Lord with the Holy Spirit, but the Holy Spirit uniting Himself with the soul of man—is its perfection. This may be infinite,—from the first longing of love (which is from God) to the intensest love of the Seraphim, all burning with love. The soul is capable of infinite increase of this. All perfection is in the intense love of God. Every religious act tends to this: to gain an increase of the love of God: to die to outward things and so live more to Him.

We cannot understand what a spirit is, therefore we have no faculty by which to *understand* God, the Trinity, or the body prepared for us hereafter. 'Spiritual body': it will not be the sluggish thing which now weighs us down.

Oh the unspeakable condescension of our God! that

He dwells in us. We could not believe it, if our Lord had not said so.

Be very watchful against grudging devotion in others. It is putting self as a standard and wishing God's glory diminished.

Covet earnestly the best gifts.

Pray for the grace seen in others.

Pray that they may have it more, and you also, to the glory of God and the salvation of others' souls.

You might do more good if you were better.

Strive more and more for intense love.

Go on cheerfully, like a little child.

Try to see the graces in each, not the imperfections. Do not compare one with another: as well might we compare one flower with another. Each have their gifts and graces from God: not to speak of inward gifts which He knows.

If you see faults in others, remember you would be just the same, but for the grace of God. In all remember that they are much better than they seem.

Pray for every defect you see in another; so shall each turn for good into your own bosom.

If ever such a thought as envy at another's grace should come again, humble yourself before your Lord, for the miserable sin; as if you did not wish for His glory, or were indeed sorry for it. Detest it, abjure it.

Pray for the person that that very grace may be enlarged in him, with the thought of His Five Wounds, and that this grace which He purchased for him, be given him.

Above all strive against this sin, which is from Satan and is his own sin—to hate God's grace in souls.

Long to be the last in the Heavenly Courts, which you do not deserve to be at all, but for His Passion.

Rejoice in any grace in another which God has not poured on you.

In these days, when devotion is so rare, we should rejoice in it in any one.

If you have a bad thought about any one, pray for that one.

If conscious of a fault in any, pray God to give the opposite grace.

Take what befalls others, as from God. Pray for them. Do not note feelings about them so much as the not praying for them.

Force yourself to praise them.

Pray for inward reverence in those who seem to lack it.

If any thought of suspecting evil in another arise, pray for the opposite grace for you both.

St. Philip Neri saw no ill in any but himself.

If we are sorry for others' faults, we shall not speak sharply of them.

It seems quite easy to prefer any one to one's self—by dwelling on the special grace in everybody, one's straightforwardness, another's gentleness, and so on.

People are like flowers—one a lily, another a rose, another a violet; each have their separate grace more developed than another.

When I was in London there was a great ugly wall just in front of where I sat, but when the sun shone upon it it became all-glorious. That is like us: we are ugly, but when the grace of God shines on us we become very different. There now, look—see that wall! it is ugly enough in itself: now see! how resplendent!

Compare self to others, but for self-abasement.

See evil in self: God's good in others.

Love God's grace in others.

In all thoughts of others, pray for them: so the distraction will issue in prayer.

On Temptation.

It is better to dismiss thoughts, e.g. in curiosity, 'What does it signify?' in pride, 'How stupid!'

That evil thoughts return is no token that they have not been subdued.

On Self-Love.

Try to throw yourself out of yourself, by throwing yourself into other's minds, and into books, and above all by thoughts of God.

Self-love is like being in a mist, you cannot get rid of it directly; all you can do is to seek to rise above it.

God cannot give His gifts till this is subdued: it would do harm, not good.

Self tries to persuade it is *best* to speak of self.

Be very strict not to speak of self except when asked a question.

Be more resolute than ever against speaking of self. Think, 'Is it *necessary*, or can it be avoided?' Take examples from the lives of Saints, anything except self. Choose silence.

Seek not so much to forget self as to think of God. Not so much to forget your body as to think of your soul, and of the account to be given to Almighty God.

Fix the heart on God, and so forget self.

To get rid of 'I,' the one object.

Regard speaking of self as you would touching hot iron. As this is overcome, it is to be hoped other things will mend.

To watch self-consciousness and think of self is like stirring up mud to clear a river, or to hunt motes instead of letting them settle. Best to think of something else.

'To lose all consciousness of self,' St. Bernard says, 'is one of the highest graces: happy they who gain it even for short intervals.' Not to speak of self would conduce to the gaining of this: it would be a great spiritual benefit.

Try to throw yourself into others' minds, to sympathize more with them, and not to express anything which their words suggest, of your former or present self.

Take the continual thought of self as a punishment from God for your long sins. Remember you have no more right to complain, than a man who has become lame in a drunken fit, has to complain of his lameness.

Uproot every remains of desiring man's praise.

To speak from any exaltation of self, aggravates self.

Be very careful not to say anything to excite displeasure against another.

Pray to keep from harsh judgement, or anything unloving.

About historical persons, if you know nothing good, just say nothing.

There is no more stringent command in the Bible than our Lord's words, "Judge not."

"Speak not evil one of another."

Never tell stories of others' follies or faults, thinking how the Holy Angels regard such, and how it is against humility and love.

If you fall into speaking evil of others, break off suddenly with confusion.

One said to me, 'I used to ask myself, "*May* I say this ill of my neighbour?" and I always found a reason for it. Now I ask myself, "*Must* I say this?" and I *never* find a reason for it.'

Give no opinion against others if not a duty.

It is well to repeat anything good [of others].

Take care not to speak of others in a way they would not like.

In telling a Sister's fault, think if it is from love to her.

It is a bad sign only to be seeing faults.

To speak of character with a person in one's mind is virtually 'judging.'

Never say anything which might foster an unkind feeling: or of any one what does not tend to love.

Be careful not to avoid speaking to any one in particular, from any slight dislike.

Excuses may be viewed in two ways. It is higher not to excuse self at all: but in an imperfect state, perhaps it is better to say how a thing happens, as it is against love to vex another by letting things seem to be done carelessly.

Be careful not to say anything about a fault hurriedly or eagerly. The rule (of the Sisters of Mercy) 'not to reply' is very valuable: it leaves no impression on receiving no answer.

If fault is found by way of question, then to reply very quietly is quite well.

Take all reproof as from our Lord.

Try to find out the thing, however small, which may have led to it, even if the main point seems undeserved. If not 'very angry,' yet, most likely, not so calm as your Lord wills.

It is of more value to you to know of one ounce of wrong in yourself than to have a hundredweight of praise.

Gather up the least fraction of blame: it is of such value to you.

Contradiction and blame are not pleasant, but they are the caustic to our wounds.

The being sore at reproof may be, and is in great part, from the love of God: that we are sorry to see ourselves so imperfect, so far short of what God wills. But there is pride in it too.

Be very careful against excusing yourself at the time: make a strict resolve to say nothing: to receive it as God's Voice: as His means of burning out proud flesh; and if blame is not deserved, take it as a means of humiliation.

Rejoice to have that discipline (of being reproved) continued, which in the world ceases: there, no one tells of real faults, yet all see them.

True, what is found fault with is not always very, very bad: but every, the least fault is desired to be removed.

If not expressing love damps it, it would be better to return to its expression.

Try to interest yourself in what others think and are speaking of. Do not think of anything like it which you know, but go on with their train of thought. This is far more effort and far more loving.

In doubtful cases, when a thing seems suggested, do what is most loving.

Be very tender about ——; she may feel excluded, and so the more liable to 'feel things.'

Little acts of love, foster love: such as asking of the other's health.

Pray to love others so as to grieve for any fault in them, and earnestly desire their perfection.

If you feel not to like any one, remember you wish to be with that one in heaven. The little thing you see amiss is, after all, but the slough which God will do away before entering heaven. Think of the good and beautiful in that one.

To feel irritation and not give way to it, is victory. A person might tremble with anger, yet if he repressed it, it would be victory.

In irritation, 'I' comes in. It is what 'I' bid which vexes if not done.

I always say, 'Look on any one who vexes you as a benefactor.' Such an one gives you an occasion to exercise meekness.

Many seek humility, but we hear very little about meekness.

Speak to others as you would like to be spoken to.

Give way to one younger when you can.

Give way to all, rather than dispute.

Be glad to find out one grain of being in fault, rather than a hundredweight of being right.

Be careful of sharp words.

To look greedily or curiously at things is bad, but it may be an involuntary action of the eyes.

The heap of sins within will not hurt whilst it does not come out into acts. It is as a lion within bars. To fret all day from curiosity to see a letter, or from greedy wishes, would be no harm if you took no food greedily and did not satisfy the curiosity. The *act* does harm, for it is sin. Else to be without this conflict would be to be without temptation: so should we never be perfected.

We pray, 'Transform us,' that is, this mass of corruption and sinfulness, into His Image.

When the sense of your corruption comes to you, pray 'Make me what Thou wouldest have me to be,' and then go on cheerfully.

Do not brood over falls, but pray to God to forgive and change you.

When you gain collectedness and the mastery over over-activity, things will go better.

Are you making curiosity a combat?

Quell curiosity, and everything which hinders the love of God.

Curiosity seems slight, but there must be a great deal in it, as it was part of Eve's sin: it lets in distraction, against which, if dead, the soul would have so much the less battle.

If God in mercy takes away outward temptation and so removes a battle, yet we must have some, and it must be against negative things, as curiosity, being more thankful and humble, &c.

Entirely extirpate curiosity.

Ask for nothing you can do without, or is for health.

Of course, never do the least thing against conscience.

To ask leave for little things is being like a little child.

To dislike asking from one particular person is to be avoided: it might breed dislike of that one.

Complain of nothing. To complain is to assume that you love yourself better than God does, and could do better for yourself.

On Obedience.

Do things simply because you should obey your Superior, and give up what you think would be right.

To subdue self-will is the great thing. To be put out at contradiction is worse than to eat meat twice a day.

Affectation of manner cannot be removed at once. Try to do each thing simply as you are told to do it: without improving upon it: and leave the rest to God.

An affected tone is not perhaps in your power. Try to fix your mind on the person you speak to, and your subject, and not think of yourself.

Pray often, in thought of the Blessed Wounds, 'Lord, all to Thee alone.'

If your bottle is full of self, God cannot pour Himself into it: empty it of self, and God will fill it.

The Religious Life.

Having given up all for God, do not be fixed to little trifles: for example, flowers.

In writing, you seem what you would wish to be: in reality you appear what you are.

Do not do things on the idea of your 'holy vocation,' but simply to please God. Think in each act what would please Him. Pray to do better, when you try.

Strive after simplicity: to do all to please God.

All here are come to live to God alone, and should be loved with superhuman love.

Do not talk of your 'life,' but live in good works.

Watch, lest self glide into joy at vocation. Speak not to others that of it which they would mistake. Pray for those who condemn you, as losing, in not perceiving God's gift. A humble person would be pained at being made something, whilst being nothing.

For you now it is best to look on the past as one fullness of God's mercy and your own sinfulness—and to live in God.

Union with God is sealed by the vow of celibacy. Obedience and poverty are accidents: it is the vow of chastity which makes a *Sponsa Christi*.

This may be carried out in the world, if it is impossible to leave a dependent parent.

'Crucify me, with Thee, to myself.'

On Recreation in a Sisterhood.

When reminded of God's Presence each half-hour at Recreation, think how it has been [spent], and set off anew. Begin Recreation with a firm purpose to be more collected. To pray before speaking would tend to collectedness. In any pause, examine yourself and begin afresh, rather than think of something to say.

On Sundays and holy days be more than ever careful not to let self go: to be under restraint. On holy days, having more liberty, strive to remember more and more the Gift received.

On Fridays, laughter and loud talk are specially inconsistent. To come from fasting and those very solemn prayers [on the Passion] to laughter!

Watch against speaking of things of the world, especially anything you might feel vain of.

To go on with anything that vexes another is to turn a holy Home into something worse than the world: for even there a polite person blushes and turns the conversation when it annoys another. This is not the way to mend a fault, but to aggravate it.

The remedy for faults at Recreation is to lift up the heart to God.

Recreation is given for amusement: do not let play go too far.

Never tell of any good you ever did: it is losing God's praise for man's.

In Recreation tell of what you have read.

Satan is very busy at Convent Recreation: he thinks it is his best opportunity.

ON MORTIFICATION.

Be very watchful not to eat the least thing out of meals: it is Satan who would long to mar fasts, and it shows that the least thing is of consequence.

Anything which crosses self is better than those self-denials in which there may be self-importance.

Looking about and curiosity are great hindrances: also wishing to know, and examining.

It is very bad to look at things while worshipping God.

To speak slower, and pause first, would cut off many faults. It is a long lesson; well, if it is learnt in ten years.

To speak ever with prayer is a long lesson. Be not discouraged at failures, but thankful it is no worse. Make it a special aim.

Acts of self-mortification are not such proofs of love as taking what occurs as His Cross: such as disappointment or contradiction.

Leave God for God.

St. Philip Neri never denied himself to any, whatever he was doing: and so for you: if you have to leave Christ for Christ, beg Him to be with you, and He will make up your loss by Himself.

The want of any spiritual consolation is a very severe punishment.

Outward mortifications may have an inward satisfaction in them, so that the very pain would be a sort of pleasure, as a proof of sincerity and a doing something. Mortification of speech is the most severe, and would best suit you: it would involve the most continual self-denial. All spiritual writers agree in denying people outward mortifications, by which they would kill themselves, and in saying that mortification of speech most perfects.

To do all things more slowly and calmly and gently would be a great good to try for. To try to pray before passing from act to act: from child to child. Not to do things against time: better do less, than hurriedly.

Food.

Take food as daily medicine against daily decay.

Seek to live as simply as possible: offer meals to God before, during, and after, and take each thing as from Him.

Do not talk of food. Complain of nothing.

Give yourself up, about food, to your Superior, and take just what is given you.

In food, a little taken slowly does more good than much eaten quickly. Quick eating may be from inattention, or idleness, or greediness.

DEATH.

The departed are to be prayed for as yet to be judged: as in a state whose bliss may be increased by prayers; how, we know not, but leave to Almighty God. Martyrs went straight to the Beatific Vision, and yet will be more blessed after the Resurrection. Ordinary Christians are not equal with them.

What the ineffable glory and delight of the first view of the blessed world will be, no soul can think.

We cannot realize the circumstances of our death: but think of that moment when all here, all man's praise, will be nothing and God ALL. Think of things, 'What should I think of this, how do this, at my last hour?'

We cannot foresee our trials nor God's grace.

In sickness, thoughts of death come, for every sickness is an anticipation of the last. This life is the time of grace. It is now we must gain the love of God. Our future capacity for loving Him depends on what we gain now.

If any one is serving God we should wish them life, that they may serve Him more:—fill up the measure of what God wills for them. Pray for this.

St. Paul, Apostle as he was, was in a strait, not knowing whether to wish for life or death; rather inclining to death, but with no wish.

For yourself, value life, as having so much to do in your own soul.

It is a very solemn thing to bear about one any illness which seems God's messenger for death.

Death may be desired from love: 'Oh, if I may but see and love Him, I would not care to be the lowest in heaven.' Another, too, for love, may say, 'I would endure any length of time on earth so that I might love Him better for ever and be more near to Him.'

There are degrees in heaven: the soul here acquires a capacity of love, though there to be infinitely enlarged. Some will have their place amongst the highest, some among the lowest Angels. Each will be rewarded according to their works.

The duty of each, then, is to leave all wholly in God's Hands: to pray Him with intense desire to do with us what He sees will most further His Will for us. He will then do what the desire prays, whether giving life, or vouchsafing death.

Try to take every the least thing from the Hands of God. Every pain, every cough, every degree of weakness, every refreshment, sleep, waking, medicine, each, one by one, from God.

When exhausted, say, 'O Jesu!' not 'Dear me!'

When tormented with vain imaginations, make the cross and turn to some Psalm or good book.

When tormented with anticipations of food, say, 'Jesu, Bread of life, be Thou my Food.'

Nothing can have been more blessed than the death of dear ———. Her one desire and thought seemed to be to live to God: to be with Him. She panted for something beyond her, which she now has: and you too may rest in Him, even here, in your measure, as she does above: whether in toil or in rest, it may be to Him.

Very blessed it was that through giving up her own thought she received the Body and Blood of Christ on her last day, and departed so in peace.

And now one of this Sisterhood is in Paradise, let the others love one another more and more, and strive that by no thought (as far as your own thoughts are in your own power) or word or deed you may displease your Lord ; or do that which at your last hour you would wish undone. Love one another so that you may have no thought or word to remember which you would desire had been otherwise, when those words shall be said over you, " Blessed are the dead which die in the Lord ; for they rest from their labours, and their works do follow them."

www.ingramcontent.com/pod-product-compliance
Lightning Source LLC
Chambersburg PA
CBHW020234240426
43672CB00006B/526